☾ EXHIBITIONISM ☀

for the shy

_____

by Carol Queen

Down There Press

EXHIBITIONISM

for the shy

Contents

☾ Dedication

This book is dedicated
- to Natalie, who first said, "Just let me watch you";
- to Robert, who said, "Talk dirty to me" (then gave me plenty to talk about);
- and to every pair of voyeuristic eyes that focused on me in the peep show...

Without all of whom I'm sure I'd still be shy.

Foreword

by Nina Hartley

I'm thrilled beyond words that Carol Queen's amazing book, *Exhibitionism for the Shy,* is finally being reissued. As a long-time fan of her and her work, I simply loved the book the first time around, recognizing it instantly as an important contribution to the ever-growing pile of sexual self-help books. Why? Because it covers the basics and spells out how to build a strong foundation from which to explore and experience sexuality and erotic pleasure in a positive light.

It's hard to fathom this about me by looking at my career, but I, too, am a recovering shy person. I'd have given anything for this book to have been around when I was in high school, when I was struggling with all sorts of desires and fears about sex, sexuality and sex with partners. I figured it out on my own, eventually, but I'd have appreciated some help, as it would have cut down on some humiliating experiments! I'm thankful that it's available now for people of all ages. With Carol's singular voice leading us through the wilderness of shyness into the magical clearing marked "confidence," anybody who's motivated can find his or her own sturdy center, from which a satisfying sex life can be built.

In order to be "good" in bed, a person must first be at home in his or her skin. To really let loose with fantasy and to accept another's fantasies (to say nothing about being able to communicate these fantasies and desires with a partner), becoming comfortable with one's physical self is essential. Until we experience our bodies and ourselves as beautiful, strong, unique, sexy and powerful, we'll be forever fearful of others, easy prey for unscrupulous partners. This book helps with all of that, and more. Carol's tone is warm, kind, knowing, supportive, encouraging and spot-on. You can tell that this is a path she's made for herself and wants to share it with others so that they, too, can get more out of life, love and relationships. Oh, yes, and from sex, too! That's the beauty of this book: by overcoming one's shyness from the inside out, whole new worlds open up: social, professional, personal and sexual. It's truly amazing and transformative.

Even if you never, ever, perform for an audience comprised of more than just yourself, you can benefit from this book and the wisdom it contains. By doing the work she suggests, each reader can, and will, learn more about him- or herself – and knowledge is always good. If you develop to the point of having an audience of one, you'll be amazed at how splendidly your newfound confidence triggers a greater positive response from your partner, creating a wonderful, lusty feedback loop that will only intensify your fun. If you've ever had the desire to have an audience of more than one, then every insight you learn here will prove vitally useful to your endeavor.

In short, this book has something for everyone. If you're an old hand at taking off your clothes in front of people, you'll learn some new tricks of the trade. If the very idea terrifies you, this book will calm your fears and help you along. If you've wondered why anyone would ever want to show off in front of others, this book will reveal just why that can be so much fun.

In the end, the person who stands to gain from reading this book is anyone with a body to call his or her own.

Thanks, Carol, for your vision and persistence.

Nina Hartley has spent the past 25 years as a sex entertainer, performer, educator, advocate and Carol Queen fan. The author of Nina Hartley's Guide to Total Sex *lives in Los Angeles with her husband and co-conspirator, I. S. Levine, and continues to perform in adult entertainment.*

Preface to the Second Edition

What a difference a decade and a half make when it comes to opportunities for exhibitionism! Do you know, boys and girls, that in the old days, people often had to actually go *outside* to find someone to admire them as they showed off? Now, of course, friendly strangers are a mouse-click away, teens are getting busted for "sexting" (who knew that kiddie porn laws applied to actual kids having supposedly-private communication? Who can pin down, today, what privacy actually is?), and ever more people seem to be, like me, formerly shy. But body image issues do not seem to have gone away, even with the advent of wonderful role models like Big Burlesque and its zaftig dancing girls. Where body tyranny rules, plenty of people still have reason to be shy... or think they do. My original *Exhibitionism for the Shy* interviewees are joined this time around by new experts in show-offery, and I cannot thank them enough for taking the time to share their thoughts and experiences. Especially big thanks to Margaret Cho – she's exhibitionism's biggest 21st century success story to date, if you ask me – and to the ever-inspiring Nina Hartley for contributing her thoughts to the new introduction.

This time around, instead of having a resource chapter whose contents will before long be out of date, I'm introducing a website – www.exhibitionismfortheshy.com – where I can let you know about show-offy resources like places to do it and things to wear – and you can let me (and other readers) know about resources you discover! Please, though, check to make sure the listed places remain in business before you make a trip to shop or stay.

Finally, more thanks are due: To Mary Branscombe and Simon Bisson, without whose astonishing post-millennial computer skills the previous edition would still be stuck on a little piece of plastic, unable to speak to my fancy Macintosh gizmo that I now use; to Nellie Wilson, who made sure the old manuscript was edited enough to be made new; to Kat Sunlove and Layne Winklebleck, who offered their house in the country as a crucial writing refuge; and always to Robert, who has given me so many opportunities to be a show-off in our twenty years together, and who puts up with how bat-shit I get when I'm working on a deadline.

Grazie too to Patrick Hughes, without whom the new edition would never have happened; his support and business inspiration were crucial to getting the book back into print. Speaking of which: without my wonderful new publishers Aaron Silverman and Molly Maguire, there would be no second edition either. And it would be less readable without the redoubtable layout skills of Janet Hardy and less beautiful without the fantastic new cover design by Johnny Ink.

Laurel Sharp took the back cover photo at the same time as the pic that appeared on the front of the first edition of *Exhibitionism for the Shy*; I always sort of regretted not appearing naked on that book, and I'm so pleased to be able to right that counter-intuitive situation this time! True, I don't look exactly like this any more – but exhibitionism still gives me a one-of-a-kind thrill. I hope it does you, too – if not now, then very soon.

Finally, my deepest gratitude to all the readers of the first edition – not only for supporting the book, for which I'd owe thanks enough, but for telling me that it made a difference in your lives, your erotic comfort, and your willingness to take sexy (but one-step-at-a-time) risks. Thank you for trusting these ideas about erotic comfort... and your own desire to be a more erotically comfortable person. I hope you don't mind if I imagine you (nearly naked, maybe?) cheering the book's new readers on.

❋ 1 ☾

Recovering from Reticence

You have an unselfconsciously erotic person hiding inside. How do you coax it out? You want to induce your sexually comfortable and outgoing self to come when you call. You want to become more playful and spontaneous with your partners. You want to feel more joyful and at home in your body and your sexuality.

There are many ways to get more comfortable with your body, your fantasies, and your partners. Two especially effective and fun ways to do so, sexy talk and sexual exhibitionism, are the subjects of this book.

You can enjoy erotic show-offery and talk whether you're male or female. In some species males have the fine, sexually suggestive plumage; in our culture today women are more likely to dress up to attract others.

But exhibitionism is more than dressing up, more than catching the eye of a mate – or a playmate. Exhibitionism involves presenting yourself in an erotic way, whether through dress, speech, or behavior. This book is about exhibitionism that turns us on, that makes us feel hot and erotic, full of pleasure and self-confidence.

You can explore hot talk and sexual exhibitionism regardless of your sexual orientation, and I wrote this book with heterosexuals, bisexuals, lesbians, gay men, and everybody else in mind. The only prerequisite for reading it is a desire to enjoy sex and spice things up. And it doesn't matter whether you're solo or partnered, young or old.

Exhibitionism For The Shy is the first book to be written about erotic exhibitionism and the only book to teach you how to explore it by yourself or with a partner. It has grown out of the many workshops I've led, for the shy and not-so-shy alike, about exhibitionism and erotic talk. This book deals with physical and verbal presentation, but it isn't just a guide to dressing sexy, or learning to do a strip-tease or give good phone sex. I'll help you reach inside yourself to find the sexual persona most appealing to you, the one you're most comfortable with and turned on by.

The whole point of *Exhibitionism For The Shy* is to assure you that, no matter who you are or what you look like, your sex life and sexual self-image can be enhanced by learning to be more erotically outgoing. Here you'll find exercises, tips, and techniques you can use by yourself or with a partner, and encouragement to believe in yourself. I've also interviewed a number of people who love exhibitionism and hot talk (a few names have been changed to protect the not-yet-completely exhibitionistic), including several new contributors to the second edition. Some may already be household names to you, like Margaret Cho, Nina Hartley, Annie Sprinkle, Violet Blue, and Candye Kane (to name just a few of our guest experts and celebrity exhibitionists). Others are ordinary sex-positive people who were glad to share their thoughts on showing off. They'll provide inspiration and an array of suggestions and strategies. You can construct your own exhibitionistic self from the building blocks that best match your personality, fantasies, relationships with partners, and experiences.

Maybe this book's title caught your eye because you are, in fact, shy. If you're painfully shy and looking for a way out, the idea of erotic exhibitionism may be inspiring and alarming all at the same time: you may be thinking, "I could never do that!" But that's part of the challenge of shyness, you see; I think you can, but you'll have to come to believe it too, if you're going to get out of shyness's grip. Of course, no book can fix shyness all by itself. But if the idea of erotic exhibitionism intrigues you, you'll find encouragement here to take the first steps toward overcoming your reticence.

A lot of qualities go into good sex, and you don't need to talk a blue streak or swing from the chandelier with no panties on to enjoy it. For those whose overall self-esteem is low, no lexicon of dirty words or exotic-erotic wardrobe alone is likely to raise it – though a competent, compassionate therapist probably will.

Shyness is not always the same thing as low self-esteem. Especially in the sexual arena, shyness is sometimes a behavior pattern left over from our younger years when we weren't yet self-assured enough to be adventurous, or from an upbringing that left us nervous and insecure about sex or connecting with others. Shyness can accompany a life-change, like ending a long-term relationship or quitting drugs or alcohol. Particularly for some women, reticence in bed can be a way to preserve our sense of ourselves as "good girls," or to maintain an image for our partners that we're not "too" experienced or "slutty." But sexual shyness affects men as well as women; many men become strong, silent types partly because they just don't know what to say. Be assured that in your fantasy life or subconscious resides a part of yourself which relishes pleasure, or believes that it can. I know this is true because you chose to pick this book up in the first place. That character is your best ally when it's time to come out of your shell.

The pleasure-loving side of each of us may need to be coaxed out, or it may already be in charge of our priorities. It will take different forms in different people, for none of us develops alike in our eroticism any more than in our physical bodies. For some, the erotic self emerges as a stud or a bombshell; in others it is as playful as a child. In some it will be imperious and dominant; in others it will be eager to please. For many of us, a number of erotic archetypes lie under the surface of our personalities, waiting to be asked out to play. If you've lived this long under the impression that there's one (and only one) normal, correct, proper way to live in your sexuality, it's time to shake off that notion right now. You can emerge from shyness into a full, lively, rich sexuality, but to get there you will follow your own path, guided by cues from your fantasy life and subconscious.

Of course, you may not be shy at all. The first time I did my workshop for women called "Exhibitionism for the Shy," some of the participants crept in nervously – clearly, they were the audience I'd envisioned. But others roared in like gangbusters, wearing brightly colored or provocative clothes, outgoing as could be. They were so enthusiastic about exhibitionism that they hadn't even bothered to read to the end of the title!

Facilitating this crowd felt like trying to row a boat with one oar. The actually-shy women could barely get a word in edgewise – and I could only hope that their more gregarious sisters would give them some tips and some inspiration. Since then I've split the workshop into two parts, one for the shy and one for the brazen, to try to meet each crowd's particular needs: for the shy ones, suggestions and support; and for those brazen hussies, a chance to swap stories, get new ideas, and compare favorite ways to create flashy, sexy outfits. Elements from both workshops found their way into this book.

How I Became Bold

People usually don't believe it, but I am a recovering shy person. How did I go from shy and tongue-tied to the head of the class? A lot of things worked together to help me get over that painful, embarrassing state in which I could barely talk and wanted more than anything to disappear: supportive friends, a wonderful therapist, meaningful work, just plain growing up, and my relationships with lovers. Besides, being shy made me unhappy. I didn't for a minute think it was a natural state. I didn't want shyness to impede my social life or my sexual life, and I could envision how much more satisfied I'd be if only I could find a way to change.

Doing so on my own wasn't easy. It felt humiliating to make a stab at coming out of my shell, only to scuttle back in when I felt rejected. I had a number of sexual partners – I often managed to be in the right place at the right time to get sexual invitations, and I benefited, if that's the right way of putting it, from many boys' tendency to persist despite the possibility of sexual rejection. Still, I was usually speechless in bed. When asked what I liked, I would murmur, "Oh, everything you're doing feels wonderful," whether it did or not. I just could not find the words to give explicit directions – even after beginning to masturbate, which provided me with an idea of the sorts of touch to which my body would respond. More often than not it felt like there was a wall between me and my partners.

Part of my sexual reticence had to do with my fear that I wouldn't measure up to some ideal of sexiness I couldn't even really envision. I grew up influenced both by sixties-era notions of sexual freedom and by the flowering of feminism in the seventies. While I didn't think you had to look like a centerfold to be sexy, I wasn't sure what did go into making sexiness, and was even less sure that I'd have it once I figured out what it was.

In my attempts to move toward sexual comfort I compiled a list of sexy qualities. I gathered these from various places – reading and watching movies, studying attractive or successful role models, comparing my better experiences with my worse ones. I was never tempted to emulate models with whom I had nothing in common; fortunately, "Be yourself" was an important tenet in the philosophy of the day. In fact, I slowly evolved my sexual persona from exactly the right source: deep within myself.

It turned out that my shy self's weaknesses were the mirror image of my erotic self's strengths. My shy self was uncomfortable receiving too much focused attention from others. My erotic self, which was much bolder, loved and thrived on attention. My shy self feared that no one would want me enough to give me the kind of sex I craved; my erotic self reveled in being made love to. My shy self worried that I was too inexperienced to proficiently make love to a partner, but my erotic self just said, "Show me how!" and dove in to practice. It was almost as if my shy side had developed to hide the qualities possessed by my sexual side. Conversely my erotic self, when it began to fully emerge, knew how to heal the hurts my shy self had sustained and to assuage its insecurities.

Beginning to assemble the parts of my ideal sexual self was important, but so was finding a partner with whom to let that outgoing persona grow. I was used to falling passionately in love – and certainly in lust – with people who didn't want to have a relationship with me. This had some of the same salutary effects as masturbation: it let me practice my own feelings of desire and lust without getting too muddled up with someone else's responses. I probably never would have learned to reach orgasm if I hadn't discovered that through self-pleasuring I could focus on my own physical responses, uninterrupted by the unpredictable moves of a partner; similarly, having crushes got me used to feeling in love.

Eventually, though, I had practiced being in love so hard that it was time I tried it *à deux*. I met a woman on whom I developed a raging crush - and lo and behold, this time I managed to aim that desire in the direction of someone inclined to want me back for more than an evening or two. I finally had a place to get comfortable enough to learn about sex... with a partner who'd never been shy.

Not only had Natalie never been shy, she had always been orgasmic, had masturbated as far back as she could remember, and was very accustomed to making the first move. She talked during sex and did not take "Oh, anything," as an answer to "What do you like?" She told me clearly what she liked and asked me specific questions, putting me through a crash course on Opening Up Sexually. This turned me on as much as it terrified me.

Natalie's sexual pleasure with me depended on our being able to communicate. For my part, her insistence that I open up and tell her the truth about my desires and responses served as proof that she really wanted me. It was healing as well as hot that my lover insisted on good sex.

There was nothing medicinal about this, though for me it was certainly remedial. My sense of myself as sexy and desirable soared. I became more responsive and orgasmic - not surprisingly, for I had given her information about my sexuality that I'd kept secret from everyone else until then. I also became more secure in my prowess as a lover as she taught me how to pleasure her. I could finally use those mental notes on sexiness I'd been keeping in case I ever had a chance to blossom.

If my self-image had been truly impaired, this rapid awakening would not have been possible. Natalie gave me permission and inspiration to become the sexual self I'd yearned to be, but she didn't create my newfound comfort in my sexuality. If I'd spent my life up until then convincing myself I'd never be sexy, never be loved, never be wanted, it would have taken a miracle - or at least a good therapist - to restore my sexual birthright to me. Sure, I'd feared all those things, which reinforced my shyness, but I didn't carry them like a life sentence.

One profoundly useful reason to get comfortable with explicit sex talk has to do with communication. After I had comfortably mastered "verbal intercourse" and we were on fairly equal footing guiding each other in pleasure, we began to tell each other about some of our fantasies.

Fantasies are the most private parts of our sexual makeup, and often the parts for which we get the least amount of support. At first I couldn't disclose some of my fantasies to Natalie simply because I wasn't yet aware of them. As my erotic comfort level changed, I let more of them come to consciousness.

We acted out some fantasies. Others we narrated while making love. For me the act of speaking the hidden and the forbidden felt erotic no matter what the fantasy's content. Hearing Natalie's felt like a real privilege, and sexy to boot.

One of Natalie's fantasies proved particularly important for me. She liked to watch. She loved it when I dressed erotically, and early in our relationship she began buying me lingerie. It turned out that I felt very hot in garter belts and stockings, so dressing up spiced our sex just as talking did.

But she wanted more than to see me in lace – she wanted to watch me masturbate.

I panicked. I didn't think I could do it. Masturbation was so intensely private. Finally I solved the problem by doing it with my eyes closed tight, making her promise to be quiet so I wouldn't be distracted and could keep my fear and self-consciousness down.

Ironic, isn't it, that one of my secret masturbation fantasies involved being discovered or peeped at while in the act?

It took me a long time to get comfortable touching myself in front of Natalie. The biggest step was when we decided to do it together. At first the sight of her masturbating was shocking – then I found it turned me on a lot. Natalie had now introduced me to voyeurism.

I knew I had undergone a radical turnaround from my shyness after the night I spread out on her bed, head thrown back, and purred, "I feel like Marilyn Monroe!"

Five years later, when Natalie and I parted, I had made great strides in changing my sexual self-image. I was rarely shy, and an excellent therapist had helped me sort out issues that weren't based in my sexuality but which affected it. I was ready to make sexuality more than a private interest, and I moved to San Francisco to work towards a degree in sexology.

San Francisco is a sexual world unto itself. It's not that the rest of the country is devoid of the sexual diversity San Francisco boasts - far from it, as I learn anew every time I travel outside the Bay Area and am welcomed by homegrown sex communities of every stripe. But San Francisco, in its eccentricity and civic pride in tolerance, allows all kinds of people to make a home here without resorting to the secrecy much of the rest of the land requires, to one degree or another, of those with varying sexual interests.

In this tolerant environment I began to explore new curiosities and fantasies. Not long after I'd begun graduate school I followed my fascination to a group safe sex party where only masturbation was permitted. Of course, there are infinite ways to make masturbation interesting, especially when you have help! I wound up on a sofa jilling off (that's like jacking off, only female) with several enthusiastic, competent assistants and a semi-circle of people standing nearby watching. I found myself coming again and again - a sure sign that I was on to something, since I had never been multiply orgasmic in my life. Since I had been masturbating - alone - to a similar fantasy for years, it's no surprise that it worked wonders when I finally got to try it out. I began to identify myself as a sexual exhibitionist.

I met my next two lovers at parties like the first one, ensuring that my desire to explore sexual adventure and exhibitionistic behavior was supported. With the second lover, Robert, I found my voyeuristic, fantasy-loving match. We evolved the intense and erotically rewarding practice of talking each other through fantasies. He knows my fantasy hot spots, I know his, and we can trade them back and forth whenever we want - over the phone, during lovemaking, driving in the car.

My explorations led me to work for a year in a peep show, North Beach's famous Lusty Lady Theatre - the kind of place that invites you, in neon, to come "talk to a real live nude girl!" Thanks to Robert I was getting pretty good at talking; by the end of my tenure at the peep show I felt downright expert, given that every time I opened the curtain of my booth to a new customer I looked a new set of fantasies and desires in the eye. We did much more than talk, however, and I found that mutual masturbation with a stranger, a pane of glass between us, felt wildly exciting.

LIVING IN – AND LEARNING FROM – A DIVERSE SEXUAL WORLD

I do not mean to suggest by my story that you must summon the courage to masturbate in public if you're ever to throw off the chains of shyness. Nor do I want to imply that only an experienced, supportive partner can waken us timid Sleeping Beauties, transforming us into successful sexual beings. This model has some implications that are not at all empowering. It closely resembles, for instance, traditional female sexual socialization, whose scenario of "someday my prince will come, and so will I" puts our erotic awakening entirely into someone else's hands.

I, like many women, have been swooning over, fighting, and compromising with this script all my life. It's important to emphasize where our sex histories depart from it. For me, learning to masturbate and focus on my own self-pleasure, developing ways to nurture my sexual self even when I was too shy to flaunt it, and choosing a same-sex partner all played important parts as I carved out my own sexual path, not the one I was raised to follow. For some women and men, partnering actually hampers the process of erotic individuation, and if communication difficulties and sexual incompatibility plague the relationship, erotic growth can be stifled altogether.

On the other hand, criticizing sex-role socialization only takes us so far. If you are inspired to new erotic heights by your Prince or Princess Charming, embrace that growth. We are, after all, social animals. It may help to remember that sexual mentoring is important to many people's erotic maturation. In erotic literature it is as often the man being initiated by the experienced woman as the other way around; much gay erotic literature embraces a same-sex version of this scenario. In fact, "teacher" and "novice" are powerful sexual personas for many of us – because or in spite of our socialization.

Your sexual path surely differs from mine in many significant respects. The greatest unacknowledged sexual secret in our society today is how different we are in the specifics of our responses and desires, not to mention our sex histories. What's entirely natural for one person is often quite the opposite for another. We direct much-needed attention to ethnic multiculturalism in our attempts to deal with the stormy legacy of the "melting pot." But it's less often acknowledged that we also live in a sexually multicultural world. People who don't fit the standard sexual mold, whatever it is in any given era, can experience misery and rejection, even oppression, because of their difference. Humans naturally exhibit a rainbow of erotic diversity in both behavior and fantasy, but societal mores often restrict free expression.

Another important lesson from multiculturalism also applies to the sexual world. We are different, but we also have many things in common. As a non-monogamous bisexual female discovering my own erotic pleasure and strengths, my experiences are unique to me – but many aspects of my sexual journey may feel familiar to you even if you're not bisexual, female, partnered, or a resident of San Francisco – maybe even if you've never been shy. Often we believe the experiences of those who are "too" different don't have relevance for us, but we almost always have commonalities that give us opportunities to learn from each other. Keep this in mind as you learn about others whose sexual lifestyles seem at first very different from yours.

The point of becoming more comfortable with exhibitionism is to help you become more comfortable with who you are, not to transform you into someone you're not. If anything about sex and eroticism inspires you, you have all it takes to become more sexually outgoing, even if getting more exhibitionistic or learning to talk dirty was your partner's idea, not your own. You may also get support from friends who are not your lovers or partners; maybe you know other people who are exploring these issues too. You can learn all sorts of specific skills to please somebody else, from gourmet cooking to skiing, but if you're not having fun, why bother?

Good Sex: Information, Communication, Creativity

A contrary point of view demands to know why sex needs to be enhanced in the first place. In this view of sex, spontaneity does not need any sort of additional fuel; lovers tumble into one another's arms, sparks fly, and no sex toys or guidebooks are ever part of the picture. This is a good point, especially if the person raising it is actually having such light-my-fire sex. Many, of course, are not.

Try thinking of sex as play. The games one can devise may be as complex as chess or as simple as solitaire. At least for some of us, pleasure in sex increases substantially when we can laugh, wear costumes, let inner selves out to play, and indulge in a grown-up version of the creativity psychologists say kids engage in whenever they pick up a toy or invent the rules of a game. In other words, insisting on or waiting for that swept-away feeling can rob sex of some of its potential pleasure.

Further, many of those "sex is sacred, special, spontaneous" types don't actually find their sex lives very enjoyable. The fact is, the majority of us sometimes need or want to try something interesting or exciting or new to keep sex fresh. Sex therapists earn their livings advising couples to keep their sexual communication open and their fantasy lives active.

But more than that, a great number of us need sexual enhancement and, more basically, better sex education, before sex begins to get good at all. It is a pernicious myth that sex comes naturally. This may be true in cultures in which families are open about sex, and children spend their young years accumulating correct information about it. Far too many of us have no such luck. Studies indicate that primates (presumably including humans) don't, in fact, even know how to mate instinctively. In some species the young learn how to mate by watching adults – but of course this is an enormous taboo in many human cultures. No wonder we can benefit from sex manuals, watching explicit movies, and listening to friends.

Even when reproduction seems to come naturally, sexual pleasuring skills do not. Good sex consists of knowledge, skill, and chemistry; participants in good sex need to feel comfortable about their own sexuality. In a society where young people are supposed to respect chastity, rather than the giving and receiving of pleasure, it's a wonder that any of us develops high sexual self-esteem and the requisite skills.

The most important thing I've learned from my study of sexology is that the social climate in which we grow up impairs many of us in our adult search for sexual happiness. In a fundamentally sex-negative environment we face curtailed access to information; erotic difference is portrayed as wrong, which threatens individuals' self-esteem. A sex-positive outlook can help repair the damage to our psyches which results from all this. And the single most useful tool as we search out both information and compatible, sex-positive partners is communication.

It's true that hot talk is a powerful turn-on for many people, and that's an excellent reason to use it. But more importantly, erotic talk lets you communicate about sex without sounding clinical or detached. Today I can ask for exactly what I want sexually, as well as learning my partner's preferences via direct questioning and fantasy talk – as well as through non-verbal ways of communicating. I know that communicating this way will maintain – even heighten – our level of arousal. Overcoming the tendency to stay silent about one's own preferences and avenues to pleasure is the very best reason to conquer sexual shyness and learn to get comfortable with explicit language.

GETTING STARTED

Sometimes getting the words to come out isn't the whole problem. "My partner really doesn't want to know," "I might ask for something s/he finds unacceptable or doesn't like," or other concerns like these may be the real reasons the cat has our tongue. These are issues of sexual communication that may have nothing to do with language. If you know your communication leaves something to be desired, read on. You're in a perfect place to begin to do something about it.

Successful communication about sex depends on several factors: timing, including both your and your partners' emotional states when you talk; how you interpret your partner's reactions; your ability to acknowledge both your own and your partners' feelings and go on talking just the same. Even if you're not in a sexually compatible relationship now, you and your partner can build one together. Learn to communicate honestly about your needs and desires, try to be nonjudgmental about each others' sexual interests, and abandon assumptions you may harbor about what constitutes "normal" sex. This way you avoid stigmatizing one another's desires. If you're willing to declare good sex a priority you can learn to please each other and experience some wonderful new turn-ons along the way.

Exploring exhibitionism and voyeurism together can help both of you open up sexually, feel more adventurous, and help you feel a little less hidden emotionally. If you're shy, you'll get appreciative feedback about your erotic self. Having a responsive partner can be truly healing – so many of us who are shy about sex carry the belief, as I did, that we will never get the kind of sex we want, and it positively alters our self-image to be proved wrong.

Most importantly, you'll get to experience sexuality as if you already were more adventurous. Once you get used to that feeling, it will come more easily to you all the time. The same goes for exploring erotic talk. It will enhance your communication about the hard and wet realities of sex, and it will give you practice establishing an open, communicative erotic environment. Hearing bold words issuing from your own shy lips can be a pretty amazing experience, helping you break through the shell of your self-image.

What if you try it and you find you don't like it? You can try it a few more times and see if you warm up to it, or go on and try something else you're curious about. There are no guarantees that you'll find any one sexual practice hot, but even if you don't enjoy something, you've grown from simply trying it: you probably learned more about communicating, and now you know better what you might prefer. Be open to the feelings that come up when you try something new, be honest with yourself and your partner, and please don't let one unenjoyable experience deter you from experimenting.

If exhibitionism, voyeurism, talking dirty, or listening to sexy talk are the erotic créme de la créme for either you or your partner, getting into them together will be extraordinarily hot and powerful. There's nothing quite like the feeling of sexual awakening, and you can have those feelings even if your virginity is long gone. If you're willing to explore new kinds of play and new fantasy scenarios, you can renew those fluttery, excited sensations as often as you want.

What if the prevailing climate around you is hostile to open, adventuresome sexuality? Can you somehow turn your bedroom into an oasis of positive eroticism?

You can. First and foremost, think about what you need in order to heighten your sexual comfort level. Do you want to be more self-assertive? Do you need communication skills? Are you uncomfortable about your or your partner's sexual desires? Do you need a support group? Help with overcoming a painful or non-consensual sexual history? Do you need to get out of a current relationship, to get over an old relationship, or to find a new partner?

If a source of nonjudgmental information and a supportive person to talk to about sexual issues would make a difference in your life, you can call San Francisco Sex Information and discuss your situation with a trained volunteer. You may also have friends close to home with whom you can talk; to find out which people in your life may be likely confidants, start by bringing up sex-related topics on a social, not a personal, level. Their response when you say, "I just read an interesting article about safe sex" or "sexual communication in marriage" or what-have-you will probably tell you whether you feel comfortable telling them things about your own sexual life or thoughts. In a situation like this, disclose only as much as is comfortable for you and your friend. Is s/he supportive? Can you trust this friend with confidences? This process of sharing with a friend will be similar in some ways to opening up with a sex partner; both kinds of disclosure can have emotional rewards or consequences.

After determining what you need for the growth of your sexual comfort level, start looking for resources that can help you. Read material that presents sex in a positive light. I've included several suggestions for finding these on the *Exhibitionism for the Shy* resource website (see chapter 14). Supportive friends may suggest others.

Make having good sexual feelings a priority. Share this positive view of sex with your partner or partners, enlisting their participation in creating a sex-positive climate within your relationship. You can give each other support for letting go of feelings of fear and shame around sexuality; you can agree to learn more about sex together. Share this outlook with your friends, as well.

Exhibitionism For The Shy is about overcoming sexual shyness and reticence and projecting your sexuality in a confident, erotic, arousing way. It's about finding your inner turn-ons and expressing them. Exploring erotic exhibitionism and talk lets your fantasies and your own sexuality blossom, especially when you learn how to find and play with compatible partners. These forms of erotic play will help move you past shyness and into your own rich, confident sexuality.

Everyone deserves and can find pleasure and fun in their erotic lives. *Exhibitionism For The Shy* shows you how.

2

What Exhibitionism Is – And Isn't

Maybe you're uncomfortable at my suggestion that you become more exhibitionistic when you've only heard exhibitionism described as a problem. Don't people get arrested for that sort of thing? Don't people who are unbalanced resort to it for attention?

Talking dirty is one thing; you can do that in private. Am I going to recommend that you undress in front of your open window, or what?

We have a problem with language here, because the term "exhibitionist" has indeed been used to describe people who engage in nonconsensual behavior and who may fall afoul of the law for doing so. Ignoring the limits of consent creates problems – I recommend you practice your exhibitionism only where you know it's appropriate and wanted: in front of the mirror, with your lover(s), and in groups of like-minded show-offs and voyeurs.

THE INVENTION OF EXHIBITIONISM

Along with a lot of other words for differing sexual interests, the term "exhibitionism" traces its history to the nineteenth century, when scientists began to scrutinize human behavior in order to describe and categorize it more precisely. (A very interesting analysis of this time period is found in Michel Foucault's *The History Of Sexuality, Volume One*.) The medical profession itself became differentiated into those who dealt with the body and those whose studies emphasized the mind. Doctors started to consider certain behaviors as diseases that until then had been regarded as simply sinful or criminal – when special notice had been taken of them at all. In studying these behaviors, hoping to learn what "caused" them and whether they could be "cured," the doctors coined many new words and paid very minute attention to their patients' sex lives. Nice work if you can get it, eh? But many of them, for all their learning, had the same opinion of sexual variation that clergymen before them had: "It's deviant! If we can find a way to stop it, we will."

Dr. Richard von Krafft-Ebing spent a great deal of time in the late 1800s observing patients in insane asylums. Since virtually all the patients he saw masturbated (in public, since of course they had no privacy), the doctor determined that he had found the cause of insanity. Victorian families hadn't exactly been pro-masturbation even before he came along, but for some years after, his theories carried the day; children could now be threatened with insanity and the asylum if they persisted in what was termed "self-abuse."

Other sorts of sexual difference were reconceptualized and transformed into illness. People who desired partners of their own gender got a name: homosexual. People who weren't homosexual received the label "heterosexual." Some people didn't fit in those opposing categories; the term "bisexual" eventually evolved to help the doctors fit them into the schema.

Various sexual interests were observed and called "fetishes." This term mainly described erotic longing or arousal provoked by an object, a substance, or a physical characteristic. Shoes, fur, legs, and countless other things thus became classified as objects of desire – and desiring them, the doctors determined, constituted mental disease.

Books of case histories filled up with the symptoms of all these spicy new illnesses. The term "exhibitionism" was coined during this flurry of naming, and was paired with a matching deviation: "voyeurism." These were defined as "unnatural love of exhibiting oneself" and "unnatural love of watching," respectively. These exhibitionists usually did things like pulling their pants down at the dinner table, masturbating in church, or exposing themselves to unsuspecting passersby in the park. Voyeurs, for their part, never seemed to be around when an exhibitionist wanted to drop his or her drawers – they peeped almost exclusively on the unknowing or the unwilling.

No wonder these unfortunate folks came to the attention of the law and the doctors. Instead of getting their kicks with each other, they bothered unconsenting people – who found what they did not erotic but upsetting!

The many varieties of psychosexual orientation have been buffed and polished by the followers of Krafft-Ebing and his kind. Today they are called not illnesses but "paraphilias," which still implies deviance, since it means essentially "love or desire that is out of the ordinary." (To my mind, the question is, "Deviance from what?" since plenty of people engage in many of these essentially harmless behaviors.)

In the 1960s and 1970s some of the "deviants" began to speak out. Pressure from gay activists, angry that psychiatry considered homosexuality a maladjustment, led to a vote in 1973 at the American Psychiatric Association convention that removed same-sex attraction from the books, so to speak. *The Diagnostic and Statistical Manual* (DSM) is the psychiatric profession's reference book for mental illnesses and deviations. Now members of the S/M community – labeled by the nineteenth-century doctors as "sadists" and "masochists" – find themselves in a similar dialogue with mental health professionals. In 1994 these sexual lifestyles, practiced consensually, were removed from the DSM-III, and as I write these words another DSM revision is expected soon, probably with new alterations reflecting changing medical understanding, and cultural opinion, about erotic variations.

DESIRE AND CONSENT

Today a person will probably not receive the diagnosis "exhibitionist" from a psychiatrist or psychologist, suggesting s/he is pathological, unless their behavior is uncontrollable or, especially, nonconsensual. This really makes a great deal of sense – a person who forces their attentions on the unwilling suffers at best from pathologically poor social skills (and ignorance of the fact that they could get their erotic desires met by a consenting partner). At worst, they commit sexual abuse or rape.

If this society understood voyeuristic desire and could separate it from the issue of unwanted advances, sexual harassment, and other nonconsensual behavior, exhibitionism would seem less dangerous. But the flawed conclusions of those turn-of-the-century doctors still carry a lot of weight. Many still believe there are types of sex play that are inherently "unhealthy." Instead of decrying sexual fantasy, voyeurism, and people who enjoy being exhibitionistic, we should all recognize the real culprits for inappropriate behavior: nonconsensuality and poor communication. Bad sex education has a role here, too – it doesn't teach people that their sexual desires might be met positively by a consenting partner. When people are basically ashamed of sexual desires and unaware of sexual options, nonconsensual behavior can be the result.

So I exhort you to perform exhibitionism only in a context of consensuality partly to keep you out of trouble – some parts of the country have laws against things you might decide sound like fun – and partly to keep you from pestering the locals who aren't as adventurous as you and who don't want to see your underpants, much less what they cover up.

If you practice exhibitionism without the consent of the viewer because you think no one would ever willingly look at you, I'll bet you're wrong. No one is too old, too plump or skinny, too plain or unconventional-looking – in fact, too *anything* – to find a willing audience for their exhibitionistic desires. This book can help you figure out how to find that audience. Besides, is it really satisfying to show off for people who don't want to watch?

When I worked in the peep show I had a few visits from a dyed-in-the-wool exhibitionist – in fact, probably a card-carrying one, for he was on probation for exposing himself, which meant he was a registered sex offender. A well-dressed older businessman, he didn't look at all like anyone's stereotype of a sex criminal. He visited the peep show to get the dose of sexual attention that kept him going. He didn't behave any differently than other pleasant, polite customers, so I was happy to oblige. After all, I could help keep him out of jail.

But he told me that if his therapist learned of his peep show visits, he'd be found guilty of violating probation! This is too ironic for words, not to mention for good sense. A good sex therapist would have written this man a *prescription* to visit a peep show booth – but he had fallen afoul of the law and into the clutches of a backward-thinking court-appointed psychiatrist. Too many of the people in practice today read Krafft-Ebing's outrageous masturbation-makes-you-crazy book, *Psychopathia Sexualis*, as part of their training. Through the 1950s, and in some places even later, the book was standard reading at medical schools.

One caveat about therapeutic matters is especially relevant here. Beware of therapists or groups that specialize in treating sex addiction. Addiction is a concept that relates to the effects of chemicals in the body, and many professionals use the term irresponsibly – in the worst cases, manipulatively – when it comes to sex. Sexual compulsion may be an issue for some people, but it frequently disappears when they find an appropriate partner or venue for sexual satisfaction; sex addictionologists, though, will more likely attack the sexual behavior than help you find someone who wants to do it with you. Exhibitionism, voyeurism, and even masturbation are on many of these counselors' warning lists. They are part of an industry whose understanding of sexual variety is only half a degree removed from the simple-minded logic and Victorian moralism of Krafft-Ebing.

EXHIBITIONISM AS CULTURE

When we consider art, history, and fashion, thinking of exhibitionism as a problem, much less a "paraphilia" or a disease, makes very little sense. Exhibitionism and voyeurism are far from unusual. They are woven into the fabric of a great many cultures, from old Japanese paintings which show a third person peeping around the shoji screen at a pair of lovers, to today's billboards featuring pop stars in skivvies. Sexual showing off has added cultural spice since ancient times; in some contexts, as in the erotic rituals of some Goddess-worshiping cultures, it has even had religious significance.

We might agree that all sexual art has an exhibitionistic component, and certainly those who view it are voyeurs of a sort. Our mores may forbid blunt sex talk in polite society, but our museums and theaters provide the defense of high culture to nudity and sometimes explicit sex – hence Robert Mapplethorpe, who produced lush photographs of sexual images that turned him on; Annie Sprinkle, who performed an autoerotic ritual on stage; and the many other artists whose work is inspired, at least sometimes, by sex.

Then there was Cicciolina, former porn star and Italian parliamentarian. She was refused entry into the U.S. because of her high profile in the sex business – until she married artist Jeff Koons. Then she visited in high style, along with her new husband and his show featuring nude portraits he painted of her. What a life for an exhibitionist! (They've since broken up, but she is undoubtedly on to other adventures.)

Yet the sexual content of explicit art is said to be acceptable because the artist has alchemically transmuted base material into capital-A Art; and the runway's ever-shifting array of alluring, skimpy, sexually suggestive clothing can be purchased for Fashion's sake, not to send an erotic message or get a thrill. Many a voyeur has been confused by a sexy package of clothing containing a very sex-negative person! We can't always tell whether the eroticism is incidental or the whole point.

"The Exhibitionist Species"

Writer Brian Alexander has recently spent many months combing the country to take the temperature of its current sexual mores. To hear him tell it, he's seen elements of exhibitionism pretty much everywhere.

"We are, the sociologist and sexologist Pepper Schwartz told me several years ago, 'an exhibitionist species,'" says Brian. "After having traveled all over the United States in search of the many and varied ways Americans are thumbing their noses at our reputation for being repressed prudes for my book America Unzipped, I have to agree. I suppose you could argue that most species are exhibitionist – I mean those red rumps on chimps and all that bird plumage are there for a reason – but people are generally taught that showing off your sexual self is a bad thing. There are laws, you know.

"But to one degree or another most of us do it. Some of us do it with Porsches, some with cleavage-baring tops and Wonderbras, some with a sweat sock in their man briefs. A few do it by getting naked and/or having sex more or less in public. For example, one night in a Seattle sex club I watched a couple *in flagrante* on a chaise. Now, of course, this couple could have simply done exactly the same thing they were doing at home and not had to listen to Trent Reznor screaming over and over again while they did it. Or they could have rented a nice hotel suite and ordered up some bubbly from room service. But that would miss the point. They *wanted* other people to see them doing it. They wanted witnesses.

"Schwartz, a professor at the University of Washington, told me why," Brian continues. "'I think to some extent people feel underappreciated, especially in a more urban society. It's hard to feel sexually special, and so I think a lot more people want to be ogled whether they are handsome or beautiful or not.'

"Susan, another exhibitionist I met, and whom I profile in the book, explained it to me this way. 'Something I am not interested in is losing my sexuality.' But middle age was upon her and though she is attractive, she is not holding her breath for that call from Playboy. Keeping hold of her sexual persona is a goal. 'For a woman, that is more of a fight,' she says. So she takes pictures of herself and places them online or trades them with like-minded people who shower her with compliments. For Susan, and I think for many other exhibitionists, witnesses make their sexual adventures more real, affirm their allure. Exhibitionism is like a signal flare saying 'I'm here and I am hot.' This can seem desperate, but I didn't get the impression Susan is an especially desperate person. Or if she is, she has lots of company.

"Every summer on Lake of the Ozarks, in Missouri, hard-drinking boaters gather in a place called Party Cove. By noon, many are naked. Sex isn't unusual, though both nakedness and sex are illegal in public and you could go to jail. Yet it's very tempting, apparently.

"Mardi Gras in New Orleans has come to seem as much about women pulling up their shirts as it is about jazz and the coming of Lent.

"In October, Key West hosts something called Fantasy Fest, a sort of exhibitionist's paradise.

"In the United Kingdom, exhibitionistic sex is often called 'dogging,' and so much dogging is going on in some locales that public parks have been closed.

"There is now so much exhibitionism going on that I sometimes think it might be refreshing if everybody just kept their shirts on. I know that may not be what you want to hear in a book that is all about exhibitionism, but after spending a year wandering around the United States meeting people who are enthusiastic exhibitionists, I began to miss the allure of seduction, the slow tease, the mystery. That makes me horribly old fashioned among sexual hipsters, some of whom seem to think I am making a moral judgment. I'm not. If you want to show off to people who are willing to see you show off, have at it. But so many women are now lifting their shirts, with the slightest encouragement, that some of the fun has gone missing.

"I wonder sometimes, if, instead of desperation, there might not be a little 'me-too-ism' going on. Once a critical mass of people break a taboo, nobody wants to be left behind. Twenty-five years ago any talk of oral sex was radical. Now it's sitcom fare. Performing sexually for an audience is still certainly radical for many people, probably most, but it is now common enough that everyday folk have become gleeful crotch flashers and a few happily perform live acts.

"The term sexologists use to describe this sort of mainstreaming is 'permission-giving.' Well, there is a lot of permission-giving going on. We have given ourselves permission to declare to the world that we are sexual beings. It's not exactly the reading of the Declaration of Independence on the courthouse steps, but exhibitionism is, certainly, a public declaration of one's sexual heat."

Brian ends, almost mournfully, "I'm just not so sure such declarations are that interesting any more" – and he may be right, culturally. Surely we're no longer the prudish nation he set out to visit, knowing in his heart, I think, that this was one myth that wouldn't be hard to debunk. We're less prudish, in fact, than we were the year *Exhibitionism for the Shy* was first published, in 1995. Back then, the book rode a wave of social change as the US began to recover (especially in my town, San Francisco) from years of conservatives at the top and fear and repression everywhere (because of AIDS, if for no other reason). Perhaps the pendulum might have swung back again after the Clinton years – if it hadn't been for the Internet. Now we are a different country, sexually – well, we're not, in fact, but we *are* more open, something Brian found in every region, in large cities and small towns, when he went out searching for the sexual USA of today.

In one way, though, I disagree with his conclusion – because even in a friskier and more open society, some of us remain shy. Not reserved but dedicated to the arts of seduction and the tease – *shy*, painfully so, with far less access to sexual fun and erotic community than our more brazen sisters and brothers. If everyone else seems to think it's their birthright to be on *Girls Gone Wild*, the least we can do is try to give you greater access to your own sexual power and pleasure. And it may be that you're a little shy even with yourself... so first, you'll need to hop into the shower, soap up sensually, and serenade yourself with a heartfelt rendition of "Getting to Know You."

THE IMPORTANCE OF WHAT TURNS YOU ON

Just as some people are more homosexual or heterosexual than others, some have more or less of the exhibitionist in their makeup. I'm using the term now as I defined it earlier, "deliberately presenting yourself in an erotic way" – and I'll add an important component, "for your own enhanced sexual arousal." Our own enjoyment and arousal in exhibitionism make it erotically powerful for us, as opposed to something we engage in simply to please or attract another. Emphasizing our own sexual response also helps differentiate erotic from fashion and from the sort of outgoing, show-offy behavior – like Britney without underwear – that, although it may have nothing to do with eroticism, sometimes also gets labeled exhibitionism.

It's part of the misunderstanding handed down from the Victorians that we think exhibitionism is nothing more (or less) than willy-wagging done in broad daylight in the town square. On the contrary, you can be a sexual show-off even if no one ever sees you. You can enhance masturbation with an exhibitionistic frisson; you can engage in erotically outgoing behavior with only one partner. This continuum extends to multiple partners and/or public play – but most exhibitionists will never go that far. Please do not think your exhibitionistic "credentials" depend on your exceeding your own comfort levels!

For people who fit my above definition, exhibitionism - like voyeurism - can shape sexual identity. For us, erotic delight in being viewed is a deep, gut-level component of our sexuality. If we were unable to have it, our experience of our sexuality would be substantially diminished.

Preferences for any aspect of sex that we find exceedingly important or crucial to our erotic response define our sexualities far more completely than labels like gay, straight, and bisexual. Knowing only a person's sexual orientation can create mistaken, downright stereotypical assumptions, made worse if we base our suppositions on gender-role biases. It helps to know more about a person than whether they like men, women, or both - particularly if they're a potential sex partner!

Take the classic foot fetish, for example, and imagine a foot fetishist who's a heterosexual male. We could show him a porn video that a wide range of other heterosexual men have rated as very arousing. But if all the women in the video wore shoes, and his arousal depended upon seeing a woman's bare feet, he would probably not find the video a turn-on. Perhaps he wouldn't even find an individual woman attractive unless he saw and liked her feet. Attraction to feet is as central to this man's sexual make-up as the fact that he's male or that he's heterosexual. I would call foot fetishism part of his sexual identity.

Or, central to the theme of this book, consider a woman who finds it a turn-on to dress provocatively in public, seductively eat a meal with her fingers while her partner watches, and keep the lights and her garter belt and stockings on when they go to bed. The gender of her partner may not matter, since heterosexual, lesbian, and bisexual women alike may engage in exhibitionistic behavior. If this woman ends up with a partner who finds her outgoing antics shocking, anti-feminist, or too overwhelming - or even one who simply doesn't like to watch - she may find her sexual response affected if she tones down her exhibitionism to please her partner. Or she may lose her partner because they're not sexually compatible.

This type of sexual incompatibility is common. Too often we don't even try at the outset of a relationship to determine whether our partner's sexual style will match our own - in fact, many never even think in these terms at all. We figure love will find a way – and sometimes it does, but often it needs some help. Lovers who find themselves fundamentally incompatible in this way will need to identify together what they do share and strategize ways to satisfy the desires they don't. As an alternative to going through this process, it's much easier to know which erotic activities are central to your happiness, and look for a partner who wants to share them with you. It's also easier to talk about these early in a relationship than to let a long-time partner in on your sexual secrets, since the person who has loved you, and thought they knew you completely, often finds a years-late revelation more than just shocking: this can feel like an insulting blow to the very heart of a couple's intimacy.

The Courage to Value Sexual Satisfaction

It would require some radical changes in our culture's ways of thinking about sex and relationships for everyone to agree to the importance of this kind of sexual compatibility when we couple. Yet if this value became much more widespread, think how many of the painful dramas of partnered life might lose their fuel. Especially today, when authorities encourage us to avoid sexually transmitted diseases through monogamy, sexually incompatible couples face cruel challenges that too many find themselves ill-prepared to meet. (Personally, I don't suggest monogamy alone as a strategy to avoid AIDS or other STDs. Ostensibly monogamous people have contracted HIV from their partners. Sexually transmitted diseases can be avoided by getting good at, and insisting upon, safe sex, and a couple with great communications skills is in far better shape, monogamous or not, than a couple who can't bring up difficult sexual subjects with one another.)

What would have to change for us as a people to prioritize sex partner compatibility? We'd have to give more priority to sexual pleasure and satisfaction for everyone. We'd also have to get over our hesitancy regarding sexual communication. Somehow, with no official encouragement to say anything more than "no" (except when we're supposed to say "yes"), we are expected to develop the ability to communicate intimately and in detail with a partner about a subject many people have never heard discussed aloud in anything but a joking tone. Too many feel shame when sex doesn't go right or isn't as exciting as we thought it would be – isn't good sex supposed to come naturally when we meet someone we love?

We hear mixed messages about sex today: women learn to be sexy to attract a partner, but we're still not really supposed to explore, or act sexually knowledgeable or assertive – in many cases it's not even acknowledged that we have our own erotic needs and desires. Rather contrarily, both men and women are supposed to be sexually sophisticated, but too much of that is still considered immoral or kinky. Many of us lack access to good, factual information about sex, which gets in the way of whatever sophistication we aspire to. We get sex information from pornography, which is stigmatized and in danger of censorship by the same folks who fight the dissemination of good sex information, especially to the young. Young people who have consensual sex are oftentimes still punished. When we hear youth and sex mentioned in the same breath, the young usually appear as victims. Women, too, are often portrayed as victims of male sexual urges, as if we do not have sexual desires of our own (and as if most men don't control what my mother called their "urges" perfectly well). The culture is sexually schizophrenic, obsessed and repressed, and even those of us who have personally escaped sexual repression have to live side by side with people who vilify our comfort.

Exploring sexual fascinations can greatly heighten the pleasure we get from sex, and heightened pleasure in sex can have a positive effect on our entire lives. Worrying if we're normal, measuring ourselves against an arbitrary standard, is less helpful than asking, "Am I happy?" "Am I injuring myself or others?" or "Do I feel supported in my sexuality?" If you really want to know what your neighbors are doing, chances are they're wondering if they're normal, too. Since this is such a commonly asked question, the answer is probably yes!

I have a theory that many people who don't enjoy sex much have some key component to their sexuality that they have either not discovered yet or that makes them so uncomfortable that they avoid experiencing it, maybe even resist thinking about it. In a society which doesn't give much support to either the sexual "deviant" or the ordinary person who just wants to explore sex openly, it can be hard to muster the courage it takes to make sexual happiness a priority. The kind of erotic preference I'm talking about here functions as a sexual sparkplug, and people who cut themselves off from its energy because of fear or repression shut down the supply of the stuff that makes their engines run.

If you or a partner haven't yet found your source of erotic energy, exhibitionism or voyeurism may inspire you. Maybe sexy talk will do the trick. Any outgoing behaviors can help you sidestep your reticence and dive right in. You can enjoy exhibitionism and voyeurism regardless of what else is important to you sexually. You may also find important clues to your sources of arousal in your sexual orientation (the gender/s you erotically desire), your own gender identity, your fetishes and fantasies, and any preferences you have about dominance and submission or other forms of erotic power play.

The fantasy personas you access in your talk and play may provide important clues to your core turn-on, if you don't repress them or the information about your sexuality they can provide. Remember, sex is not rational; our desire taps into the same kind of deep, half-hidden sea from which our dreams come. Besides being arousing, erotic talk can help you put words to fantasies, give life to aspects of yourself you haven't really met, and access submerged ideas in the well of your secret imagination.

It wouldn't surprise me to hear that you fear the well is full of monsters; so few of us get encouragement, even from our lovers, to really explore sex. Society doesn't respect us for it, and in most of our minds the bugaboos from the pages of *Psychopathia Sexualis* still lurk.

"Don't think about it, don't look at pictures of it, don't try it, don't associate with people who do it": the gist of the message most of us get is clear. The single most common question we ask about sex in this country is "Am I normal?" The bats in our belfry are all those "cases" whose sexual desires fascinated and repulsed Krafft-Ebing.

In fact, each man or woman who bulldozed through the rigid boundaries of Victorian sexual propriety could be considered a role model. Their sexual satisfaction was so important to them that they had to find ways to gratify it, even when this exposed them to societal scrutiny or legal consequences and otherwise disrupted their lives. Today we're more fortunate: we do have more support than they did. Since their day, social movements have arisen which advocate for our right to experience our own sexuality, not mold it into somebody else's idea of what it should be. Each of the doctors' solemnly-named labels describes a set of erotic possibilities that we who are sex-positive can let out of the asylum and potentially revel in.

Those sexual identities the sex scientists named – not only heterosexuality, homosexuality, lesbianism, and bisexuality, but exhibitionism and voyeurism, masochism and sadism, the various fetishisms, and many other fascinations – can all be lived out today in relationships with consenting (in fact, enthusiastic!) partners. Unlike the institutionalized Victorians who gave different sexual preferences their bad raps, we are in control of our own sexualities. We have access to information and support – the availability of which in those times might have been enough to keep the fetishists out of Krafft-Ebing's line of vision and happily living their own lives.

Happily, too, youth culture today seems far less hung up in sexual judgment than at previous times – though this communication-savvy generation has created its own mores, since most of the people in high school, college, and beyond were subjected to terrible sex education, non-pleasure-oriented and larded with sex-negative attitudes.

Exhibitionism is about projecting and feeling our eroticism. It's true that society still doesn't give us much credit or show us much esteem when we do; in fact, we may have to muster up enough courage to transgress the boundaries of propriety our family, religious background, and community claim to uphold. The promise of sexual satisfaction, though, can help us jump a lot of fences – and arousal and gratification are the direct payoffs an exhibitionist seeks. We are worlds away from the asylum-bound exhibitionists the 19th century doctors studied (though if you think dropping your pants and jacking off in church is a hot fantasy, I don't blame you); we're in charge of our own sexuality, and we're going to learn to show off with a lot more finesse.

3

I Like to Watch – And Listen

One way to start getting to know your bold, erotic inner self is especially easy for shy people; you can watch, exploring your responses to the boldly sexy people in your life. In other words, to learn more about becoming an exhibitionist, watch others who already are. Become a voyeur.

Voyeurs and exhibitionists are made for each other. People who like to talk dirty have natural mates, too - the French call them *écouteurs*, or "listeners." This has implications for you in your search for partners, of course, and for your sexual possibilities in already-existing relationships. Sometimes to get the most out of your erotic charge on exhibitionism you have to help awaken your partner's voyeurism. It may be easier to do so if you understand and enjoy voyeurism yourself.

IN SEARCH OF SEXINESS

What do you look for? Start with people, no matter how they dress, who carry themselves unselfconsciously, even proudly. Some women and men have a natural eroticism that does not rely on sexy clothes, makeup, even their degree of physical attractiveness. If you don't consider yourself very attractive, try especially to tune in to the sexiness of people who don't conform to the rigid "young-thin-pretty"/"tall-dark-handsome" cultural norms – if possible, people who look something like you. If your physical self-image is low, perhaps you can team up with a partner or a friend and get them to point people out to you.

So far you have people whose erotic attractiveness resides especially in their bearing and how they appear to feel about themselves. Now look at modes of dress and presentation. What kinds of clothes are sexy, and how do the people you notice wear them? With dress, we begin to notice people who are more than likely exhibitionistic, not just attractive or self-assured. Common modes of exhibitionistic dress include tight, body-conforming clothes; bright colors and/or patterns; unusual materials like leather, shiny metallic fabric, and fur; and clothing that shows lots of skin, whether because it's skimpy or because it's sheer. People wearing these draw attention to themselves, usually erotically.

Long, flowing, billowy clothes can have an exhibitionistic effect too, even though they're the opposite of short/tight/skimpy garb. It's all in the fabric – and the way the person wears it. Sometimes gender-ambiguous dress also has an exhibitionistic – and, depending on the viewer, an erotic – effect.

To illustrate the importance of how a person feels inside his or her clothes, see if you can also spot people who look uncomfortable when dressed erotically. This isn't hard to do these days, since many popular styles have been skimpy and sexy, and not everyone wears them with equal aplomb. Never wear something you don't feel good in just to be erotic – it will work against the effect you're trying to create.

Finally, note exhibitionistic behavior on the street. Lovers who kiss long and lingeringly, right out in front of God and everybody. People with an especially sexy walk. People who look directly at you and smile as they pass. When you go out to a club, you can easily pick out the exhibitionists on the dance floor.

This is far from a dry research project if you go about it with some inspiration. I'm not suggesting that you look for exhibitionistic role models and simply copy their style – though you could get lucky, I suppose, and find the perfect person to emulate, or you could mimic so well that the style you borrowed would seem perfectly natural to you. Some highly attractive, "put-together" people have undoubtedly done exactly this – researched clothes and make-up and demeanor to the degree that they become expert at attracting others. Whether they personally get any pleasure from it is another matter.

Let your inner voyeur out to play. Who doesn't occasionally walk down the street and notice someone magnetic to watch? We are a visually-oriented species in a very voyeuristic culture, and all of us have plenty of opportunity to explore the responses we have to what we see. Mother may tell us, "Don't stare!" – but most of us are sometimes inclined to disobey her, and I recommend that you seek out opportunities to do just that.

Your mission: discover what you enjoy, what attracts you, and what you respond to erotically. You can do this in many, many contexts. If you fear your brazen stare will get you in trouble when you ride public transit (and it might, if you don't stay aware of propriety and consent issues), you can visit a burlesque show or an exotic dance emporium, or go to feast your eyes on Boylesque or the Chippendales when they come to town. If you feel too shy to turn your voyeuristic gaze onto live people who might notice you looking, you can practice with movies, TV, the Internet and photos. You don't have to seek out sex magazines to see beautifully-posed erotic pictures these days – major companies use striking, sexy images to create pleasant, even erotic, associations with their brand-name products, and you can find these pictures in virtually any general-interest publication.

LEARNING TO LOVE IT

Many of us have been warned away from looking and the potential pleasures of the erotic gaze. Whether or not we heeded Mother's admonition, many cautions and beliefs have influenced us. It is still common, for instance, to hear that women don't respond sexually to visual stimulation as men do, although statistics estimate that thirty-some percent of women do report such stimulation. That number, from a study conducted fifty years ago, when women had far less access to sexually suggestive or explicit imagery, is doubtless very low. Since then, some feminists have suggested that voyeuristic looking "objectifies" the person being observed and somehow harms them – at least in the case of males looking at females.

Some people incorporate beliefs like this into their sexual reticence. "Why should I pursue exhibitionism?" a heterosexual man might wonder.

"I've heard that women won't respond to me anyway; touching and romance are more important to them." Or a woman might hesitate to explore exhibitionism because she fears she will thus contribute to her own objectification and possibly even compromise her own safety.

It may help a hesitant person to understand the pleasures of sexual looking "from the inside" before it feels safe or permissible to play the companion role of exhibitionist. Accessing the pleasures of voyeurism can help make exhibitionism seem more natural.

Becoming more voyeuristic can teach fledgling exhibitionists more about the chemistry and turn-on between themselves and voyeurs than they could learn from exhibitionism alone. An understanding of the voyeur's response can help us get the kind of exhibitionistic attention we crave. Proficiency in any kind of sex play can be more easily achieved if the one doing it knows how it feels when it is done to them; so a show-off looking for a responsive partner will have more luck, and presumably more pleasure, if s/he knows what to play to. Proficiency aside, it can increase our arousal to know from experience what our partner is responding to and how it feels. The complex interplay that creates good, fulfilling sex gets fuel from this sort of sexual sharing.

Of course, it's important to remember that any aspect of sexuality has many facets; your voyeuristic turn-ons may not be exactly like anyone else's, just as different individuals prefer very different kinds of genital touch and engage in very different fantasies. You'll want to communicate with your partners about what you like and what they like. But the depths of your understanding of each other can increase if you both know from experience the basis of each other's response.

This advice cuts both ways. If your partner is primarily voyeuristic and encouraging you in your exhibitionism, you have a wonderful opportunity to grow into sexual boldness with an appreciative partner. But has he or she ever showed off for you? The two of you can ease into voyeurism and exhibitionism together by leaving the lights on and your eyes open when you make love, being naked around each other more often, or by watching each other while you get undressed. Of course you can explore your voyeuristic responses with a sex industry professional or pictures on a page – but why not explore them with your lover or a friend as well?

This holds equal relevance for talking and listening. To help conquer reticence about uttering dirty talk in bed (or elsewhere), we can explore our own turn-on about listening to explicit words and spoken fantasies. You're far less likely to think, "I can't say those words!" when those words have contributed to your own arousal and orgasm.

Let's consider some examples of learning to be a voyeur to see how it can affect exhibitionistic sexuality. Suppose a woman decides she wants to learn striptease as a way to attract her lover's focused erotic attention. She goes to a class or buys a how-to video, and this teaches her the moves, but she wants to do more research. She decides to have a little adventure, and one day she leaves work early, meets her best girlfriend for a drink, and they go to watch the show at an upscale strip club.

She wants to know, for one thing, how the strippers dress and what kind of music they dance to. She finds that she has a favorite kind of costume – she likes the dancers who come onstage looking rather demure, but who wear lavish, sexy lingerie under their dresses. She has a button-down dress that would be perfect, she realizes, and she knows a shop that sells lingerie she'd feel very sexy in. She doesn't like the music some of the dancers use – too fast and loud – but others have recordings of older jazzy tunes that perfectly complement their acts.

She watches the dancers rather dispassionately at first – interested in their outfits and moves, but not turned on to any of the women. Finally a dancer takes the floor who exudes an eroticism she can't help but respond to. The dancer flows with the slow, throbbing music she's picked; she strips very deliberately and makes plenty of eye contact with the members of the audience, who all seem mesmerized. Our dance student's skin prickles as she realizes how much the stripper has aroused her – then smiles, because it's exactly the way she plans to make her lover feel when she does her own private striptease at home.

Here's another scenario. A rather shy young man is having the most wonderful affair of his life; his new sweetie has had more sexual experience than he has, and she's made it clear that she'd like him to talk while they have sex. But this request makes him uncomfortable. He's seen porn movies in which the men talk dirty, and they're always telling the women to suck their big cocks and things like that; he doesn't feel like ordering his partner around. In fact, he'd rather she told him what to do occasionally. So he resists.

Then one day she rents a porn movie for them to watch together. One of the actresses talks a blue streak, and our tongue-tied friend notices something different about it – she doesn't follow the "Suck my clit, fuck my cunt" formula; instead she simply describes what she's doing and feeling and what's being done to her. "Ohh, you're touching my pussy!" she croons. "Oh, you're sliding your wet fingers inside!"

The presence of his lover, the eroticism of the actress, and her sweetly-spoken dirty talk cast their spell on our shy friend, but what really makes him hard is his realization that what works for the actress will work for him, too. Soon he whispers in his lover's ear, "Baby, you're touching my cock! It feels so hard and ready for you! Oh, if you stroke me that way I'll come!"

He can tell from his sweetheart's response that his shy days are numbered.

PRACTICING ON PORN

It's no coincidence that our shy man found in porn the key to his erotic inspiration; pornography is made for voyeurs and calculated to arouse. This doesn't mean that every image and scenario in porn will arouse you: probably quite the contrary. But visual porn can be the ideal exhibitionist while you learn to watch; it doesn't talk back, get shy, have expectations, or object to being looked at. I don't mean that it has qualities that make it a superior choice for you as a voyeur, just that in the beginning of your voyeuristic career watching porn movies and looking at erotic pictures are great ways to get comfortable with looking and getting aroused, without interpersonal distractions. You can transfer these skills to your relationship with a consenting partner later; you can watch or be watched to your heart's content once you've gotten comfortable in these roles.

If you've watched little or no pornography, you may have heard that it is rife with scenes of violence or abuse towards women. In fact, while acted-out abuse can be found, most of today's porn is simply sexually explicit. Porn has been widely criticized for violent-seeming content and most producers of porn responded to the criticism. Look for story-based porn or research the genre with the help of Violet Blue's book *The Smart Girl's Guide to Porn.* The real heroine of today's heterosexual porn is the sexually assertive and responsive woman, and there are too many examples of this kind of sex film to name.

In porn targeting gay men, of course, there are no female characters at all. Years ago I felt uncomfortable watching heterosexual porn yet loved the male-on-male variety, and I've heard many other women say the same. And bisexual porn tends to feature the good-looking younger actor who's a staple in gay porn, plus women. For a genre with something for just about everyone, it's surprising not to find more bi movies on the shelf.

You may want to restrict your viewing, at least at first, to certain porn genres – lesbian, all-male, women-made, or those featuring types of sex you particularly love. In this culture, where sexual curiosity too often mutates into sexual shame, we often find our first exposure to porn uncomfortable or shocking. After all, we know it's supposed to be dirty. We haven't had the opportunity to get used to the sight of people fucking right in front of us!

Over time, though, those shameful feelings can fade – unless, of course, we've incorporated them into what we like about porn. Some folks don't want to watch at all if they can't revel (or even wallow!) in how nasty and naughty they are for watching such filthy stuff.

If you're new to porn, just pay attention to your feelings as you begin to watch. You may prefer to do this all alone – if so, remember that many people use porn as an adjunct to masturbation, and you might want to see how that feels. If you have someone in your life who likes porn or is willing to supportively experiment with you, you may prefer to view with him or her. On the other hand, if having someone with you makes you feel embarrassed, self-conscious, or defensive, consider starting solo.

Notice what you find erotic. Do the performers engage in sexual practices that interest or inspire you? You can get plenty of fantasy material from porn without ever having to try specific activities yourself – that you like to watch it on screen is enough. Your sexuality, alone or with partners, can be enhanced by those images: even if you've never been in a gang bang or had anal sex, you can still think about it while you masturbate and talk about it in bed while you play.

Notice what you find anti-erotic too. If something really pushes your buttons, you can choose to avoid images of it and let your partner know it's not something you feel comfortable sharing in fantasy. Alternatively, you can try to figure out just what it is that bothers you, maybe learning something important about your sexual responses in the process. Sex educators often recommend watching more of the button-pushing material so you can become increasingly neutral about it, and this might be a particularly useful strategy if you're bothered by something that means a lot to your partner. If some of the images you find distressing are also turn-ons for you, it's possible you've stumbled onto something you're deeply ashamed to find erotic. Remember that a tremendously wide range of fantasy material can sexually arouse humans, and finding something erotic is not the same thing as wanting to do it in real life or even endorsing it! You might benefit from reading more about fantasy and the part it plays in sexuality, and Dr. Jack Morin has published a wonderful book called *The Erotic Mind* which examines people's attractions to things like shame, fear, and guilt: elements of experience you'd expect to damp down eroticism, but which for some people do the absolute opposite.

Also, notice *whom* you find erotic. This can tip you off not only to enticing fantasy partners and characteristics you'd find alluring in real life – it can also lead you to dig deeper into the substance of your attraction. What do you like about this character (either the individual or the qualities s/he displays)? Her red hair? His big dick? The way she strokes her own nipples while she's getting fucked? The way he insistently holds his partner's gaze? Her tone of voice? The things he says? Her resemblance to your best friend's mom, whom you always had a crush on? His gentle demeanor? The way she's dressed? You get the idea.

You can like – or dislike – all kinds of things in a porn movie. Don't analyze it like fine cinema (generally, it isn't). Pay attention to the things that erotically move you or interest you. You can find yourself attracted to characters, their body types, the way they talk or move, their timing, the erotic roles they play, the environment, the kind of sex they have, and the way they have it, among many other things. These are all fantasy building blocks, and the more of them you recognize, the richer your fantasy life can be. When you want to show off your eroticism, you'll have a clearer sense of what you think looks and feels erotic. When it's time to talk dirty, you'll have a wealth of things to say. Lots of phone sex workers – professional hot talkers – watch porn to give them ideas. I suggest you go one step further and comb porn for the elements that make it hot for you.

Here are some signs that your body is responding to one or more of these many elements. Look for erections (if you're female, did you know your clitoris gets erect when aroused, like a penis does? If you touch it you may find it's grown firmer and feels bigger than it does when you're in an unaroused state). Wet pussies, too, of course – though women are very different in the amount of vaginal lubrication they produce. Other signs of arousal are feeling squirmy or fidgety, a flushed, warm face or other body parts, clenching or fluttering pubococcygeal or other muscles, and changes in your breathing and heart rates. Even if your head tells you you're not turned on, if you notice these bodily responses, the porn is doing something right!

Notice one more thing – with whom do you identify? I don't just mean "males" or "females," although that's useful – and don't think that a woman can't erotically identify with a man and vice versa. Maybe it has nothing to do with the character's gender – you just like the erotic personality the actor presents: a prowling sex fiend, a tender virgin, an insatiable temptress, a sexual athlete who can fuck all night. Maybe you want the kind of sex they get to have; many heterosexual men like to watch lesbian porn not because they fantasize about bursting in and fucking all the women (though that can be a fun fantasy, too), but because they perceive woman-woman sex as more sensuous and full-body than the mostly penis- and performance-oriented sex men get to have in porn films.

On the other hand, maybe you easily identify with an actor's gender and the way he or she expresses it. You may identify with a character of your own gender based on the way s/he expresses gender characteristics you find especially erotic. For example, a shy man may identify with a sexually assertive man, or a reserved woman with an insatiable woman. You may identify with actors who present themselves sexually the way you feel you already do.

Alternatively you may have a transgender fantasy, an erotic curiosity about "how the other half lives" (this need not be an indication that in real life you want to change your gender, by the way). You may have a fantasy in which you trade in your sexual orientation for a moment by imagining yourself the other gender (the way I did when, watching male-male porn, I fantasized that I was a gay man). In your fantasy you may see yourself without any gender at all, or feel like both at once, or some gender other than male or female. (If this idea intrigues or feels librating to you, I recommend the fun, charming, thought-provoking work of Kate Bornstein, especially *My Gender Workbook*.)

EXHIBITIONISM VS. OBJECTIFICATION

I am certain that my pleasure at working in the peep show had to do with the fact that there I could indulge my voyeurism and my exhibitionism at the same time. I had already discovered that I loved masturbating watching porn videos. I had also discovered the pleasure in being watched while I masturbated. I hadn't done a lot of exploring both pleasures simultaneously, though, until I was ensconced in my little red booth where I put on shows for customers who simultaneously put on jack-off shows for me. Without exception, I had less fun and was less turned on with those customers who wanted only to watch. It was a complex response loop – not only did I get to indulge in voyeurism with the customers who jacked off, I also got – ahem! – hard evidence that they responded to my exhibitionism. I enjoyed those few customers who wanted only to be watched while they showed off for me, but something was missing when they didn't want to watch me too.

I had the same experience there with talking dirty. It was always more fun when they talked back.

Perhaps to really relish a peep show or porn career you have to be a dyed-in-the-wool exhibitionist; for some people, it would be discomfiting to know that strangers are masturbating to memories or pictures of you. The fear of being sexually pleasing to another person in that way – without a relationship, without mutuality – is at the heart of many women's worries about exhibitionism and objectification. This fear has also become the seldom-acknowledged basis of some feminists' political stance about these issues.

Do women in the sex industry suffer from the attentions of voyeurs? Is it a negative experience to be "objectified" in this way?

I have framed the question in a way the people who object to objectification never would. Note that I specifically called the folks who pay to watch strippers, peep show workers, and porn models "voyeurs." Sex work critics are much more likely to call them "men," and to imply that watching porn and staring at women's bodies is integral to male sexuality. This neatly sidesteps the fact that many sex workers are men, too. It's true that most female as well as male sex workers' customers are men, for sociological and possibly socio-biological reasons (but some women certainly do enjoy client-side participation in the sex industry). However, they are mostly voyeuristic men – they share a particular sexual interest, a strong focus on watching. Many other men express little or no interest in this sort of sexual entertainment. Further, who ever suggests that exhibitionism is one reason some sex workers like their work? Those of us who find potential for pleasure and arousal in our work situations can be expected to have a different take than those who don't.

Certainly not every woman – or man – in the sex business is an exhibitionist. Some of the women at the peep show found nothing arousing about the situation except the paycheck. But many who assume it would feel degrading to fuck before a camera or dance naked for strangers are not the least bit exhibitionistic. How, then, could they understand that such activities could be exciting to those of us who do eroticize sexual show-offery? (Some of them may also be ashamed of their own voyeuristic turn-on.)

There can be no doubt that some phone sex workers, erotic video performers, and exotic dancers are the most professional and effective exhibitionists in the land. Later we'll talk to some of them to learn which tricks of their trade are useful for "civilians." I introduce you to them to give shy and brazen people alike an understanding of the special skills and pleasures of people who are sexually outgoing.

Maybe you're thinking, "How can this help me? I'm too old or too fat for anyone to want to look at me; I can't even dance. Thinking about strippers and porn stars just makes me feel inadequate." For now, remember that you're learning to watch – for pleasure, to find your own hot spots in images, characters, sexual situations, and types of language, and to check out behaviors and fantasies you may want to incorporate into your own life. The purpose of looking at the experience of sex workers isn't to urge you to compare yourself to them, but so you'll take a closer look at what they do. Phone sex workers can be expert erotic sirens no matter what they look like – you didn't think those handsome men and buxom beauties in the phone sex ads are the actual people who answer the phone, did you? Sorry to burst your bubble!

And please don't be too convinced that no one wants to look at you. Some genres of porn rely on over-50 women, plus-plus sizes, hairy bodies, and many other physical styles that the culture as a whole does not code as automatically desirable. Exhibitionistic sexuality does not depend on youth, physical perfection, or any particular visual cue. Dwelling on what you look like is a great excuse for neglecting to explore how erotic you can feel. That feeling, not the specific visual you present to the world, is the source of your pleasure, and if you focus on negative thoughts about yourself, you'll miss it.

Porn movie star Nina Hartley is the most outspoken and articulate spokesperson for exhibitionistic sex workers – those who are frank that their performances give them sexual pleasure, and that they eroticize performing. Nina is one of the top stars in the nation because, besides being an attractive, sexy woman, she enjoys her work as only an exhibitionist can. I once attended a workshop of pro-feminist men as they agonized over pornography. (Was it harmful? Did it objectify women?) One brave guy spoke up in favor of porn, and said the reason he'd learned to feel comfortable with it was Nina. He had heard enough about her to know that he could respect her progressive politics – probably a more important point in this crowd than in others! – but he loved Nina's performances because she so clearly brings joy and enthusiasm to her work. Seeing her on screen, he said, he could really tell that she wanted to be there. He didn't feel guilt about watching her perform because it was so plain to him that she was doing what she wanted to do.

I told Nina this story. "That means a lot to me," she said. "Once I acknowledged I had a need for the level of attention porn movies and dancing naked afford me, I got – and continue to get – a real charge out of helping people out or entertaining them in that way. When people look at me they usually then behave in a sexual manner. That's really gratifying. Plus I was always fascinated watching porn, and I knew that other people had to be watching it with the same intensity and detail that I was. So I'm also aware of the educational value in what I do."

This whole debate reminds me of President Jimmy Carter's confession that he felt lust in his heart. I think he was talking about objectification. I've grown very familiar with that feeling of lust, and I find it a pleasant experience that enhances my sexual feelings. I need never encroach on others – my "lust objects" – with my sexual desire. I think folks who decry sexual objectification simultaneously decry fantasy, for the vast majority of people, men as well as women, do nothing more with their voyeuristic crushes than masturbate and fantasize.

WATCHING AND LISTENING – MORE IDEAS

You can get a lot of material from porn that will help you talk dirty, even if the visuals don't especially attract you. You will hear some of the characters talking explicitly. You can respond to words and vocalization on top of noting what kinds of scenarios make you hot. You can close your eyes and just listen, making your own pictures in your head. If you're alone you can talk back, or join in the action in your imagination. You may want to describe porn scenarios to your partner later, or use them for a fantasy jumping-off place. "Hot talk" audio may also interest you, as may expert phone fantasy professionals. One-on-one chat lines provide a good forum for the écouteur, but the person on the other end will probably expect you to talk back. If you just want to listen, you might look for a party line where a number of people call in for a sort of telephone orgy. A sharp-eared wallflower at a "gathering" like this can learn a lot. Online versions of this exist as well, though hearing actual voices is, for the hot talk student, better than just watching sexy comments scroll by on your computer screen.

You may prefer other sex-industry options for watching and listening, like peep shows, phone sex lines, exotic dance clubs, and so on. Or you may prefer to watch erotic, but non-explicit, movies. Plenty of films have scenes which voyeurs will find delicious to watch and exhibitionists will find inspiring; some films even have scenes where characters watch others and/or exhibit themselves as part of the plot. A scene in "The Incredible Lightness of Being" features one woman photographing another, and I bet it will inspire you to get out the camera!

You may find you'd rather read erotic stories and supply the visual details in your mind; porn books can provide you a rich source of dirty words in action, too. You may enjoy looking around your everyday world with a voyeuristic eye to its erotic potential. You may already have an enthusiastic, exhibitionistic, sexy-talking partner to share your explorations with. In all cases, if you want to learn from voyeurism how to be an exhibitionist, if you want to learn from listening how to talk, stay alert to the many facets of your arousal, and with what and whom you identify. These will teach you what you want to do and what you want to say.

☾ **4** ☀

Learning To Show Off

Now that you've begun to explore the pleasure that can be had in erotic looking, it's time to delve into the pleasures of being looked *at*. Becoming comfortable with this has two steps, each of which can involve any number of permutations. First, you have to overcome your reticence – which for many of us distills down to fear that others won't really find us sexy, and furthermore that we'll look silly and embarrass ourselves if we try to present ourselves erotically. Second, you need to figure out which forms of exhibitionism work best for you. How do you feel most erotic, confident, and, most importantly, turned on?

THE FEAR OF GOING TOO FAR

Perhaps you've had experiences with voyeurism and exhibitionism that weren't pleasant for you. You saw a flasher in the park and felt frightened. You were pressured into watching explicit material and didn't enjoy it. A partner masturbated in front of you when you weren't expecting it and you felt uncomfortable. Someone pressured you into showing off. You dressed erotically and felt unpleasantly exposed.

All these situations are fairly common. What differentiates them from the sorts of experience we're exploring in this book is comfort and consent.

I don't recommend you do anything that makes you feel uncomfortable and to which you do not consent. If someone has pressured you into something, you might not have said no, but neither have you given clear consent. That's different from being nervous about doing something new, yet wholeheartedly willing to try it. The whole aim of this book is to help you identify things you'd *like* to try, even if the idea of doing so frightens you a little, and give you support for continuing them if you want to.

Remember that exhibitionism entails first enhancing your own erotic feelings. Then you can turn your attention to arousing a special someone, a few others, or everybody else, if that's what you want. If you begin by trying to please others you may succeed – but if you're not finding any pleasure in it, why bother? Fortunately, believing, or even pretending, you're something special lies at the heart of showing off, a feeling which can automatically pull you into the erotic moment. No matter how shy you are, if you can let erotic pleasure take you over anyhow, you become more sexually present and powerful – in short, you *become* someone special.

You can ease into exhibitionism, and you can go only as far as you want and then stay there happily. The most successful anti-sex lie told to us to curb our urges to explore – "You'll go too far! You won't be able to stop! You'll lose control!" – is nonsense. Conscious sexual development involves knowing when you want to stop just as much as knowing when you want to go. If what you want to try is in fact dangerous or risky, keep it in fantasy or strategize ways to minimize your risk. It only feeds obsessive behavior to think you have no control over your own sexual choices.

You can be an exhibitionist without ever conquering the fear of appealing to strangers. Just because you want to wear nothing but sexy lingerie in the bedroom, you don't have to wear it instead of your clothes while you're walking down the street. Just because you fantasize about someone watching you while you undress, you have not given anyone a license to peep through your curtains. You can be absolutely reserved in public and still be a provocative show-off with your lovers. Your desires, your boundaries, and your limits are paramount. You can decide how much of a show-off you want to be, in what contexts, and with which partners. You can explore any aspect of exhibitionism you want and never have to go further than you wish.

If someone assumes that because I'm exhibitionistic, for example, I must be willing to have sex with him or her, I let them know that's not the case. If s/he persists in this belief and behaves accordingly, they've crossed the line into nonconsent. And have I asked for this treatment? No, because I can and do get the same sorts of clumsy invitation when I'm *not* dressed in a frisky manner; it's not about me, it's about the social skills of the person issuing the invitation.

You can cultivate your own erotic enjoyment in being viewed and in showing off your sexuality at your own pace; in fact, you can be a happy exhibitionist without ever showing off for anyone.

EXHIBITIONISM FOR ONE

Start by coaxing your shy-but-exhibitionistic self out of its shell when you're all alone. You don't need to worry about what your partner or strangers on the street will think, because right now, no one will see you. You're going to derive your enjoyment in showing off not from being watched, but from the pure fact that you're doing it. You'll simply focus on how you feel.

The next time you're undressing for bed or taking a shower, imagine that someone has found a way to secretly watch you. It can be anyone – a stranger, your partner, a dream lover. Pick someone you'd *want* to have watch you – if the idea of your neighbor peeking through a hole in the wall upsets rather than arouses you, alter your fantasy scenario accordingly. Remember, becoming exhibitionistic doesn't necessarily mean that you want everybody and their dog to line up to peep under your blinds! Rather, imagine that someone who turns you on knows you want to be watched and has made an end run around your shyness to do just that. If you want to embroider the fantasy with details – where your mystery guest is hiding, what will happen next – go ahead. But the fantasy doesn't need to end with your dreamboat crawling out from under the bed and having you right there on your pile of clean laundry. It doesn't have to go anywhere. Instead, focus on your feelings as you imagine being observed.

Fantasize next that your admirer watches you very openly. Again, add any details you want, but keep track of your feelings. What elements of these fantasy situations arouse you? Is it the feeling of being furtively watched?

Of so enjoying your body that it doesn't matter whether anyone is there observing? Or being frankly and appreciatively stared at?

I like showing off even more than being watched because it helps me tune in to a heightened awareness of my body. When I pretend someone is watching me I become aroused not so much because someone could ostensibly peep on me, but because of what I'm doing. In other words, thinking, "I'm running my soapy hands all over my tits, showing off, all alone," is hotter for me than "Someone might be watching me through that keyhole!" You too may find that you respond more to one or another angle of the fantasy.

Let's explore this further. For an experience that isn't all in your mind, choose some music that you like, preferably something you consider sexy and something you can move to. Now, again all alone, dance to it. Feel your body move; disconnect your head from any worries about how you look, and concentrate on letting the music sink into your limbs. Express the music with your physical self. If there are no obstacles in the room, close your eyes for part of the time. Dancing by yourself has many delights – you can sing, you can be far more expressive with your body than you might dare to do in public, you can touch yourself.

Dancing can lead to altered states of mind, and it can lead you into your body perhaps further than you've ever been before. For these reasons dancing has been part of erotic rituals for millennia, from its place in the Goddess' ancient temples to the part it plays in the courtship rites of sweethearts. At the age of fifteen I read a book for teens about sex and was shocked and very titillated to find the author advising me to "go through the motions" of sex on the dance floor! At that point I didn't have the nerve, except on the dance floor in my room, door safely closed, but my solo dancing suddenly got much more erotic, and pleasurable.

Warmed up yet? All right, now dance naked. Or with scarves. Or dressed erotically – whatever erotic dress means for you. Needless to say, if your thoughts turn to a special voyeur, raptly watching your undulations, thrusting hips, and flowing body – go with it!

Hopefully the experience of dancing awakens not only a heightened consciousness of your body, but also of pleasure in your body. The combination of music and motion warms your limbs. You don't have to feel the least bit awkward about not knowing the steps, because you invent them as you go. In dancing, you communicate physically and often emotionally with the music in a way that's rather similar to the physical communication you have with a partner when you're making love. And after a while, you've exercised enough to have produced endorphins, your body's own drug, which give runners, dancers, and lovers alike a euphoric high.

Now get a mirror, preferably one in which you can see your entire body. Cue the stereo up. It's time to have an auto-exhibitionistic experience: dance for yourself.

When you do, it's important to retain the body-based pleasure you have in moving and communicating with the music. Don't look at yourself critically, as we so often do when confronted with a mirror. Banish every thought that remotely resembles, "I look ridiculous." "God, I've got to lose weight!" "I'm too old for this." "I could never do this in front of someone else."

You don't have to ever do it in front of someone else, though if you later find yourself happily doing just that, don't be too surprised. Now, though, simply see yourself in motion, moving erotically, sensuously, experiencing physical pleasure as you do, and stay alert to see signs of that pleasure.

Maybe you will see it looking into your own eyes. Maybe your pelvis has developed a mind of its own. Maybe your body has chosen to move very slowly, as if through water. Something about your pleasure in the body will look pleasing to you. If you find you get distracted from your dancing, close your eyes for a while and go back into it. Then peek. If you can't get into looking at yourself, pretend you're looking at somebody else – in a way, you are, for the you that moves with the music probably differs from the you who looks at yourself critically.

Wear clothing you feel attractive in. Wear no clothes. Wear a costume. Once you've stopped feeling shy around yourself, become your own voyeur. Show off for yourself. Discover how it looks to move in certain ways; see how the things that feel sexiest to do often convey the most sexiness. Do a striptease for yourself. Pose. Play.

Sex is adult play, and one of the biggest detriments of shyness is that it so often short-circuits our playful feelings. As kids, we get to dress up and take on any number of roles – and then when we hit puberty all that is supposed to stop. But as Robert likes to say, even if they forgot to tell you, when you turned 18 you finally became old enough to become a grown-up version of the playful kid you once were. So turn your mirrored room into an erotic playpen where you can mingle your adult feelings of sexuality with the sort of play-acting at which children excel. Play "Let's pretend": if you don't feel sexy, ask yourself, "How would I look and feel if I did?"

BODY IMAGE

It's very important to maintain your focus on the feelings in your body as you simultaneously watch yourself. Few of us have bodies that would look right at home in *Playboy* or *Playgirl* or onstage at a strip club: most of us think our parts are put together in an inferior way to those of the paragons in ads, movies, and erotic pictures. Astonishingly, lots of perfectly gorgeous people consider their looks badly flawed. If beauties wail about their looks, it stands to reason that all we ordinary folk might be substantially more beautiful than we feel. In fact, when people fall in love with us, they usually act as though what we thought was a sow's ear is really a silk purse. Have you ever noticed how much better you look to yourself when someone else is in love with you? Why not, then, begin to act as if someone – no, make that several someones! – are in love with you all the time?

Finding fault with your physical appearance tends to distance and distract you from that glorious erotic being who lives inside your skin and wants only to luxuriate in pleasure. If you can stop the clamor long enough to let that being get the upper hand, you might find that it teaches you a thing or two about beauty.

My friend Bayla recently attended a sex party. The great variety of people she saw there, she says, "blew the myth that only stereotypically attractive people have dates. I saw people who I thought were less attractive than me getting the kinds of things I want. After that you can't say, 'Well, it's because I'm not attractive.' It makes you reevaluate attractiveness to the point where what is shoved down our throats by society doesn't mean anything anymore. It just means nothing at all. Because you see people having lots of fun who break all those rules."

Social standards of attractiveness are foolishly narrow. That's bad enough, but another layer of the problem makes things worse. Too many of us have a prevailing belief that only the beautiful can truly attract love and sexual attention. We suffer from that mistaken notion especially when we are young, and it can poison our self-image. Only a minority have body types and faces that match the look Madison Avenue, even more than the adult industry, decrees to be attractive. That number shrinks the older we all grow, for it's been axiomatic in our culture that youth is beautiful, while age is not. These standards seem to weigh more heavily on women than on men, to be sure, but plenty of men are concerned about conventional ideals of male attractiveness, and men too can be struck by panic as they age and begin to see themselves as less sexually desirable.

Plenty has been written and spoken about these issues. I want to remind you here that most people have their own versions of any worries you have about your own physical attractiveness. Also, I want to emphasize that the pleasure of exhibitionism is not reserved for the young and beautiful. True, you may have to look a certain way if you want to do erotic exhibitionism for a living, but that's not the case at home – you can spice your sexuality with it all you want and for as long as you desire.

Many exhibitionistic people don't conform to narrow standards of beauty. One woman I know is at least eighty years old. She attends parties dressed only in stockings and a merry widow corset, and she exudes such a sense of comfort with herself that no one snidely whispers, "I can't believe she's dressed like that!" I know other exhibitionists who are, by contemporary social standards, overweight or out of shape. Each time I see a person who doesn't meet cultural standards of beauty enjoying their sexuality in an exhibitionistic way I rejoice: it gives every one of us more room to enjoy and love ourselves when they do.

Julia Trahan is a performance artist whose work often deals with her own sexuality and with the effects on her life of a childhood accident which left her disabled. "You know, I think people really don't know what they look like," she muses. "I think who I see in the mirror is someone totally different from the person you see. When I'm in public, feeling self-conscious, people are seeing the whole picture, but my head is full of specific body parts." Julia has to make a point of overcoming this self-consciousness whenever she goes on stage, but the effort she makes to do so rewards her with the attention of her audience – which makes her feel more in her body and more powerful.

"We women are constantly at war with our bodies," says performer Margaret Cho; "it is hard to find amnesty for ourselves. I did it by dancing naked for a couple of years with 'The Sensuous Woman.' [More about this and Margaret's experiences below.] I think the best way to get over your body issues is to just flaunt your body at every opportunity. It is hard because the urge to criticize ourselves is overwhelmingly strong. I don't know why that is. I think that all bodies are beautiful in millions of different ways – but I get down on myself too! Since I became a dancer, I have felt much better about myself. I even did a naked photo shoot myself not too long ago, with my favorite photographer Austin Young. My friend Suhaila was there for moral support and she has done a lot of modeling. She gave me some good advice. 'When you are being shot, try to think of a secret. Something beautiful. Something only you know. A secret. Hold onto that. Let them see the secret in your eyes. Feel it.'"

Juliet Anderson is well past sixty. She became a porn star when she was forty years old, and she was wildly popular partly because her fans were so grateful to see a vital, mature woman on screen enjoying her sexuality. Who better than Juliet to comment on exhibitionism and the older woman or man? "Sex is between your ears," Juliet says. "Realize that there's a lot of life left. One of the healthiest things you can do for yourself is to get the sexual juices flowing. Maybe the plumbing doesn't always work like it used to, but who cares? Your whole body is sexual. The quality of your life can improve tremendously.

"It's our fear that stops us. We're more afraid of our fear than of what's actually going to happen. We say, 'What if...?' Don't even worry about 'what if.' Just say, 'I have a right to pleasure in my body that does not hurt anybody else.' You have a right until the day you die, and you'll live a lot longer and a lot healthier if you take charge of your own sexuality."

Juliet has made (and stars in) a movie called "Ageless Desire" in which she puts this principle into explicit practice. Through her exhibitionism she seeks to teach and inspire, especially older women and men who rarely hear supportive messages from the culture about their desirability and continued right to erotic pleasure.

Another form of body image issue has to do with genderedness – not whether you are male or female, but how masculine or feminine you are, and whether your sense of yourself in gendered terms matches the rather narrow ideas in our culture about how women and men "should" look and behave. This may or may not have anything to do with gender identity or sexual orientation – plenty of straight Wyoming farm wives are pretty darned butch, for instance – but mainstream social messages insist that people who don't conform to these gendered norms are less attractive than others, and until and unless such a person finds people who find him/her/hir sexy just the way s/h/ze is, body self-love and -comfort are sometimes a challenge.

"For me," says theatre artist S. Bear Bergman, the entry into body-comfort "was boxing – as a kid I was shipped off to dance class and called graceless, but in boxing being big or fat or masculinely gendered is good, and it's graceful, much like dancing – but the expectations of what that means are totally different. It changed my ability to move and really be in my body. I remember being so surprised and delighted that that was possible. After boxing I took dance classes, because I had learned how to move."

PLEASURE AND SELF-PLEASURE

Watch a few porn movies with an eye to noticing the difference between those attractive bodies who clearly enjoy what they do and those who spend all their time on screen straining for a flattering camera angle. See what I mean? Erotic enjoyment is contagiously attractive; it doesn't depend upon looks. Even great looks can't infuse erotic energy into someone who isn't enjoying herself or himself.

Just as the mature voyeuristic eye prizes signs of sexual energy and pleasure more highly than Playboy dimensions or movie-star looks, the exhibitionist has more immediate thrills available to her or him than expressing physical perfection. If I had to choose between pleasure in the body and fabulous looks, I'd choose the former every time.

You can't very well show off your erotic self if you don't feel grounded in erotic feelings. Ensuring that you have enough sexual and sensual pleasure in your life is the quickest and most thorough way to get that grounding.

You may have already discovered how richly you can enhance your life by taking care of your own needs for sex and sensuality through masturbation, fantasy, and other sorts of self-pleasuring. I don't mean perfunctory jacking or jilling off here, though masturbation can relieve tension like nothing else can. I mean, rather, truly sensual, leisurely self-exploration, where you set the mood, take time to explore your physical responses, and devote yourself to your own pleasure. If you haven't made this sort of self-loving experience part of your life, or if you haven't masturbated at all, I recommend you read Betty Dodson's remarkable book *Sex For One*.

Self-pleasuring has its own bountiful rewards, including heightened self-esteem, feeling more alive and powerful, more sexual satisfaction – and orgasms, too! If you've been hesitant to masturbate, or do so but feel uncomfortable about it because it's not "the real thing," let me assure you that not only are *you* the real thing, but also that through masturbation you will bring more of yourself to your partnered lovemaking.

Many women, influenced by sex-positive feminism and the work of Betty Dodson, Lonnie Barbach, Joani Blank, and others, are familiar with these ideas. Ironically, many men, even if masturbation is an everyday part of their lives, have a hard time changing their attitudes about what so many guys see as a quick J/O. There's nothing wrong with quickies, but if you're a man who has never taken the time to give yourself long, lingering pleasure, please join your enlightened women friends in exploring the benefits of self-loving. *The Joys Of Solo Sex*, *The Multi-Orgasmic Man*, and other books can inspire you to give yourself more erotic bliss and take your sexuality in hand, too – did you know that the most common exercises for men who want more control over the timing of their ejaculation and orgasm involve masturbation? You may also find inspiration in the DVDs of Erospirit founder Joseph Kramer.

Set aside as much time as you can allow for a self-pleasuring experience. Set the scene in a way that turns you on – do you love the sensuality of a candle-lit bath, or would you prefer to rent a couple of raunchy videos? Take all the time you can getting aroused. Read an erotic book, if you like, or get out some sex toys, or call a phone sex line. It doesn't matter how you choose to make it special for yourself, but do something.

Now settle down in front of the mirror you used in the dancing exercise. If you can move the mirror, try bringing it close to you, perhaps propping it at the end of the bed or wherever you've chosen for your self-pleasuring. As you begin to touch yourself, watch yourself in the mirror.

As in the dancing exercise, you're acting simultaneously as your own voyeur and exhibitionist. Look in your own eyes; watch your hands on your body; see the signs of your arousal. Your nipples may get hard, your skin flush; women may see their genitals getting swollen and moist, and men may see their cocks getting erect. Fantasize about anything you want, but keep watching. Observe yourself. Turn yourself on.

This exercise has infinite variations. Watch yourself use a vibrator. Fuck yourself with a dildo and watch. Masturbate to orgasm. Watch yourself in different positions. Wear lingerie or any sort of clothing that feels erotic to you. Wear street clothes, and see how you'd look sneaking a masturbation break at work!

Notice which visual images of yourself please you the most. If you've never watched yourself being sexual before, you may find yourself surprised at how erotic you look. "Some of the best masturbation I ever had was with a lighted makeup mirror between my legs," says my friend Sybil. "I did Kegels, watched my cunt move and change color. Talk about being your own private exhibitionist! It was so hot!"

Add fantasy variations. Imagine someone peeping secretly while you masturbate. Someone watching you brazenly. Someone watching you and finding you so hot that they have to masturbate, too.

If you have an adventuresome partner who supports your forays into exhibitionism, now you can involve her or him. You can act out these fantasies of being spied on or openly watched; you can masturbate together, watching each other. You can situate a mirror next to your bed so that both of you can watch all your antics.

If you find yourself still too shy to let your partner watch, perhaps s/he will agree to be blindfolded or "watch" you with closed eyes while you strip or pose or masturbate in front of him or her. You can get comfortable with your partner's presence and at any time you can say, "Open your eyes now." Alternatively, you can wear the blindfold and focus on your body instead of seeing an intimidating pair of eyes watching you. That way you are aware you're being watched, but the blindfold can distract you and let you relax into it. Of course, the aim of these exercises with your partner is to get so aroused from her or his presence that you will *want* to see those eyes.

MASTURBATION, TALKING DIRTY, AND FANTASY

You can also adapt these masturbation exercises to your purpose if you want to learn to talk dirty. My first clue that erotic talk could be hot for me came during masturbation; I found myself talking as my orgasm neared, and it seemed to heighten my arousal and hasten and intensify orgasm. Even when I did not think I was fantasizing – I had no linear scenario running like a porn movie in my head – I talked dirty, usually as if I were addressing a lover. My shy first forays were nothing spicier than "Oh, yes!" (the same words I managed to first squeeze out with a partner), but they escalated to the truly salacious before long, and I would cry "Fuck me!" probably loud enough for my neighbors to assume someone was with me doing just that.

If you're so shy that words just won't come out, start with sounds. Erotic moans and murmurs can turn a lover on as much as naughty stories, and they're a wonderful way for you to get used to making some noise. You can incorporate this into masturbation. Especially if you think erotic words or phrases while you coo and gasp, you will find that as you get more turned on, the words will superimpose themselves onto the sounds. Like magic, instead of vocalizing "Uhn! Uhn!" you'll find yourself saying "Yes! Yes!" – then maybe "More! Harder! Give it to me!" Then try graduating to "Fuck! Fuck me!"

Masturbation allows you an appropriate place to practice words, gestures, and fantasies, but I recommend it for another reason too. When you introduce erotic variation to yourself first, you allow yourself the opportunity to erotically fix on it. Masturbation can serve as your lab, where you explore your own sexual responses to ideas and sensations. Remember that fantasy need not be a prescription for behavior – just because you like the thought of something during masturbation doesn't mean you have to, or even want to, try it in real life. At the same time, a fantasy that evokes a good response during masturbation will likely please you more during partner sex than one that doesn't register on the Richter scale of your solo arousal.

What if you enjoy masturbation, but can't get comfortable fantasizing, or don't know what to fantasize about? You don't have to. Plenty of people don't. Many people think a fantasy has to have a linear quality, like a movie script, while their heads are filled only with fleeting images or one still picture. They may have no visual images at all, only a soundtrack. This is just another type of fantasy; not everyone's brain is tuned to exactly the same channel!

If you want to engage in more detailed fantasy and your brain isn't coming up with new material, try reading erotic stories, watching sexy movies, or listening to "hot talk" CDs. Let the scenarios, characters, words and images infuse your consciousness while you masturbate. You'll know when you've hit upon a fantasy that works for you because your body will respond with heightened arousal. This may be true even if you read the same story or watched the same video outside a sexual situation and got nothing out of it, even disliked it. The brain may be the biggest sex organ, but for a lot of us, it serves as an almost anti-sexual gatekeeper when it's in its rational mode. Sexual enjoyment isn't rational, and sometimes we have to "get out of our heads" and let the rational (and critical) parts of the brain go on a break. This is the same advice a sex therapist would give a person who wasn't reliably orgasmic – stop worrying about it and analyzing it, and let your body's responses get a word in edgewise!

If you have a supportive partner, you might want to enlist their help in spinning fantasy material together. Partners can do something else of crucial importance in helping you overcome your shyness and pursuing exhibitionism: they can reassure you about your sexiness.

It's possible your sweetheart doesn't even know how shy you are, especially if you experience shyness mostly in sexual situations. S/he might not have figured out that you're quite a different person in the bedroom than you are chatting at a party or giving a presentation at work or school. Let your partner know that you're nervous about coming out of your shell, and discuss together how s/he can support you and bolster your courage. Ask her or him to tell you when you look or act sexy. Request acknowledgment when you manage to go further than you have in the past. Concoct ways you can practice your exhibitionism with your partner's assistance and involvement. If he or she appreciates the new you, be sure you hear about it. Chip away together at your shyness and sexual reticence; you'll have far more incentive to do that if you receive your lover's appreciation and positive reinforcement for your efforts.

WHEN SHYNESS IS SEXY

Some people find they can exploit their shyness to heighten sexual tension and erotic pleasure. For them, an end to shyness might actually diminish their enjoyment. If this is the case for you, you can have even more pleasure if you recognize and manipulate your shyness. Here's how.

Most sex educators and therapists of the past couple of decades have been real cheerleaders for sex, insisting that people should feel positive about and unafraid of sexuality. This has helped countless people to overcome sexual difficulties. Most people do lead happier, more sexually satisfied lives when they get over the notion that sex is wrong and dirty.

However, confirming the concept of erotic diversity, other folks have managed to hitch their sexual satisfaction right to this "sex is dirty" wagon. I already mentioned theorist Dr. Jack Morin, who describes these "unexpected aphrodisiacs": shame, fear, and guilt. Many sex therapists presume that people derive less pleasure from sex when fear, guilt and shame get in the way. For some, however, these emotions actually give arousal its juice.

If your turn-on is directly wired to the naughty, the nasty, the vulgar and obscene, and to sex as forbidden and frightening and depraved, I do not suggest you simply pull the plug and try to visualize butterflies and green meadows. In the first place, it probably won't work. In the second place, there are ways to capitalize on this source of sexual heat without truly believing that sex is awful, as are you for enjoying it.

Notice whether this type of arousal causes mixed feelings for you. If so, your shyness may be at least in part a reflection of this, if not a way of covering up how depraved you believe you really may be deep down. If you exaggerate your beliefs and concerns and make them central to your sexual fantasies, you can work their erotic potential even as you dispel some of their power over your psyche.

Wallow in what a naughty, bad girl or boy you are! Tell yourself you're just a nasty slut. Make plans to confess your sins. Imagine how ashamed you'd be if anyone walked in and caught you doing such a wicked, wicked thing (you're getting exhibitionistic about it now)! What would they say? Imagine it, and say it to yourself.

This exercise is not meant to reinforce negative feelings you have about sex or about yourself. If you have feelings like these but they *don't* cause or enhance arousal for you, it's a signal that you really do feel fearful and negative about sex. If this is the case, don't play with these emotions. Work on learning a more positive and healthy approach to sex by getting more sex information or seeing a therapist.

However, if you see sex as good but are aware that you have baggage that links your feelings about sexuality to your feelings of reticence and even shame, you may find that exaggerating these feelings helps put them into perspective for you. It's harder to let these emotions control you when you're practically parodying them in your fantasies. For one thing, you're recognizing them, bringing them into the light. For another, you're mindfully using them to enhance your arousal. You are taking control of them and divesting them of their anti-sexual potential by giving an erotic spin to what may in the past have gotten in the way of your self-esteem.

Turn your shyness into a sex toy! Play with it as a conscious element in your fantasies. Instead of seeing yourself as nervous and bumbling, see yourself in the character of a frightened virgin (whether you are or not), and emphasize the erotic potential of the fear. Instead of chastising yourself for all your sexual thoughts, follow the advice of the Eartha Kitt song in which she hisses, "I want to be eee-villl! I want to be baaaad!" – and list all your naughty desires.

It doesn't matter that you may always feel a jolt of fear or badness whenever you expose your body to a lover or whisper wild obscenities into another person's ear. It matters only that this fact becomes part of the eroticism of the act, not an impediment.

It may even be true that fear, shyness, or shame is the source of your desire to exhibit yourself. It can be a way for you to overcome your fear, proof that you have taken control of your shyness, or give you something "eee-villl and baaaad" to do so that you can milk the erotic potential of your feelings of shame. In fact, there are probably as many kinds of desire for exhibitionism as there are exhibitionists – people of all sorts of sexual profiles and sexual desires can embrace exhibitionism and voyeurism, erotic talk and listening. The rest of their sexual interests will help shape the kind of exhibitionist they are.

DRESSING UP

One variation of visual exhibitionism is so common that it really begs to be discussed first: erotic costuming. Other species have special markings and coloration that attract mates; clothing serves homo sapiens the same way. How you dress sends a powerful signal of identity, status, and sexual availability or interest. And it doesn't just signal to others – it speaks directly to our own self-image. If you're having trouble breaking through shyness, changing your clothes can quickly get you out of yourself. If you want to feel erotic, try erotic attire.

What is erotic dress, exactly? As the Supreme Court justice said about obscenity, we know it when we see it; more importantly for exhibitionists, we know it when we put it on. Don't limit your possible sources of exhibitionistic enjoyment to the obvious sort of garb from the Frederick's of Hollywood or International Male catalogs; all kinds of dress can bring on the rush we get from erotically showing off.

In the first place, in what environment do you plan to wear a certain type of clothing? Will you be looking for attention on the street? at a party? at a *wild* party? or in bed? Obviously (to all but the most brazen of our exhibitionistic sisters and brothers, anyway), our wardrobe might change radically from one place to the other. Out in the world we might want to be at least discreet enough to avoid arrest for disturbing the peace, while in private, short skirts, tight pants, and shows of cleavage, all traditional exhibitionistic streetwear, can give way to the bare essentials.

Second, what sort of response do you want to evoke? Your exhibitionistic self's choice of dress will probably depend on the kind of erotic energy that fills you when you show off. Think about the different erotic messages you can send by the clothes you choose. If a woman wears a leather corset and high-heeled boots, no one is likely to expect her to act like a shrinking violet – that's dominatrix drag. If a man wears ultra-tight, strategically ripped Levis, he'll evoke a far different erotic personality (and response in his partner) than if he slips into a pair of lace panties. If we glimpse pristine white cotton undies under a woman's short, pleated plaid skirt, she's more likely to seem like a wide-eyed virgin than if she struts into the room wearing pasties and a g-string.

The power of erotic dress goes much further than arousing our partners or suggesting erotic roles. Remember my definition of exhibitionism – first and foremost, we're turning ourselves on. When I got ready for work on my first day at the peep show, I couldn't have been more nervous – but the clothes I wore into the booth, a virginal white lace blouse and white panties under a short skirt, immediately put me in the mood to be a good little girl gone bad. My nervousness disappeared because that was such an appealing fantasy for me. When I wear high heels and a garter belt and stockings to bed with my lover, the sex feels charged up partly because that outfit appeals to him, but also because I feel sexy in it – and because getting dressed meant that I was purposely clothing myself for making love.

It goes back to the basic disagreement between the "good-sex-is-spontaneous" folks and those of us who love to plan an encounter in advance, savoring the fantasy, arranging everything, dressing up, the anticipation... even putting condoms where they'll need to "spontaneously" appear later.

To explore the eroticism of deliberate planning for sex, start at your closet. What will drive your partner wild? What will they see when you take off this piece of clothing? How will you look when you're nearly naked? In bed (if you get that far) will you keep any clothes on? If so, what?

Don't be surprised if this necessitates many changes of clothes in front of the mirror, or even a shopping trip or two. Perhaps you're willing to try sexy garments but don't know where to get them. There are plenty of sources for these on the web and by mail. Or comb the shops in your town. Don't forget to try the second-hand shops; they can be full of great costume elements.

If you haven't played erotically with clothing before and you're not sure what will feel sexy, try a variety of things. You may find that different sides of your erotic personality come out when you wear different kinds of clothes. If you've always avoided lingerie, try a tux. (Or try the lingerie and see what comes up. I have one woman friend who's happiest in lingerie when she's pretending to be a man dressed as a woman!)

However, the important thing is wearing what's sexy to you. It could be tight and clinging or long and flowing, extremely revealing or covering everything but wrists, nape, and ankles (these three areas of the female body became highly eroticized during the era when women wore long dresses with high collars). It could be leather or lace or latex, completely sheer or thick and velvety. It could make you feel boyish, butch, masculine or manly – whether or not you're a man; it could make you feel femme, feminine, girlish or womanly – whether or not you're a woman. It could fit a classic definition of erotic dress or its eroticism could be unique to you. In any case, it's the right sort of exhibitionistic garb if you feel a heightened level of eroticism when you put it on.

Don't forget to dress up your feet. Many kinds of footwear can carry an erotic charge – heavy black motorcycle boots, high spike heels, girlish sandals or mary janes, over-the-knee leather or patent boots, buffed-to-a-sheen wingtips. Bare feet or open-toed pumps revealing painted toenails drive some people wild. Have you treated yourself to a pedicure lately? You don't have to be a foot fetishist to indulge in such things – though if you or your partner is, such touches can be truly hot (have your partner give you the pedicure, or return the favor). What about stockings, whether sheer and silky, fishnet, patterned, or cotton ones that are held above the knee with a garter?

Once you've chosen an outfit or two, go back to your mirror and once again do that masturbation exercise in which you're simultaneously voyeur and exhibitionist. Give yourself some visual feedback. Experience yourself the way a partner would. If you have picked more than one sort of erotic dress, do your arousal and sexual feelings differ as you change your clothes? Don't be surprised if, in dressing up and watching yourself, you get your first glimpse of an erotic persona emerging.

Your Body – As It Is and As It Could Be

With these exercises you can treat yourself as a sex object before anyone else does. The point is to increase your comfort with your body, including the way it looks, and to ground yourself in your exhibitionistic potential. You don't have to worry and wonder how you look, what kind of impression you're making, if you've taken a good look at yourself already. If you're shy about your body, you might try looking for erotic images with similar body types. Unfortunately, there is not much of this sort of stuff available for men, but if you're a woman whose body type doesn't meet present-day porn standards, check out turn of the (20th) century erotic photos, which are full of women who'd never make it on the Playboy Channel but whose guileless nude poses are completely charming. You might even want to make a little altar to your erotic self as you evolve away from shyness – all you need is a Polaroid or digital camera and a sexy outfit or two. Annie Sprinkle's wonderful work turning ordinary women into pin-up queens can be an inspiring example – look at her book *Post Porn Modernist* and her video "Sluts and Goddesses" to see how gorgeous Everywoman can be. If you're Everyman, you may have to start a gallery of your own, but these days loads of regular men as well as women exhibit themselves online, so there are images out there if you look.

Candye Kane is a sexy, torchy blues singer – and a big woman. She likes lingerie, partly because it helps her feel erotic, partly because it gives her confidence. "That would be a way for people who haven't explored exhibitionism to start feeling brave," she says. "It facilitates getting into an erotic mood, like role-playing." Once you're into the pleasure of the exhibitionistic moment, body image concerns can take a back seat to the erotic fun.

Perhaps you won't be satisfied with your body as it is. All this new exhibitionism may arouse in you an urge to diet, go to the gym, or station yourself in front of the screen with a copy of "Buns of Steel." There's nothing wrong with taking care of yourself; exercise is health-promoting and rewarding even if you don't wind up with a new improved physique.

But beware of the little voice that says you'll never be sexy the way you are. That's a very different message than "You could look and feel better." The whole point of the mirror exercises – in fact, all the ideas in this book – is to give you access to your own eroticism now, not after thirty-five pounds, a tummy tuck, and a nose job.

For those not permanently inclined, body paint, removable tattoos, and non-toxic, skin-friendly markers (especially in the hand of an artistic friend) can provide a fun incentive for showing off your body. This is great to do at home, but you haven't experienced its full potential until you've taken it to the beach or the park. It can draw lots of attention, but at the same time you feel more covered than you would if you didn't have the paint on.

Other temporary modifications to explore include shaving or shaping your pubic hair (you may discover new or changed sensation during genital stimulation when you do this). Hairdos of other types can be fun. Playing with wigs gives you lots of options without having to commit to bleaching, perming or coloring your hair.

Having your nails manicured and polished or buffed is a great way to add a small change to your appearance that can make you feel different – especially if it's something you don't usually do. And don't forget makeup – especially if you don't usually wear any. Or try wearing more outrageous makeup than you ever would under ordinary circumstances. Make your look extraordinary on purpose.

Body modification can take many forms. Perhaps you're attracted to the idea of doing something more or less permanent to enhance your looks. Breast implants and reductions, facelifts, and other forms of cosmetic surgery have been around for years. More recently, many people find they feel more connected to and in control of their body when they've marked it as their own by using methods like tattooing or piercing. This can feel like "bringing what's on the inside, out," including one's own sense of spirituality or eroticism. Some find that this gives them a whole new sense of wanting to show themselves off because such marking can feel highly exhibitionistic.

Of course, this isn't everyone's cup of tea. As my aghast mother said when I got my tattoo, "But honey, you can never take that thing off!" The image you find profound and hot today, expressing your very soul, might seem rather anachronistic in forty years – so keep that in mind (although existing removal technologies will probably improve). Then again, it might make you a fascinating oldster. As I replied to my mom, "I don't anticipate wanting to take it off."

It doesn't matter whether the visual elements you choose to help you feel more erotically outgoing are temporary or permanent, true fetishes for you, or just hot outfits. It doesn't even matter whether you make yourself look special at all. There's no one single way to be sexual! Most importantly, what enhances your erotic feelings and experience? What do you want to do? What do you want to say? How do you want to look? Beginning to answer these questions will help you bring your erotic personality to life.

MEET A DANCING QUEEN

Comedian/performer Margaret Cho made the news in the '90s when she got her own sitcom, and not long after, word on the street was that her producers were giving her a hard time about her weight. Cho is certainly not the only contemporary entertainment figure to struggle with body image issues, but she may be the only one to break through those issues by becoming a burlesque performer! I asked Margaret to talk to us about this partly because I'd heard the missing link between the old Margaret Cho and the new one was, in fact, belly dancing.

Belly dancing is a perfect art form for the person who thinks s/he's too chubby. Certainly svelte ladies and gentlemen can learn the moves and look great – but if their bodies aren't jiggling a little, their performance lacks that certain something that only a full-bodied performer brings to this super-sensuous art form. Belly, hips, ass and breasts are all integral to good belly dancing, and many a woman who've been called fat has learned a new love for her body through its sinewy twists, shakes and rolls. (Men, too – this is by no means only a women's dance, at least as it's practiced in the US.)

And Margaret was one of those girls who'd been called fat way before she went to Hollywood. "I was really into ballet as a kid," she says, "but when I was in a recital, my father told me that I was the fattest ballerina. I never wanted to dance again after that, and I didn't revisit the idea until I was well into my thirties. I just happened upon a belly dance convention and it was amazing. All these beautiful women of all ages and sizes dancing together and having a blast. I immediately began taking classes and even did some performing in Middle Eastern restaurants. What was the most challenging and exciting part of belly dance for me was learning how to communicate without words. Belly dance is all about the simulation of intimacy, beyond words and in a way, beyond movement. It is also a very intricate and complex dance form, but one that exercises emotions as well as the body. That was the scariest for me, learning how to expose my emotions. As a comedian, I am able to use humor as a shield, so I can keep people from really knowing me. As a dancer, people have to be able to see inside you, which is extremely exhibitionistic and terrifying, and then totally exciting!"

In her blog, Margaret wrote about a recent belly dance intensive class she'd taken with her favorite teacher, Suhaila, echoing how the alchemy of music and movement can awaken the body's own wisdom and sensuality: "My favorite part was watching everyone else do the moves in their own way. The choreography was gorgeously transformed by each woman's body, defined by her own style and way of understanding movement... I just want to have mastery of this format, and be able to stand up there with all these secrets inside me, to reveal and conceal my mysteries at will, in order to express all that the music has to offer, to give a home to the rhythms and the notes, so the seat of the song can be in my hips and my heart, not just my mind."

From belly dance, Margaret segued to New Burlesque, and today, besides performing, she's also a producer, taking her Sensuous Woman Show around the country. I asked her to talk about the social (including sex-and-gender) messages she wants her events to convey, since, besides showcasing ecdysiast and comic talent just like the burlesque halls of old, her gigs are full of surprises. Her show might feature a male belly dancer, a crossdressed comic performer (like Kelly, whose "Omigod, Shoes!" song is a huge show favorite), a midget doing flawlessly-costumed, old-timey burlesque – Margaret puts together gigs that hearken back to the first half of the 20th century with a very 21st century appreciation for diversity. "I wanted a place for women to feel safe, to feel seen, to be sexy, to feel good about themselves, doing their thing," said Margaret about the show when she introduced it in her blog. "We will have some burlesque, from first timers to stripping superstars, belly dancers of all denominations, the best comics and God only knows what else." And it's 21st century in other ways: some of her first Sensuous Woman performances benefited Hurricane Katrina rebuild efforts, and now when she takes the show on the road she usually partners with a local non-profit.

"I love burlesque," Margaret says. "The best burlesque dancers are similar to belly dancers in that they reveal not just the body, but the emotions as well. Burlesque is very feminist art, in my opinion, because it is women using their sexuality on their own terms. We own our bodies and we are using them the way we want! For me watching burlesque healed me from a lifetime of eating disorders and body issues because I got to see all different kinds of women, with different body types, including those I had not seen in a sexual context, being beautiful and proud. Really strutting their stuff! That is powerful!"

"What do you think of the way the media portrays female sexuality (and sexuality in general) these days?" I asked her. "Is your work in any way an antidote to or critique of that, or do you see it as more of a continuum?"

"I think we see only a very limited view of female sexuality," Margaret replied. "It is boring and pretty sad. The sexual female in the media is one with a very narrow view of what beauty is – one defined by fashion and men's magazines. I don't know what is sexy about that. I think that female sexuality is so powerful and magnificent that the media is afraid to portray it with any dimension because then, how could it be controlled? It might make women see how important and amazing we are!"

Through her performances and exploration of body-based art forms like belly dancing and burlesque, Margaret Cho has joined the ranks of happy exhibitionists, and her story suggests that even if you start out only dancing for yourself, in front of a mirror, there are lots of things to be gained from taking it outside and, at the very least, giving your all at a dance class. I'll let her have the last word: "I am an exhibitionist because it frees me! I feel so good about my body from showing it off. The approval and validation I get from an audience is vital to my own self-esteem. I have been down on myself for so long – finally exhibitionism has given me a reprieve from my own negative self-talk!"

Too Shy to Talk?

"Talk to me," your lover whispers in your ear. "Talk dirty to me."
I use the phrase "talk dirty" not because I think explicit sexual language is dirty or bad in any way, but because for most people the phrase conjures up blue talk, all those delightful four-and-more-letter words you may get a thrill out of exploring. I alternate the expressions "dirty words" or "talking dirty" with less charged phrasing like "erotic talk" or "hot talk" to blur any barriers the phrase "dirty talk" might provoke. If Anglo-Saxonisms turn you off, look for alternate language that turns you on – the turn-on, and the communication it facilitates, is the whole point.

While I'm on the topic of four-letter words: you've probably noticed that I occasionally use them as I write. I feel casual and comfortable about words like "fuck" and "pussy," so please be assured I'm not using them for shock value. If sexual slang is not part of your everyday speech, these may jump out of the text at you. Try to read them as simply descriptive. You can be a terrific erotic talker and never use them.

Auto-Erotic Talk

Let's get back to your lover's request. You open your mouth – but no sound comes out. You're tongue-tied. What can you do?

You can start by practicing alone. Do you worry that explicit words will sound shocking, silly, trite or embarrassing coming out of your mouth? Begin by desensitizing yourself enough that you can actually speak them out loud. If there are specific words you routinely choke on that you want to include in your pillow talk, pick a time when you're undisturbed, maybe involved in something else – washing dishes, say, or driving the car – and just say them! Don't bother, yet, to string them into sentences. It may not seem highly sexy to chant "fuck fuck fuck fuck fuck" while you're unloading the dishwasher, but don't worry. The erotic drama and punch will return when someone is listening.

In fact, it will probably return earlier than that. When the words no longer stick in your craw, take them into masturbation. As you get turned on, say them. Make them into short sentences (or long ones, if you're feeling really talkative). Try to talk right up to and through orgasm. If you've never done this before you may find it highly exciting, and it will accustom you to hearing yourself talk dirty in an eroticized situation.

I have a friend who discovered a whole new territory when she began to do phone sex for a living. She liked talking so much that she taped herself talking dirty while masturbating (not forgetting the juicy sex sounds – punctuating hot talk with moans and sighs heats it up for the talker as well as the listener), then played it back and used it as a sound track the next time she masturbated. Getting really creative, she got another tape recorder and recorded herself listening to (and talking along with) the first tape, creating a tapestry of auto-erotic sound. Wouldn't that help jolt you out of your shyness? The tape would make a great surprise to leave under a special someone's pillow, too.

What should you say? Anything you want. Especially as an addition to self-pleasuring, you can talk as blue a streak as you wish, and you need concern yourself neither with what your partner might find a turn-on nor what would drive your mother to wash your mouth out with soap. Masturbation is your own erotic time, and devoting it to your most intense turn-ons will not only loosen you up for sharing with a partner, it will be its own reward.

Listen to yourself talk while you masturbate – or even at other times when you have the privacy to talk to yourself. This is not a great exercise to do on a crowded bus, but if you can make solitary time, use it to get accustomed to hearing deliciously naughty things coming out of your mouth. As you get more comfortable you'll likely find that your arousal increases, since for many people the freedom to become emotionally as well as physically turned on depends on how comfortable they feel.

Next go back to the mirror and watch yourself say those words. Watch yourself masturbating and talking. If you're comfortable doing so, aim a digital movie camera at yourself as you talk. Watch it later and talk back while you watch. Tape yourself talking while you masturbate. If you find you don't enjoy this or can't feel comfortable, don't worry. You don't have to keep it up – you gave it a shot. Unlike the sorts of exhibitionism displayed by people who want to be watched, your preferred form of exhibitionism, talking erotically, doesn't require you or your partners to be visually oriented. This kind of showing off can be done in the dark!

IN SEARCH OF WORDS

Perhaps you simply don't know which words you find erotic in the first place. You may feel you haven't really discovered your own sexual interests, much less the words and phrases you associate with arousal. At least some of what you will find erotic on a fantasy level will also sound sexy when you talk about it, so as a next step, explore the realm of erotic fantasy, searching for your hot spots. This means, among other things, trying not to censor yourself when sexual thoughts flit into your head. Instead, note which erotic ideas or images grab your attention. If you're sexual with other people, what sorts of play do you like best? Dwell on this and see where your mind takes you. If you find yourself responding to anything with physical signs of arousal, that will also be a clue.

Porn movies are one place to start. Images of explicit sex are extremely arousing for some people, not so inspiring for others. Try watching a few to see whether one or several engage your erotic imagination. Some porn videos feature talkative characters; if you can find these, you have the advantage of hearing sexy words spoken. With others you'll need to come up with more of the language yourself. You'd think porn actors would talk a blue streak, but often they don't... one picture being worth a thousand words, and all that.

Once you get a bit more comfortable with speaking up, porn videos make a great prop for talking, because you can describe what's happening on-screen.

Especially if erotic talk is your aim, you might find more inspiration in hot talk CDs – and on the printed page. After all, you can watch sexual scenarios for hours and be as incapable of stringing a sexy sentence together at the end as you were when you began, but erotic stories are composed of the building blocks you want to play with – words. Besides, you'll be providing the mental images you find hot, and you may find your creative fantasies flow especially easily because of this.

You can get fantasy as well as vocabulary ideas from lurid romance novels and trashy porn books alike – the latter are a particularly rich trove of those words your mother would consider really filthy, hence a delightfully nasty source of inspiration if you want to go for hard-hitting dirty talk. However, your erotic talk need not be peppered with four-letter words to weave a very powerful spell around you and your partner. Some talkers never utter an explicit word; sexuality and subtlety can certainly go hand in hand.

Sexy scenarios from Nancy Friday's fantasy compilations (feel free to skip the armchair psychology), erotic anthologies, Victorian bawdy novels, cutting-edge 'zines, and the "good parts" from mainstream novels all might get you going. If you have a kinky bent you might like what I used to read in college – old psychiatric case study collections. (Heavy on moralistic judgment, but oh, those perversions! Until you've masturbated to *Patterns of Psychosexual Infantilism* you haven't lived). A classic source for scenarios and lingo is the "Letters" genre; Penthouse publishes a magazine with mostly heterosexual vignettes (these have been collected into books as well), and there are similar publications that cater to other erotic interests. If you prefer your erotica on the literary side, you might appreciate *Yellow Silk*, any of the many collections of upscale, more highly literary erotic writing, or the seduction scene from a well-crafted novel.

For some people, hot writing is by definition trashy and poorly written, with lots of four-letter words and characters screaming "NnnnghAAAAAAHHHHHHHHHH!!!!" at the moment of climax. Other readers find this a turn-off. (Of course, it makes a great difference to some of us if we read this while we're masturbating! If you think you don't like the trashy stuff, give that a try.) Some readers and porn viewers want their one-handed reading or fantasy-inspiring material to be as kinky or sleazy as possible, while others are fans of romantic or sensual work.

The bottom line? Everybody's different; if you haven't sampled other peoples' favorite genres of sex writing, how can you know for sure it won't get you hot? Arousal is unpredictable. Check out a variety of written porn and see what floats your boat. The more you explore, the wider your potential for arousal may become.

TALKING WITH YOUR PARTNER

This point has special relevance if you and your partner like different things. Both of you can give each other's favorite material more than a cursory try; if either of you doesn't share the other's turn-on, it's time to negotiate. Maybe you can take turns picking out a bedtime story; maybe you'll agree not to share this material with each other at all, although you can still use it as inspiration for erotic talk.

What if you still feel reticent with your partner? Perhaps you're not sure what sort of language or scenario will go over well with her or him; if you're new to exchanging fantasies and talking explicitly, you may worry about what your partner will think of your new language skills. You may have stage fright at the thought of getting started. I used to fear I'd sound silly, not sexy.

There's a step you can take in learning to talk erotically that can happen either in or out of bed. Before you start in on the scary four-letter words, begin to talk about sex more often, and more explicitly, with your partner and your friends, using non-"dirty" words. This way you separate two possibly challenging aspects – talking about sex, and taboo words – and tackle them one at a time.

If you and your partner don't talk about sex much or aren't in the habit of trying new things, the fact that you're going to suggest learning to talk erotically might make some waves. Don't be too worried: they might be very good waves. In general, introducing such changes goes more smoothly if you put things positively: "I find the idea of talking while we make love really sexy," rather than "I just think we need something to spice things up."

It is very possible that your opening up the topic of new ways to share sex will inspire your partner to tell you what s/he has been secretly craving; with luck, you'll have all kinds of new activities to enjoy!

If you are both novices, neither of you will know ahead of time exactly how the changes will feel, so it's not surprising if you're both a little nervous. You can let your partner know you feel nervous about bringing the new idea up: "I'd like us to experiment sexually, and I'm not sure how you'll react to my ideas – can I ask you to listen to my suggestions without responding to them right now? Just listen, and we'll have a conversation later." This way you can get your ideas out on the table without worrying s/he's about to say something to reject them. Ask yourself before you begin: How can I broach this subject in a way that will feel safe for me? How can I encourage my partner to suspend his/her judgment and hear me out? How can I try to make it feel safe for her or him?

Share this book with your partner. Tell him or her the ideas you like. When you begin to experiment, agree that you won't criticize each other's performance, but that afterwards you'll have a conversation to check in about how it felt. Encourage your partner to talk back to you so you feel it's a mutual experiment. Ask how s/he would like to receive feedback from you and state how you'd like to receive feedback yourself.

Erotic experimentation can feel emotionally risky for both of you. Be especially attentive to each other's need for support. Ask for support yourself, if you need it. Remember, you're learning something that can be erotic and fun. That should be a strong incentive, even if you feel nervous at first!

Now's the time to share your collection of erotic writing with your partner. You can do this in a variety of ways: leave a stack of books and magazines with a note saying, "Please mark your favorites;" liven up a car trip by telling each other what stories and fantasies you each liked best; or pull out all the stops, design a fantasy weekend in bed, and start reading to each other. Obviously, this technique requires that you both be at least willing, if not avid, readers.

Sharing your favorite erotic material will do more than just begin to clue you in to your own and your partner's favorite dirty words and phrases. It will also help you both get more familiar with the other's erotic hot spots.

You may discover erotic desires you want to explore together; you may uncover fantasies only one of you prefers and that you decide to restrict to a verbal role in your lovemaking – if you share them at all. Any one of many reasons may dictate that you decide to talk about something rather than try it – safe sex or monogamy considerations, fear, wanting to keep it hot in fantasy (some people fear that trying out a fantasy will ruin it, and once in a while they're right), even the small matter of physical impossibility! This is all perfectly okay. Some of our most potent fantasy scenarios never get closer than words whispered in our ears, but they are no less powerful sexual experiences for that.

Do It On the Phone

Another useful trick when beginning to talk with a partner is to do it live, but over the phone. You will have a cloak of privacy that respects your shyness yet doesn't shore it up. Arrange a time you can feel comfortable exploring telephone play. If your partner has requested phone sex or dirty talk, great – but you might still want to talk about it before you start dialing, if only to reassure yourself that the timing is right and that your lover's response will be positive. Otherwise, you run the risk of putting your partner on the spot, perhaps rendering him or her as tongue-tied as you're trying to learn not to be!

Phone sex can be very smutty, highly romantic, or anything in between. Nasty and starry-eyed, naughty and nice, aren't either/or options – they exist on a continuum. In fact, who says you can't be naughty and romantic at the same time?

Even if you and your partner have never masturbated in each other's presence, you might want to try it over the phone. Touch yourself and describe what you're doing; ask him or her to direct you; direct him or her. You can pretend you're together making love, or you can pretend you're strangers. You can ask for things you're shy about when face-to-face; you can describe your ideal lovemaking to each other.

Of course, you can do all this in person, too. Picking up the phone first, before the face-to-face encounter, is optional – but it often helps if you find that in person you get too easily distracted by all your wonderful options for non-verbal communication. As fabulous as kissing is, it's hard to make yourself understood when your lips are pressed against your lover's. Phone sex forces you to talk – or at least moan and sigh – because you can't touch or see each other's expressions. Besides, phone sex is a hot alternative whether you're shy or bold.

You can also practice your phone skills with an actual stranger – via either paid-for phone sex or a chat line. In the first case you'll be conversing with a professional who talks for a living; in the second, with an enthusiastic amateur. In either case, you'll have a more satisfying experience if you approach your phone pal with courtesy. If you've never called a professional line before, 'fess up and tell your phone fantasy facilitator that you want to learn new talking-dirty skills, either by example or by direction. This will distinguish you from the other callers somewhat, and you'll be more likely to get useful material from the call. Of course, if this situation is a turn-on for you, go for it and put your hands in your pants – everyone else does.

A hint – most phone sex workers find it very annoying when a caller grills them about their state of arousal, their personal lives, etc. Remember, it may be just a job to the woman or man on the other end of the line, but at least you're talking to a pro! And some phone professionals do love to talk dirty; although these people will likely prove the most inspirational, don't underestimate the usefulness of learning tips from people who didn't start out as "naturals" – who had to learn specific skills so they could be good at this specialized job.

While talking dirty is the focus of this chapter, I should also mention another possibility you may find you enjoy – writing dirty. I don't mean becoming an erotic writer for publication, although once you get started, you may want to do just that. I mean writing explicit notes to your lover, or penning vignettes or journal entries to turn yourself on (maybe in preparation for narrating them to someone later), describing a sexy scene from a dream, exchanging written fantasies with your partner (which you can read aloud to each other), or – most interactive of all – sitting at a keyboard and exploring the cyberworld of computer sex. If you can summon forth purple prose from your fingertips while another person waits with bated breath for your words, can increased comfort talking voice-to-voice be far behind? You should be aware that your fellow erotic adventurers in the world of cybersex may not always be who they say they are. But then, you too may find you enjoy trying on an entirely new sexual persona that does not match your physical self or everyday personality.

HOT TALK – FUN, AND GOOD FOR YOU, TOO

Explicit talk can be a fabulous sex toy. But if you need extra encouragement to take the plunge, remember that both your sexual self-esteem and your sex life are liable to get a boost from learning to talk in bed and wherever else you share sexual time with partners. For one thing, you can use hot talk to convey very specific information about who you are – what you want, how you like to be touched, how you feel in the erotic moment – in a way that feels sexy and accessible to your partner. Conveying information erotically – not just explicitly – increases the likelihood that your partner will respond positively to your feedback or request.

As an example, let's look at that hot potato, safe sex. We receive many more exhortations to have safe sex than instructions to help us negotiate it; most of us know it's good for us, but lots of us still complain it isn't any fun. Mary Poppins isn't usually quoted as an authority about safe sex, but remember what she said about a spoonful of sugar – it "helps the medicine go down in a most delightful way!"

To illustrate: which invitation would you rather respond to? "You're going to have to put a condom on that thing before we go any further" – or "Let me get a rubber on that hot cock of yours so you can slide it deep into my hungry cunt" (or whichever orifice is appropriate). How about "I'm going to drip some lube into the tip of this condom so when I slide it over your cock and roll it down with my mouth you can feel every little move I make"? Or "Look at me while I slip this slick latex glove on my hand. You're very lucky to be playing doctor with someone this experienced."

To feel in control sexually most of us have to feel that our partner hears us and is willing to respond to our limits and preferences. While limits and individual needs must be honored with or without the icing of sexy talk, the truth is that many of us get defensive and may not respond to direct feedback in a very open way. Conveying direction and preference erotically significantly increases our chances of getting not only a positive response, but a passionate one. In turn, successful sexual communication can substantially improve our self-esteem, especially if we've been feeling frustrated and silent about any aspect of our sex lives. It can also help minimize partners' defensiveness and resentment; the idea is to make sexual communication win-win, not only positive but positively pleasurable.

Most sex therapists teach a version of this strategy when a couple has become mired in resentful, difficult communication. Results improve when we communicate respectfully and positively. Instead of "You never spend any time caressing me!" wouldn't most partners respond better to "I love feeling your hands running all over my body, my breasts, my belly, stroking my back, getting me so hot"? In addition to being sexier, the second example is phrased in positive, not negative, terms. Too, when I add an extra note of eroticism to a request, *I'm* already in a more receptive mood when my request is met. Erotic talk is not just for heating up your partner, but for you too.

I don't recommend using hot talk just to get your partner to respond more positively to your sexual requests, needs, and limits. Here's why. Unless it's also erotic for you to make these requests erotically, you will probably resent having to present yourself this way to get your needs met. If it feels more like jumping through hoops than bringing both passion and easier communication to bed, take another look at your situation. Does it seem as though your partner doesn't respond respectfully to you and must be manipulated? Or, do you object to giving your partner direct feedback about sex, erotic or otherwise, and really wish that the sex would be better without your having to speak up?

If it's the former, you and your partner have a problem, and you may need to ask yourself whether there is the possibility of change. Your options range from confronting your partner and establishing new expectations together, to finding a counselor who can help both of you with your communications skills, to terminating the relationship.

If it's the latter, your problem may be with your expectations about sex itself. Read those romances and porn novels for the steamy scenarios, dear – but don't take them for the last word in sex education! Most of us have to be directive with our partners at least some of the time, and if they respond to the feedback our sex lives nearly always improve.

When you make your sexual desires known by talking erotically, you'll find not only that it gives you better results and makes the conversation easier to have - you'll find it fun and sexy, enhancing the encounter for you as well as for your partner. Remember that the main reason to be exhibitionistic is still that it enhances your own sexuality, turns you on, increases your pleasure. Learning to do something pleasurable involves taking greater control of your own sexuality, thus helping you feel better about yourself. The better, more empowered, more sophisticated you feel about sex, the better it can be.

Erotic talk can help put you in the mood as well as set the mood. Whether you talk or listen or have a lusty conversation, talking dirty helps you acknowledge the eroticism you feel with your partner, lets you signal that you're attracted to or interested in particular kinds of sex, and contributes greatly to an erotic atmosphere. It lets you put your toe into the water of an unfamiliar sexual practice to learn whether it feels warm and inviting. It also serves as great proof that you aren't as shy as you used to be!

IDEAS AND EXERCISES

Here are more ideas to help you become more comfortable talking dirty with your lover.

Take turns with your partner doing this exercise. While your partner makes love to you, describe what s/he's doing and how it feels. This might sound more descriptive than erotic at first, but give it a try. If it helps to give it some context, start each statement with "You're..." "You're touching my face gently, you're kissing my neck, you're nibbling the inside of my wrist, you're tugging on my nipples, you're spreading my legs..." and so forth. By the time the sexual encounter has heated all the way up, what you describe will sound like talking dirty, I assure you! For a nice variation on this exercise, tell your lover what to do to you. "Kiss me hard. Suck on my nipples. Stroke your hands up my thighs, but stop right before..." Besides being an exercise in erotic talk, this one can easily turn into an exercise in expressing what you like sexually.

Of course, you and your partner can do this simultaneously during lovemaking. If you still feel a little performance anxiety, try doing the descriptive exercise together, talking at the same time. Your words will filter through to your partner, but s/he will be talking over them, and vice versa; that way you may feel you have more freedom to speak out. The erotic cacophony can also be very exciting. Audiotape this, if you're both willing!

Another way to explore talking and fantasy with your lover can happen during sex, as foreplay, or during non-explicitly sexual, playful time. Simply narrate fantasies to each other. You can get them from your erotic reading, from videos you've liked, from your own fantasy life – wherever. If you need a place to start, imagine you've just peeped through a keyhole and witnessed someone masturbating, or a couple having sex, or some other erotic vision. Be as descriptive as you can, not just of the people you see, but of the kind of sex they're having.

Alternatively, you and your partner can do this exercise in the form of questions and answers. You might find this draws details out you wouldn't ordinarily have narrated. "What was he wearing?" "Where did she have her hands?"

Another really fun way to do this sort of exercise involves the two of you telling the story together. Start out by setting the stage, then let your partner embellish it. Then you take over again. Then give the narrative thread back to your partner. And so on. If you have a number of uninhibited friends who like to talk about sexual topics, this exercise is great fun when done in a group – it livens up any party!

Especially when done with your partner, this will help you flesh out your fantasy world, but it can also help you tune in to erotic detail – which can have real ramifications on your ability to take in sensually and visually exciting details of your environment in real life, not just in fantasy.

Here's a slightly more structured one. Have your partner describe the environment where the fantasy takes place (is it in a castle in Spain? On a beach in Tahiti? In a whorehouse in 17th century London?) and the characters (the fantasy could be about the two of you, about Napoleon and Josephine, about your two favorite movie stars). Now make up the fantasy. What will you have Napoleon do to Josephine in Tahiti? What are you and your lover doing in that whorehouse?

If you do these kinds of exercises when you're having sex, you may notice a curious side effect. The physical pleasure you experience from sexual stimulation may help you get over your self-consciousness about talking. But you might also feel an opposite effect. Talking during sex can distract you slightly from the physical, so some people who have difficulty achieving orgasm actually find that climax sneaks up and surprises them when they're focusing less on whether their body will work and more on erotic images. You'll find this especially true if you really eroticize talking, because then talking itself will be part of your arousal. Listening to your lover talk can be positively orgasm-inducing. In an erotic conversation with your lover, talking and listening meld into a very interactive pleasure, and you're less likely to feel on stage and on the spot.

For the especially self-conscious, all these partner exercises can be done with your eyes closed, in darkness, even blindfolded. Sometimes this helps free you up to talk because you then focus less on being listened to or observed. Alternatively, you can do them sitting back to back. I once observed a phone sex conversation roleplayed by two women who were sitting this way, and the position seemed to add an exciting element for them – it seemed that they put more into the words because they couldn't see each other, the way phone sex tends to distill the whole encounter into talking and listening. Yet they were right next to each other, not alone. Doing this exercise gives you your partner's presence, but pares away some of the distraction and hopefully some of your shyness.

Erotic talk need not be narratively-oriented, though telling stories is fun and story-telling can provide helpful structure and context for the shy person or the neophyte. You can also give directions, as I suggested in the exercise above. You can focus on describing and embellishing – "your hot, sweet, dripping pussy" or "his hard, straining, rampant cock." But one of the most effective sexy talkers I've ever met was an absolute minimalist, and the only complete sentence he ever used in bed was, "Ohhh, I'm gonna come!" This phrase punctuated the sighs, moans, and heavy breathing of our sexual encounters to devastating effect, for I always had the impression he was so overcome by the power of his impending orgasm that he simply had to announce it. I found this habit of his extremely exciting.

Robert talks all the way through his sexual encounters, spinning a web with his voice and his words that carries his partner in its escalating passion. He pays as much careful attention to his tone of voice as to his choice of words; his inflection weaves the erotic spell. The other crucial element in his hot talk repertoire deserves special mention: he pays close attention to his partners' hot spots, fantasies, and desires, sometimes asking direct questions to get more in-depth information, and he stores up every tiny fact to use later. This is a very effective tactic. I like hearing sexy talk even when I suspect the person says the same thing every time, but when Robert talks I know he's talking to me because he's bringing in elements meant to turn me on.

So when you do partnered explorations of erotic talk, pay attention to your lover's language and to her or his fantasies; look for recurring themes, favorite words, and heightened arousal. These are fine points that will help guarantee you get the response you want when you begin talking to your lover. After all, hearing yourself talk is all well and good – but most hot talkers I know feed off the passionate energy of an aroused and appreciative audience. For best effect, talk about something you both find highly erotic. When you do this, you'll find that the words, the sounds of your voices, and all your physical movements and sensations blend together into a powerfully hot experience.

After doing any of these partnered exercises, talk together about how it was for you. What felt especially exciting and what was disappointing? What was easier/harder for you than you expected? Would you like to modify it next time for greater effect? How? Be sure both of you get a chance to express your feelings and that you clarify whose turn-ons – and difficulties – are whose.

In fact, you can do this to check in about your feelings regarding any erotic experiment. It's a great way to prevent the syndrome where one of you is thrilled with a new activity but the other is less than enchanted. Remember, better communication usually paves the way for better sex.

Dirty Talkers Speak Up

Before we move on to look at other elements of talking dirty, roleplay and choosing your preferred language, here are more suggestions for getting comfortable and practicing. I asked several people who find talking dirty an important part of their sexuality to get together and share their secrets. Here's what they said.

"It's erotic for me to talk dirty when I'm by myself," says erotic writer and playwright Blake C. Aarens. "I have this whole repertoire that I can play with in private. But I also love reading to people. It doesn't matter what. It isn't so much what I'm saying as using my voice." Blake, herself a performer, does have a wonderful voice. So does Jamie, who says she gave conscious attention to developing her voice so her erotic talk would be more effective. "I worked on my speaking voice – it's literally different now than it used to be.

"It wouldn't occur to me talk dirty by myself," she adds. "But I love making up stories with another person. I like sex improv! It's like getting a grab bag in acting class, where you have to make up a story with what you have." Performer Julia Trahan agrees: "It's just like improvisational theater. You have your action – sometimes you go onstage and that's all you have. You act 'as if,' and then this whole world is created."

Blake adds a suggestion for beginners (or anyone else) to try. "To do the grab bag exercise, get a bunch of different things that may seem totally unrelated. Put 'em in a bag and pull three out at a time. Then make up a story." You can use actual objects in the grab bag – sex toys, articles of clothing, even things that have no obvious relationship to sex. Or you and your partner can write things on slips of paper – objects, scenarios, types of sexual activity, erotic roles, places – and, randomly drawing three, use them to concoct a story to talk about.

Jackie Strano and Shar Rednour are lovers who delight in hot talk. Until they met, they hadn't always found partners with whom they could openly talk dirty and fantasize. "I love fantasy play and reading erotica," Jackie says. "We read aloud to each other while we're masturbating. I love kinky little stories – throw in all the taboos. We can have five imaginary people in the room, gang-banging away. With other lovers I've only been able to allude to fantasies like that. I always internalized it and thought I was too kinky. I've tried talking dirty with unresponsive partners, but I might as well just watch TV."

Besides liking blue language, Shar tells erotic stories. "I've eased into it by telling people that I like to do it. Sometimes I actually start with children's fantasies, where everything's always sparkly. I see how receptive they are to that. Or I read erotica. I have a book beside the bed, and say, 'Do you mind if I read you a story?' See how they respond to that. Then you can segue into your own stories."

Shar thinks one reason she and Jackie enjoy story-telling and fantasy so completely is that they're still in touch with the childlike fun of make-believe – they just indulge in a grown-up version of it now. "A lot of people get far removed from the power of imagination. They forget that all you have to do is say, 'Here's a cup of pretend tea. Here's cake. And now we have cake and tea.'"

Were you an imaginative child? If so, think back to those days when cake and tea materialized out of thin air, you transformed into Superman, or you had an invisible best friend. You'll use the same capacity as an adult – only you'll imagine more adult and sexual things. "We'll literally start something sexual by saying 'Let's pretend,'" says Shar, "which I hadn't said since I was a child." Even if you missed out on games of "let's pretend" when you were a little girl or boy, it's not too late to start now! This sort of play, besides leading you right into erotic talk, can also lead you into roleplaying games.

"Before getting into raunchy talking dirty," Shar continues, "which is so worthwhile, I recommend it for everyone – do 'let's pretend' in scenarios that you feel totally safe in. Let's pretend you're the stereotypical repairman. We fuck just the way that we normally fuck, but we talk according to the characters' roles – you'd say, 'Well, Miss, got a bedroom around here?'"

Talking can serve as a technique to make fantasy seem real; but you can also talk to make the present seem even more vivid. Blake explains, "Talking dirty for me is a way to express sensation. To let my lover know explicitly what the sensations are like in my body. Because they can't know unless I tell them. I describe how it feels. What I'm smelling, the sound, how the timbre of a voice affects me, bringing in sight and taste and touch. I love listening, too. I remember having sex with this boy in college. I was on top of him, moving very slowly. And he grabbed my shoulders, and just started saying the word 'slow.' 'Slow, slow,' over and over again."

"Part of getting somebody captivated is believing in yourself," Blake continues. "I get my partner engaged with their own ears – lowering the volume of my speech so they have to lean forward to hear me, drawing them in, making them focus. That gives them a role to play too – that of listener. That totally pulls the other person in."

More hints from my talkative friends: Try talking for short periods of time. Whisper. Turn the lights out. If either you or your partner fumbles for words, you can ask each other to be more specific or ask each other questions to draw out detail, which can help you get more involved in your narrative.

Robert recommends describing "what I did to you. What I'm doing to you. What I'm going to do to you." "What I thought about doing to you yesterday when you weren't here," adds Blake.

Use the mirror to practice. "If you can get to a point where you can say it in the mirror without cracking up, you can take anybody with you," says Blake. Shar agrees. "Practice in the shower. Talk to yourself when your partner isn't home." "Talk out loud in the car," suggests Jackie. "Do it wherever you feel safe."

Besides giving attention to sexual language you like, start developing an ear for voices. Watching movies, particularly older movies where people used their voices especially effectively, can help you tune in to this quality. It's easy to listen to your own voice – most of us own answering machines, and you can use the "outgoing message" function to practice. (If you say anything salacious, remember to erase it at the end of your practice session – you wouldn't want to nonconsensually fire up a telephone solicitor or upset your mother!) Or leave yourself a voicemail message; think of it as practice for leaving a sexy message for someone else.

"Talk about sex where you can't really do anything about it," says Jackie. "Surrounded by people in a cafe the day after you've had great sex. On a bus." "At a boring cocktail party," suggests Shar. "It's so great, when you're sitting there with your fake little smiles on, to lean over and say, 'You know, I bet you really wanna get up behind that woman and bend her over and shove your dick between her ass cheeks. I bet she has panty-hose on, and you'll have to rip 'em off. They probably smell like her pussy, since she's been wearing them all day long.'"

Talk to each other while masturbating. Describe how you masturbate, or a past sexual encounter. Read books together, watch porn together, tell each other the scenarios you like best. "You don't necessarily have to start out face to face," says Jackie; "it can be over the phone, so it's safer. To defuse the whole after-the-fact – or before-the-fact – conversation, write it down. One day we sat in a bar, just for fun, making a list of fantasies. One, having public sex downtown at lunch hour. Two, something else. We kept them, and sometimes we pull an idea out of the hat."

"Asking to be fucked is very, very simple, and it works like a charm," says Shar. "I always wanted to say, 'Fuck my pussy!' but it was this Hustler term. I was so shy to say it at first. So I started out with, 'Oh, please.' Or, 'Yeah, do that! Uh-huh, uh-huh. More, more.'

"Just remember the simple things that you learn when you're one and a half. 'Yes. No. More. More.' More means 'food,' it means 'bottle,' it means 'kisses,' it means 'story,' it means... everything." (Not to mention "don't stop"– another very hot but non-explicit phrase.) "Progress from breathing, to moaning, to words, phrases, and sentences."

The flip side of this technique is for the other partner to take over and ask questions: "Yeah, you like that, baby, don't you?" "What do you want me to do to you now?" "How does it feel when I...?" "You can tell from the way talking escalates," adds Shar. "If they're getting hotter from what you're saying, you can say even more." "That can come with time, too, and trust," says Jackie. "Knowing that if you call somebody a 'greedy little whore' they're not gonna get up and lock you out of their house."

"Saying what you like is one way to start talking," says Shar. "Tell what you used to imagine when you masturbated. You can tell what you masturbated to when you were fifteen. When you were nineteen. When you were twenty-five. When you had your first relationship, or what you think about when you're in the car masturbating, or in the shower masturbating, in bed masturbating."

What? You don't masturbate in the car? You don't have to be a dyed-in-the-wool show-off to find a place to begin. "There's a lot to be said for just starting out by saying, 'Oh...' and your lover's name," says Jackie. "Just get your vocal chords going. Describe your partner. Say, 'Oh, your clit's getting so swollen,' or, 'Your pussy's getting wet.' Describe the situation, describe their responses."

Blake had a lover with a deep, sultry voice. "When she would say my name... oh, god. It didn't matter where we were. It didn't matter what the context was. And she knew the effect it had on me. I would call that talking dirty!"

Hmmmm.... so would I.

And remember, there is no formula. Sometimes the most unexpected vocalizations are the most effective. Julia once had a girlfriend who was a gospel singer. "Whenever she was turned on, she wouldn't use words, she would sing this melody into my ear." I also met a woman who sang during sex. It was completely engaging. She made up a melody and sang little snatches of sexy nonsense.

Shar gives another example. "I had a roommate who would call up phone sex. One time he got a guy on the line who said, 'These are the only words that you can say, no matter what: "fuck," "daddy," and "please."'" So from the other room I heard, 'Oh, fuck. Oh, fuck. Oh, daddy, oh, daddy, oh, please. Ohh... please. Oh. FUCK. Oh, daddy! Oh, FUCK! Oh, please, please fuck daddy, please fuck daddy, please fuck daddy, please fuck daddy. Fuck! Fuck! Fuck! Fuck! Oh, Daddy! Oh daddy, oh daddy, oh daddy, oh daddy. Please! Please daddy, please, please, PLEASE, PLEASE!'

"I thought, 'There's an idea that's going into my file!'"

A couple of my friends use erotic talk to give themselves nerve – or permission. Robert says he uses talking dirty because it lets him interest partners without having to cross any boundaries they might have about touch. "If I can use my voice to get somebody really turned on, they're more likely to ask, 'Would you touch me?' Then I'm on it, right away." Julia is shy with partners; "If I'm describing what I'm about to do to a person, I get myself turned on, but maybe I'm actually feeling a little hesitant," she says. "But if I say, 'this is what I'm gonna do,' it means I'm going to do it! It gives me so much confidence."

Shar is indubitably outgoing and outrageous, but she gets mad when people think talking and showing off are easy for her because "she's different." "As an outspoken person and as an exhibitionist, I want to say that speaking up, whether it's a sexual situation, or a classroom situation, or in public, whether you're outspoken or shy, always takes courage. You muster up the courage, and you do it. People literally think it's easier for me! But I still have to tell myself, 'Your mom will still love you, you'll still have a birthday cake if you say "Fuck me up the ass harder!"'

"It's still scary each time with a new partner or a new situation, or with an old partner and a new situation. It's not that I'm not scared. It's not that

I don't turn red and swallow hard. It's not that I'm not nervous or shaking inside. I'm still all those things."

Her point – echoed by everyone I spoke to – is that if you want to do something, it's worth it to give yourself the pep talk, promise yourself the birthday cake, take a deep breath and dive in, nervous or no. That Shar parallels talking in bed to talking in class is very apt; you're in the process of learning, challenging yourself to stretch your abilities.

With a partner it's very likely you'll both be stretching. "In talking dirty it's really important to take care of each other," says Shar. "To make the other person feel comfortable. You can say, 'Well, if we mess up, we'll just laugh. If we totally mess up and we don't have sex, we'll have sex tomorrow!'" "When we first got together she was telling me a story," says Jackie, "and suddenly she broke out of it and said, 'Is it OK if I bring a man into it?' Because she had asked, from then on she knew that was not a taboo." While on one hand talking dirty might seem like a risk, in reality you're giving each other a lot of information, getting clearer about what's okay and not okay. It can make you much more proficient as a partner.

Everyone agreed erotic talk is a wonderful way to deepen the connection you have with your partner. Blake says, "When you're talking back and forth, and not only are you saying what you want to say, and what the other person wants to hear, but they're also speaking from their own turn-on, with an eye toward your response – it's just incredible. Particularly if your ears and your mouths are connected at the same time your genitals are connected."

"It's something people can get better at," says Jamie, "and that is absolutely worth practicing. You'll probably have a really good time practicing. But partly it has to do with connection between people." Blake agrees: "It has to do with how well you retain non-sexual information about the other person. The colors and food they like, and their history. Talk about specifics. That engages them and allows them to be drawn in and interact with you. When you bring that into your aural play, it will let you tailor what you say to that specific person in a way that nothing else will. Then they know that this is about what's happening between the two of you."

"When you figure out what somebody responds to, that kind of stuff is sacred," cautions Blake. "You have to be really respectful of it."

That's a vital point – it means no bringing it up in arguments, no using it later in a recriminating fashion. To do so is to utterly breach trust with a partner.

"When you find a partner who loves to talk too, it's like show-and-tell," says Jackie. "Somebody is looking at you bright-eyed and egging you on. That doesn't exist in a vacuum. You have to have appreciation. The call-and-response part of it brings you out of your shell."

Shar adds, "One of the pleasures of talking dirty is re-living special moments. Jackie and I play the 'how much we like each other game' all the time. I think everybody does mutual appreciation when relationships are new. You can do the same physical thing five nights in a row, tell different stories, or talk differently to each other. Then you re-live it all later, in those cafes! It helps keep your relationship really electric because you have that much more to re-live. Now you can say, 'And then when you said you were the UPS man, oh my god, I went through the roof!' Or 'How did you know that I like to be called "bitch?" It feels so nasty when you do that! Oh my god, you read my mind!'

"It really keeps communication up. You go to that very special intimate place; you're sharing communication, and at the same time you're going into this wonderful world together where nobody else can go with you."

Besides loving hot talk for its arousing and intimate qualities, Blake has a deep and serious reason to appreciate it. She was sexually abused when she was growing up. "The abuse was always done in absolute silence. So as part of my healing, I want to make noise. I want to know where I am, who I'm with, what I'm doing. I want it out there loud and clear, at all times. Talking is a way for me to get out of that silence – to this day, sex and silence drives me nuts. It's a prescription for a flashback."

Blake and I talked about the usefulness of erotic talk as an emotional reading about how you feel about having sex: right here, right now, with this person. When I start talking, I know I want to be there. I can tell I want the kind of sex I'm having by what's coming out of my mouth. "By the same token," says Blake, "you know by listening to what comes out of your mouth when you don't want to be there. You can physically do something you don't really want to, but the minute you start giving voice to it, it totally wakes you up: 'Time to put your clothes on, Blake, and go home.'"

Perhaps especially if you've felt the effects of silence in your sex life and intimate relationships, learning to talk can help you feel more powerful and more present. What shy person hasn't felt the frustration and humiliation of being tongue-tied? I'll bet you can instantly think of three times a sexual experience could have been more pleasurable if only you'd spoken up. When you learn to give voice to your erotic feelings, desires, and fantasies, you may find that your shyness melts away – but in any event, your sex life will be richer and better.

€ 6 ✸

The Librarian Takes Down Her Hair –
Awakening Erotic Personas

P art of you isn't shy. Now it's time to discover which part.
We'll explore ways to do just that by looking at the idea of erotic
roles and personas. Just like an actor, you can try on any role; if
you're a good actor, in or out of bed, you may find that you can play many
erotic parts convincingly. When a role appeals to you very deeply, however,
so deeply that it seems to be a part of you, you've probably discovered one
of your erotic personas.

There is a difference between personas and roles. You put on a
role, something like a costume which is based in personality rather than
clothing. You can also think of a role as a character you assume. A persona,
on the other hand, is part of who you are, and has more to do with feelings
that well up from inside you. You might try on or adopt a role, but you
discover a persona.

S/M – AND OTHER – ROLES

Taking on roles can be a fun, enriching part of sex and fantasy. Consider
the world of S/M (sometimes also called BDSM), or erotic power exchange,

which includes a lot of erotic role-playing. Even if you have no interest in this type of eroticism, S/M practitioners' expertise in playing with roles and clear, precise communication can instruct and inspire. Here's some basic information about S/M, in case you don't know much about it.

When I talk about people who do S/M, I refer only to those who willingly engage in dominance and submission or play with intense sensation. Couples with an unacknowledged, nonconsensual dynamic of inequality, up to and including emotional or physical violence, are something else altogether. In some couples one partner is always dominant (or, perhaps more accurately, domineering) and the other is always submissive to the other's wishes. For these couples, such behavior rarely stops at the bedroom door.

S/M, by contrast, is mutually agreed-upon and consensual; with few exceptions, S/M people do not think of or treat each other as unequal, no matter what their role preferences during erotic play. The world of S/M includes many sorts of erotic and fantasy behaviors, and a person may prefer some S/M activities while having no interest in others.

The main roles in S/M carry the terms "top" and "bottom." In very simplified terms, the top is the "do-er" while the bottom is the "do-ee." The kinds of activities each might prefer and engage in will vary radically, from restraint to spanking and beyond, but the breakdown of who does what will not change: the top takes responsibility for doing erotic, mutually-agreed-upon things to the bottom. The bottom lets the top do these things until both of them decide to stop. Within each of these basic roles, many other roles can be played and characters assumed: a bottom may enjoy feeling like a maidservant, a sex slave, a naughty schoolboy, or a trained dog; a top may wish to play a policeman, a sultana, lord of the manor, or a kidnapper. The kinds of characters each might assume are limited only by the players' imaginations and how compatible the roles are with each other.

Besides deciding what you want to do in a scene, you need to decide in what role you want to do it. Will you be a top or a bottom? The negotiation doesn't end there. Suppose I want to top and my partner wants to bottom. But my idea of being a top involves having my bottom lavish me with attention, call me "Goddess," draw me a bubble bath, scrub my back and peel me grapes. My partner wants to be a naughty puppy who wears a rhinestone dog collar with his name on it while I swat him with a rolled-up newspaper. No compatible scene here! I may end up fuming in the bathtub that I had to draw while my "puppy" whines outside the bathroom door.

Roles often come in pairs: shy but eager virgin and roguish seducer, teacher and precocious student, stern sergeant and raw recruit, streetwise hooker and horny customer, strangers in the night, to name just a few. Notice that with many such pairs you could play S/M games if you wanted, though you could also have what some S/M people term "vanilla" sex – that is, genitally-involved, old-fashioned licking, sucking, fucking, and fondling (the term "vanilla" reminds us that there are many flavors of sex to choose from). The way you and your partner relate to each other during sex, though, may be very different if you take on roles, even if you proceed to do the same physical things you always do. The roles may affect your emotional experience, what you say, the way the sex feels, and your degree of arousal. You may even like certain kinds of sex, erotic talk, and fantasy in one role but not in another.

The individuals taking on these roles might also decide to change roles from time to time – people who enjoy playing as tops sometimes and bottoms at other times are called "switches."

Even if you have no interest in S/M per se you can see that these roles might stretch to include what you do. If you ever take charge in sex and "run the fuck," that's topping. If you lie back and let your partner pleasure you any way s/he wants to, that's bottoming (unless you told him or her to do it, in which case it's also topping). However, when it's time to get out of bed or get untied or stop saying "Yes, Mistress, whatever you wish, Mistress" – in short, when erotic playtime is over – you are probably no longer "a top" or "a bottom." You put the role you assumed for play back into the toybox. You and your partner probably regard each other more or less as equals, not as dominant and submissive. A few people choose to maintain these roles all the time, but most find this quite difficult to do.

If you've been doing your reading to look for hot fantasies and favorite nasty words, you've probably come upon fantasy roles – not necessarily S/M ones – to which you respond erotically. These roles, if they "fit" you, can give you context for all kinds of erotic play, including exhibitionism and, especially, talking dirty. Sometimes words elude us until we've developed or discovered a character for whom they feel natural. If you respond with arousal to the role – if, for example, you find it really hot to pretend to be a virgin – you might find when in role that you instinctively know how to behave and what to say. Role-playing is sexual theater, and the role functions a bit like a script. Note that the role must have some sort of familiarity to you – you must have some sense of the kind of sexual personality or preference the role represents. If you're familiar with Jungian psychology, you might say these characters are erotic archetypes.

Personas: Who Lives Inside You?

Let's move now from thinking of roles to thinking of personas. If you respond erotically to a role, simply knowing when you assume it how you're supposed to behave, there must be something in you that recognizes that character and resonates with it. I'm sure you can think of roles that have no attraction for you, and if you tried to play one of them in bed you'd feel disconnected and wooden. But you may be able to think of other roles that you can drop into just like that. If not, you are likely to discover them as you continue to explore your fantasies. Frequently our most powerful erotic roles develop first in our minds.

Within a role that feels very right, you may discern something that's uniquely you. Part of you, let's say, *is* a virgin. How do you express this? Are you fearful, or hot with excitement? Perhaps you have both feelings at once. The way you feel when you're in touch with this virgin part of yourself may or may not resemble the feelings you had when you actually "lost your virginity" in real life (assuming you have). Your feelings may, instead, reflect the way you wish it had felt. If this virgin state feels erotic to you, you may call upon it during sex – or it may come over you unexpectedly, especially if you're trying something new and you do feel virginal again. Your feelings will be your own; you will not feel like you're playing a part.

The first day I went to work in the peep show I felt on edge with nerves and performance anxiety. Finally it dawned on me – I was a virgin that day. I'd certainly never had that kind of sex before. When I said, "Gee, Mister, I've never done anything like this," I told the absolute truth! From then on I had a great time because I had given erotic shape to my feelings of excited, nervous, "I-don't-know-what-to-do" – which are the feelings I always attribute to the virgin role, and this experience let me uncover a persona animated by just these feelings.

I also have a little girl persona which I experience as erotic. I am not remembering experiences I had as a child; I have no history of childhood sex play, either consensually or not. However, I do feel very young, and also very sexual, in ways that are curious and exploratory but also inexperienced. I do not believe for a minute that all or even some little girls feel this way; it is not a projection of my ideas about the sexual feelings of little girls. Rather, it is a complicated amalgam of the memories I retain of childhood emotional feelings, grafted onto my adult sexual self. When I feel like a little girl, I respond sexually to the same things I do when I feel like an adult – but the response itself feels different, because this persona has its own perspective.

Having a young or childlike persona is quite common; for some people this is erotic and for others not. You may have heard about the concept of "the inner child;" according to this theory, we retain within us the emotional essence of our childhood selves, even when we're grown up. The erotic persona I've described is not my inner child, although I do remember feeling sexual curiosity when I was little. Many people never experience their childlike or youthful personas as sexual. While some, especially adults whose childhood or youth was affected by sexual experience they did not consent to, would not dream of having sex in this persona, others find this kind of play actually feels very healing. They may feel childlike, but they are no longer powerless children: hence they stay in control by doing only what they want and desire to do.

If you have a childlike inner self, it will tell you what it wants, likes, and fears. Listening to a persona is exactly like listening to your own feelings – your persona is a part of you, and its feelings are your feelings, even when those feelings differ somewhat from the ones you're usually aware of. Personas can, in fact, once you become aware of them, assist you in having conscious access to a fuller range of your feelings.

What does this have to do with overcoming shyness? Everything. What happens when the reserved, prim librarian lets down her hair? Focusing on the erotic implications of our various personality facets, how can we access the sexy and bold parts of ourselves? It's often easier to be sexually outgoing if you try on a role or, especially, tap into a persona. There's something about finding an alternate side of yourself or a role that's not "really" you that opens the door to new ways of expressing your sexuality. Starting wherever you are, you can use your new self to access and express sexual inspiration, even if you feel, "I couldn't do that, I could never be that way." Maybe *you* can't – but you can assume a role or discover a persona who can.

Let's see if I can clarify this by means of a couple of illustrations. Suppose I'm shy and rather passive in bed (like I used to be, in fact). But I fantasize about being a self-assured, even sexually controlling, dominatrix. I dream about men falling on their knees and begging me to tell them what I want. Maybe I even give voice to this dominatrix while I masturbate, whispering, "Lick my pussy, boy!" as I turn the vibrator onto high speed.

Now let's say that I'm so inspired by this fantasy that when Hallowe'en comes around, I go to a shop that sells lingerie and fetishwear and buy myself over-the-knee, shiny black boots and a black leather corset. I put on severe makeup and a flowing black wig. My boyfriend likes me in the clothes, and playfully, I say, "On your knees!" Strangely enough, I'm only surprised for an instant when he complies! The role fits me because I've practiced it in my fantasies; I know what to do and what to say. My shyness is bypassed because it's not really me.

But this experience awakens a formerly unknown part of me. After that fateful Hallowe'en, I am more talkative in bed; I speak up and say what I want more easily. The dominatrix has, in a way, taken root – or, more accurately, I finally uncovered her. (And of course I still put on the boots and corset from time to time!)

Some people might react less than well to the idea of personas, thinking that we contemporary Americans are less integrated and whole already than we want to be. The idea of discovering personas is not to "split your personality" – if that's even possible to do voluntarily. Instead, it's a way to take seriously the voices and perspectives of the inner selves that many of us deny in our search to be "normal," acceptable, and like our peers: it's a way of letting our full self out, one aspect at a time. As you'll see below, this can lead to greater integration, not less.

When we set out to learn how to explore the up-til-now hidden facets of ourselves, it begins to click when we find a place to speak from – like doing improvisation, only deeper. Inspiration then bubbles up from a source we aren't consciously aware of, making talk, showing off, or other sex play feel completely spontaneous. Not only is it exciting to feel this way, the spontaneity can also bypass shyness completely.

Meet Two Persona Professionals

Sybil Holiday and Bill Henkin present workshops together and consult with individuals and couples about personas. Sybil also works as a dominatrix, where she gets to see her clients' many erotic personas, and Bill works as a psychotherapist. I asked Bill and Sybil how a novice to the idea of personas might access them. How do you find those parts of yourself? Sybil had a shy, awkward adolescence, yet she began dancing in a striptease nightclub in the late '60s. How did she do it?

"I could never have gotten up and danced onstage if I hadn't pretended to be someone else. I was scared! But when I was a child I found that when I went onstage in school plays, the child I usually was – who was tall, fat, smart, dressed funny, and a wallflower – disappeared. I would lose myself in the role, and all the fear went away. I thought it might also be true when I danced. So I picked music and costumes that I found sexy but that I would be afraid to wear as my mousy, wallflower self.

"When I began dancing I took a different name. After a while my old name faded into the background and everybody started knowing me by my stage name. It really became me. I no longer had to set myself aside to create this other person. The new person took over my life! Because it was ten times more fun. Because the old me wasn't really me. The person who was afraid wasn't all of who I was. I wasn't leaving me behind, I was just leaving the part that had been squashed by shyness. That allowed me to blossom."

The shy part of us is a persona, too. Many people have probably experienced their shy selves *as* themselves – "the baseline personality," as Bill puts it. "Part of me is still shy," Sybil adds, "but that part has gotten smaller and smaller. Today my shy self plays a very small role in my life because I've fleshed out these other parts."

Sybil's story illustrates something basic about finding a persona. Even though she accessed her new self by "pretending to be someone else," the dancer she discovered when she was in her twenties had a lot in common with the bright, adventurous child she was before she got "squashed" by shyness. It wasn't really someone else at all – it just wasn't her shy self.

If we go back far enough most of us will remember a child self braver and more exploratory than the self with which we went through puberty. We can make an end run around the shy one, even if it's had the upper hand for years, by putting on an outfit, assuming a role and *playing* – give the adventurous kid a chance to grow up and enjoy being an adult. Some of us will leave our shy selves behind quicker than others. A few of us will have eroticized feeling shy and may feel resistant to letting shyness go. Most of us, though, even if we feel trapped within shyness, can find ways out.

You may have lots of personas, not all of them erotic – just as you can identify with several roles at once, some erotic and others that have nothing to do with sexuality. As Bill points out, "a persona is not something you create, it's something you discover. You don't have to go through a lot of machinations – you can just see who shows up in your erotic life." Many of us already have distinct personas operating in our erotic lives, but we haven't recognized or identified them yet. To identify a persona, look for a constellation of feelings, thoughts, attitudes, beliefs, behaviors, vocal tones, and body postures. Do you have particular moods that seem to change your personality obviously or subtly? "Notice what is different about a specific mood," says Bill. "You can take any mood and flesh it out, listen to it, interact with it. You become aware of two different states at once, the one observing and the one being observed. That's two different personas."

"To access them," says Sybil, "read porn, use costumes, think of any fantasy that turns you on. Look at the time in history of the fantasy or the role you like – whether Middle Ages or futuristic or something else. Get into it through music – all the senses and their response – even if it means using a script! If something sounds sexy, use it. Practice – read it in front of a mirror."

LOOK IN THE MIRROR

Facing a mirror and talking to your reflection as if it's another person, one whose responses you're not sure you can predict, is an excellent way to meet an alternate persona. "In mirror work I see the new me, and then there's a point when it starts to deepen," says Sybil. "Then I know I've touched on something that's really me, not a role."

Here's an example of how this might work. Imagine me in front of a mirror getting to know my childlike persona. "How are you feeling right now?" I ask, and my voice changes a little, gets more lilting and little-girlish, as I respond, "I'm kinda scared." "Why are you scared?" "Because everybody's too busy to cuddle me and I'm lonely." "Oh, sweetie! How old are you?" "I'm almost five."

From there I could reassure this little girl that I'd help take care of her, ask her more about why she feels lonely, try to cheer her up by asking what she likes, or whatever. If I've been feeling vaguely lonely and unsupported in my life, this conversation with the little girl will give me valuable information about what's going on in my below-the-surface emotions. Notice that I asked her age – get information about a new persona by quizzing it about its age, likes and dislikes, and anything else you want to know. Having this information fleshes the persona out.

Don't forget to ask its name. Sometimes new personas won't have actual names; the one you just met is called the Little Girl. The Little Girl persona carries the feelings of fright and sadness that are left over from my childhood, and I met her not in bed (thank goodness), but in therapy. If I hadn't met, listened to the fears of, and reassured the Little Girl, I suspect I would never have met Carol Annie, the sexual side of my child persona.

How about an erotic example? I'm talking to myself in the mirror because I've been feeling a little uninspired about sex lately. "Well, it's no wonder!" says the persona who's popped up to talk to me. "You never do anything exciting." "What do you mean?" I ask. "You always wait til late at night and you make love the same old way. You should leave the lights on! You should wear something sexy! What about coming home at lunchtime and doing it in the middle of the day for a change?" "Are you telling me you're bored?" I ask this obviously frisky persona. "Yes! I want to dress sexy! I want to do something exciting!" What this persona is telling me – in a voice that's not quite my own – is obvious: I've let sex get a little humdrum. If this persona takes over in bed, she'll no doubt liven things up a bit!

In Chapter Four I recommended you use mirror exercises that utilize dancing, dressing up, and masturbation to see yourself in a newly erotic way. This is different. Here you're looking for one part of your personality in the mirror so you can get to know it – as if you can look into the mirror and see your persona reflected there. You can use the mirror to converse or get more information about your persona, as I illustrated above – in effect, to be two people. Of course, the earlier mirror exercises may also have exactly this result – behaving erotically in front of a mirror can call out a specifically erotic part of you, a persona which you can get to know as the repository of your sexual boldness. But this is more interactive than the earlier mirror exercises – it has more in common with talking to yourself, the way many of us engage in private solo conversations when we're pondering something. In fact, you can use talking to yourself to recognize personas, too.

Sometimes the persona in the mirror will look different from the way you usually do, and not only because you may have dressed differently for the erotic exercises. You may see expressions you don't recognize. You may see your face change subtly. It's a new facet of yourself – a new persona.

One effective way to do mirror work with your newly-discovered erotic persona will also help you in your quest to learn to talk dirty: when addressing the persona in the mirror, talk about sex. Talk about the kind of sex the persona likes. Ask it questions. Tell it what you like. Spin out sexual fantasies, talking out loud. As you recognize different personas, notice how their sexual language and their desires may be different from your own – and from each other's. Try not to feel shocked or judgmental – remember, the persona's ideas about what's erotic may be very different than yours. Your sex life can be enriched by your persona's sexuality without your ever having to physically do any of your persona's desired activities. In a way, some personas can be understood as an erotic fantasy, embodied in you – except more likely than a fantasy to have a mind of its own!

More Ways to Flesh Out Your Personas

Beyond naming them and getting an idea about their sexual desires and preferences, use visual cues to get to know your personas. Costume can be one of the easiest ways to meet them. Do you suspect you might have a slutty stripper within who won't quite reveal herself when you wear jeans and sneakers? Get her some lingerie and makeup, for heaven's sake! Do you harbor an S/M top who feels naked without a leather jacket? Is your inner virgin cheerleader just waiting for you to take off your work clothes and buy her some snow-white ankle socks? Dressing according to role, or dressing up your personas, doesn't need to be expensive – you can do it at thrift stores, if you want – and it serves at least three important functions.

First, dressing in appropriate garb helps you visualize personas. Now when you look in the mirror you see a more fleshed-out alternate self; you find it easier to believe in yourself as sexy and bold if you look that way. Clothes don't make the persona, but they can help one emerge.

Second, clothing associated with an erotic persona will very likely have some fetishistic appeal for you – wearing it will turn you on, even if no one else ever sees it.

Third, you give your persona a cue that you believe in it, and its erotic potential, if you let it present itself the way it sees itself. Because your persona is one facet of yourself, the message you send is essentially, "I trust my erotic self."

Accessing personas or roles through props, including costume, has much in common with improvisational acting, and is another great way to draw on your subconscious strengths and leave your shy self behind. For practice (or a fun way to get into play), use the grab bag exercise discussed earlier, collecting a variety of props and then picking three. How will you incorporate these items into an erotic context that makes sense? What roles (or personas) will emerge to use them, and what will they choose to do? This exercise can remove your preconceived notions about sex, making you tap into a newly creative sexual realm.

No, you don't need special outfits, props, and sex toys to explore erotic personas and roles – your biggest sex toy, after all, resides between your ears. You and your partner can whisper to each other when you're making love and be anyone, anywhere, in the universe. But clothing serves our species as a powerful signal of identity and status, and changing your clothes is one of the quickest ways to alter your self-image.

Fantasy gives you access to the inner sexuality you may never have acknowledged, but only if you pay attention. If you've lived this long without listening to the perhaps alternate desires of your personas or your subconscious, you may have a difficult time accepting that parts of yourself want to do things you've never thought of yourself as desiring. Especially if you grew up believing that some kinds of desires are "wrong" while others are "right," you may have packed any "wrong" desires that came up into a cupboard in your brain, closed the door, and never looked at or even acknowledged them. Now what?

It turns out when you finally get around to peeking into the cupboard that you have a persona in there, at least one alternate self with a very different fantasy life. It wants to have sex outdoors, or be on top, or explore bondage, or have sex with a partner you consider inappropriate, or leave the curtains open when you fuck. Are you going to let it take over your life?

"When you let a fantasy go, it's almost always going to be more extreme than you really want to act out," says Bill. "But extreme fantasies have value." For one thing, they allow you to "unpack" your taboos. What you come up with may still be taboo for you in your sex life, but really looking at fantasies can give you lots more information about your deep sources of eroticism. They may even allow you to get to know yourself better (and hopefully accept yourself better) on all levels – not just sexually.

Allowing your fantasies to go where they will, staying conscious not just of turn-on but for information about yourself, is similar to dream work, where you remember, write down, and analyze your dreams. It makes little sense to think of "rejecting" our dreams – we accept them for what they are, usually, even if we find them unsettling. But it's common for people to reject their fantasies. Accepting that these come from the depths of our psyche, like dreams, helps us accept the fantasies themselves, and then we can look at them, flesh them out, get more details.

You can even try writing a script of your fantasy. This lets you get into it deeply and look at it more closely, and it also gives you a record of it to look back on later. You can do the same by writing about it in a journal.

You may have personas whose desires seem to contradict each others'. You may have personas whose desires surprise you. You may have personas of different ages, sexual preferences, even different genders than your baseline self. As in Jungian psychological theory, we may discover an "inner male" self if we're female or an "inner female" self if we're male – Jungians would call them "animus" and "anima." In fact, you may have more than one of these. Each persona contains something of yourself; the erotic ones hold the elements of your sexual potential. The more you allow them to come into your awareness, the richer your sexuality can become.

Your other-gender personas, if any, may not prefer the same gender you do. Either homosexual or heterosexual feelings (or both) can reside in a persona of either gender. For instance, if I were an exclusively heterosexual woman, I might have a male persona who desires women – so all the desire I feel for women is actually my male persona's desire. Of course, I might also have a male persona who desires men; when I as a heterosexual woman have sex with a man, I feel like a heterosexual woman, but when my male persona has sex with a man, he feels like a gay male. A gay man might have a female persona, but only desire women when in that persona – so that, on top of being a gay man, he has a lesbian persona. If he has sex with a woman in this female persona, it won't feel like heterosexual sex – even though he's a man (physically) having sex with a woman. In his emotional body, his persona, he is a woman having sex with another woman.

And of course a person might have a number of personas which are different from one another yet always have the same gender and sexual orientation as the baseline persona.

Confused yet? Don't be. As you explore personas, it's only confusing if you try to superimpose your pre-existing notions about yourself and about sexuality on the perhaps new information and insights your personas provide.

You may find that you have a persona or two that you only get in touch with when you're with a certain partner. Just as a specific partner can "call out" one persona or another, you may find another's response inhibits you from letting out one or more inner selves. Ideally you'll find your partner – and your partner's own personas, if s/he's in touch with them – are erotically compatible with yours.

Look for the overlap between what turns you on and what arouses your partner. Here you'll find the most fertile, immediately accessible area for play. Remember, whether exploring roleplaying for the first time or introducing a newly-awakened erotic persona, your partner will be meeting someone slightly (or very) new and different from the you s/he already knows. Give yourselves time to get to know each other's newly developed selves, just as you probably had to get to know each other when you first became lovers. There's no need to rush this process – and don't be surprised if the area of overlap grows larger as time passes.

When you and your partner explore personas, roles, and characters, verbally or through costume and other kinds of play, you will deepen your knowledge of each other and very possibly increase the levels of intimacy you can share. Even if only one of you instigated this exploration, both of you will have opportunities to take sexual pleasure and compatibility more seriously. And you can experiment, separately and together, with the erotic images that have meaning for both of you.

So don't be surprised if your explorations with a willing partner take you further than you ever expected to go. On a related note, if your partner suggests a particular role or fantasy that you don't think you'll find interesting, wait till you've seen her or his erotic response to it before you completely write it off. That response might persuade you to open up to sexual enjoyment you'd never otherwise have experienced.

SELF-AWARENESS, GROWTH, AND INSPIRATION

Sybil offers another reason to look at your personas: "If all the parts of yourself align, each persona's growth informs all the others'." This is true of all personas, not just erotic ones, but the erotic ones are as good a place to start as any – maybe better, because your growth includes more possibility for sexual pleasure. If you manage as a shy, erotically retiring person to find that you can have sexual agency, possessing the emotional wherewithal to go for what you want, breaking through those barriers you thought you never could, it can inform your non-erotic sense of self, too, investing it with a whole new level of energy and confidence. I've seen this over and over when a person meets a new, outgoing partner, or in some other way has the opportunity to have new experiences and stretch their assumptions about him- or herself sexually.

That's ample reason to follow your sexual fantasies and fascinations into erotic encounters with your personas, but beginning the process may still seem frightening. What if your response to the things I suggest you try is "Oh, but I just can't"? A very common source of resistance comes from within: a line drawn in our minds between life as we experience it now and what we can conceive of as possible. It seems impossible to see what's on the other side of the line and how to get there.

"If I can't do something for emotional reasons, there may be something going on for me that has to do with fear or anger," says Bill. "That means I might be able to learn to do that thing, but only if I address my fear or anger about whatever it is that underlies what I'm calling 'can't.'" Why would you want to learn to do something you're afraid of? To get past the fear; because you feel stuck where you are now; to deal with buried sources of distress; because the new activity would be pleasurable; to change your self-image from someone who can't to someone who *can*.

Naturally, Bill's recommendation that we take responsibility for what we think we can do must be tempered with self-respect. It won't help to beat ourselves up because we're not there yet, wherever "there" is. Sybil elaborates: "Don't push too hard. Take baby steps. One thing at a time. One costume, one fantasy at a time. If you feel you can't, what is stopping you? Maybe you can find the back door to it. For me the two back doors to fantasy were phone sex and visualizing myself as another person. I learned I could get into a scene more easily if I left the room and came back as someone else, like stepping onto a stage. And the more you do anything, of course, the easier it gets."

Porn star Nina Hartley echoes this. "My Nina persona is not a front over a hollow center. In the beginning, it was the idealized real me – I thought if I was completely together sexually and not scared, I would be kind, gracious, warm and giving. It was someone I wanted to be. It denoted confidence that I really wanted to obtain. In the beginning, before I was that kind of person, I had to act it."

"It's not necessary to go out looking for these personas," says Jamie. "They'll come to you. It's really important for people who are just starting out – the fact that you want to discover them means that you probably can." Blake adds, "You don't have to develop this whole repertoire. You don't have to find a whole bunch of inner selves. Because it's so much about your own turn-on. Start there, and the characters will absolutely come."

While I did almost no work connected to erotic personas while in therapy, the technique my therapist and I used, a variation of Gestalt, uncovered several personas. I would put my alternate self on a pillow and sit "facing" her, imagining her there in front of me, and talk to her. Every so often my therapist would have me switch places with my persona, giving that self a chance to talk back to me. You can do this in mirror work, too – or even talking to yourself.

What you learn in a therapeutic context about your inner selves' relationship to fear, sadness, anger, hope, creativity, power, and everything else can also be applied to eroticism; and if your therapist is comfortable discussing sex, you may meet and work with these personas in your sessions.

Arnold, another of my childlike personas, is a seven-year-old nerd. He loves science – think of him as the kid who always won the prize at the science fair but never had any friends. I discovered Arnold many years ago on a trip to the woods with my girlfriend – a figurative as well as literal trip, for I was high on psychedelic mushrooms. All of a sudden, while my baseline self watched with amazement, Arnold popped up and began expounding about the trees and the puffball fungus that grew on the oak leaves. "This is an example of a symbiotic relationship!" he said proudly, while my girlfriend looked at me as if I'd lost my mind.

I'm not going to recommend psychedelics as a means to access your personas, though if you use drugs now, you should know that the splits in consciousness they can facilitate make it more than likely you are not always "yourself" when high. Psychedelics have seen much use in many cultures for ritual and sacramental purposes, for just this reason: ingesting them alters our notion of the real and the possible.

Like the alterations alcohol and other depressants cause in our inhibitions, any personality state we can't get to on our own leaves us vulnerable to dependence on the chemical we need to reach it. My friend Bayla tells me she used to act very exhibitionistic when she was drunk – when she stopped drinking, she found she couldn't do it anymore. Her artificial means of getting comfortable was gone, and she had to start from scratch and learn to overcome her shyness on her own. That's why I would like to encourage you to get comfortable with your sexuality without chemical assistance.

That said, though, I wouldn't trade that mushroom trip for anything, because of Arnold. He emerged before any of my other personas – and he emerged at a time in my life when I felt rather uncomfortable with males. Because I couldn't deny that I had had this experience of turning into a boy, I had to begin to make sense of the apparent fact that I had a little bit of maleness residing within me. Many other things urged on and contributed to this process, but the end result – a much higher level of comfort with men – owes a lot to Arnold. I suppose I can thank him for indirectly helping me get so comfortable with men that I could erotically interact with dozens of them a day at the peep show – ironic, because Arnold is one of my shyest personas! It just substantiates that the growth and insight of one persona can spill over into all your other personas, as well as your baseline self.

Arnold began as an asexual child persona, but he didn't stay that way. He grew into sexuality when he met my lover, Robert. Arnold liked Robert from the start, because Robert knew a lot about science and would explain things to him. The fascinated Arnold hung on his every word. It reached the point where Robert could call Arnold out almost any time by starting to explain how something worked. Arnold developed an intense crush on Robert, seducing him by asking him to explain in minute detail how a guy gets a hard-on. I'm sure Robert doesn't find Arnold the most erotically charged of all my personas, but for Arnold, Robert will always be the first.

Blake has a male persona, too – Matt. "He's six-one, long blond hair, blue eyes, he's kind of a cowboy, smokes cigarettes," says Blake. "One day I was doing everything as Matt. I had on boots and jeans and my Levi jacket with white sheepskin on the inside. I got on the train and put my feet up on the opposite chair. I was wearing a dildo, so I had a bulge. This gay man sat down next to me. I was sitting there with my hat pulled down, and I did the whole bit, tipped the hat and looked at him. He's sitting with his eyes riveted on the dildo in my crotch, talking to me, and I'm Matt – I realized just how grounded I am in Matt. 'Cause I was right there with him. He said, 'If I give you my phone number will you call me?' I looked at him and said, 'It depends on what you want me to call you.' He was squirming in the seat! It was wonderful!"

Once you know one or two of your erotic personas, why not photograph them? For inspiration, look at the work Annie Sprinkle has done with alternate selves and photography. She takes very ordinary-looking people and, in her "Transformation Salon," dresses them in wild, sexy garb, helps them pick a new name, and takes pictures of the new personality that emerges. Some of the before and after shots are astonishing, and if you have a shred of doubt left that everyone can enjoy exhibitionistic sexuality, Annie's work should dispel it.

Look for the Transformation Salon shots in her autobiography *Post Porn Modernist* and her deck of pin-up playing cards. See her video "Sluts and Goddesses" for more of inimitable Annie's work along these lines – helping women access the erotic power of both the Slut and the Goddess archetype. If she comes to your town, be sure to see her; she's the perfect role model for every shy person who dreams of breaking out into exhibitionism. From ordinary Ellen Steinberg to ravishing porn star Annie Sprinkle to cutting-edge sexual healer and performance artist Anya, Annie serves as proof that setting out on the sexual path with a loving, open heart and a sense of adventure can take us a very long way.

So get out that Polaroid (if you can still get the film) and start documenting all your inner selves. Writing affirmations on the mirror is fine – "I am a radiant, outgoing, open soul who has no fear" – but a picture of one of your hot, erotic personas will be worth a thousand words. It will remind you that, even if you still seem shy on the surface, there is more to you than meets the eye – and underneath, close enough to touch, waits the embodiment of an erotic dream.

☾ 7 ☀

Finding Words That Are Hot For You

The main building blocks for hot talk are the language you use, what you say, and how you say it. These simple components present infinite possible variations. I could provide you with a formula for dirty talk, but ultimately you'll like the outcome better if you take the time to tailor your talk to your own particular likes – and those of your partner.

To develop your own personal style, think of your fantasy life and any especially erotic role models you may have discovered in the course of your reading and porn expeditions. Perhaps you've also gathered some words and phrases you like from these sources.

YOUR PERSONAL DIRTY WORDS

First, find the words that turn you on the most to say or to hear. For this project, it doesn't matter what, if any, roles turn you on or make you feel erotically powerful – just which words and phrases possess the maximum erotic resonance for you. Next, match appropriate words and phrases with the erotic personas you've discovered you like and relate to. You'll want to aim for a certain degree of consonance between your erotic persona (or any erotic role you may assume, for your own or a partner's pleasure) and the words and vocal tone you use when in that persona or role.

For example, take three separate erotic characters. Let's say one is a Victorian rogue, one is a submissive, and one is an erotically playful child. When you talk dirty in the persona of the first character, you may refer to quims, John Thomases, and rosebuds - some of the sex language you've discovered in vintage porn. In submissive mode your erotic status may reflect in your talk: you may refer to your partner as Mistress or Master or Goddess, and your speech may be peppered with "Please," "I beg you," and other worshipful or submissive turns of phrase. As a curious child you may talk about weenies and cunnies, "down there" and "doin' things." Each character's language sounds appropriate to it - but if the rogue begins to talk about weenies, the child about Cupid's Highway or pizzling, the realism of their talk will suffer, as will the magic their words weave for themselves and their partners.

Before we delve more deeply into talking from a persona's perspective, though, let's get back to the words themselves, with some suggestions for identifying the hot talk that turns you on. For most of us, dirty words - at least *some* dirty words - carry a charge. We may feel uncomfortable with them or we may love to drop them at times when their sound resounds in a conversation - times when it's not quite "appropriate." If you're not used to speaking them aloud, getting started can be challenging. Read them aloud and practice words and phrases you find hot when you're alone, especially when you're masturbating.

You may find that some words or phrases do nothing for you, while hearing or speaking others makes your arousal soar; you may find, too, that some words or phrases are a distinct turn-off. You'll want to identify the ones with a positive, sexy charge and leave the language that you find anti-erotic alone. But what if you don't know which ones you find hot?

Reading erotic literature, as I've noted before, may be the best place to assess your hot spots and favorite words and phrases. As you read, note the words you find most arousing, as well as the scenarios you find hottest. Write them down and later you'll have a cheat sheet.

Play some word games. Make a list of sexual words and phrases. Which ones are hottest for you? With your partner or some friends, make lists of sex words, then compare them. If each of you were going to write sexual graffiti on a wall, what would it be? Pick a word at random and use it in a sentence. Write down all the words you can think of for a particular activity or body part. List all the dirty words that start with a particular letter. As you play, you'll be inspired to make up more games.

Write various words on cards and draw them at random. Or get the great card game called "Dirty Words," which consists of three decks of playing cards, each with a word on it. Even playing old-fashioned Solitaire with these can help you learn to talk dirty! Recently I gave a set of these cards to a friend, and we proceeded to invent games using them. My favorite: lay out eight cards and have each player draw eight from the remaining cards in the deck. When it's each player's turn, they have to use their cards to make sentences or phrases, starting with the card that's already on the table. Keep drawing cards until the deck is gone or until you can't continue the sentences any more. (If you make your own version of this, include words like she, he, her, his, in, on, the, and so forth, so your sex words can be made into sentences.) Fridge Fun Adult magnets work the same way – combining and re-combining erotic words is fun and creative, and it's hard to be playful and reticent at the same time!

You can also pick words from the list in Appendix 1, which I've compiled from several sources. Many of the terms come from a list compiled by San Francisco Sex Information, which they use to desensitize phone volunteers to sexual language. Your aim, however, is not to become desensitized to them – quite the contrary!

Get pens or markers with three different colors of ink. Go through the list once and, with one color, mark all the words you know you find sexy. Go through it again and, with another color, mark the ones you might find hot under some circumstances – for instance, you might not use a certain word unless you were very aroused; you might use certain words only with a partner you trust not to judge you, or with a partner you know really likes them.

Now go through the list a third time and use the remaining marker for the words you know you don't like. These are the words you'd find a turn-off to say or hear. What's the purpose of noting your turn-off words? You can use this list to let your partners know what not to say, since sex talk you don't like can ruin your mood as fast as a clumsy touch. You'll presumably find the words you haven't marked neutral or disinteresting, at least for now.

If you have a partner to share the list with, make a couple of copies of it and do the exercise I just outlined. Compare your results. Hopefully you'll find some overlap between your lover's favorite words and your own. Notice which of your "maybe" words your partner especially likes, and vice versa; you may find your partner's response to them makes them more erotic for you. Notice, too, whether s/he dislikes any of your hot words, and vice versa. You may have to negotiate the use – or avoidance – of these.

You can tape this list of words up where you'll see it a few times a day – you can read it aloud while you're dressing for work, getting ready for bed, or doing the dishes.

There are plenty of four-letter synonyms for penis and vagina and other body parts. Note that I've grouped the words together by usage, which brings us to another exercise. Get two pictures out of a magazine, preferably nude. You'll want one of your sex and one of your preferred sex, so one can represent you and the other can represent your partner. If your partner's doing this with you you'll need a set of pictures for each of you. If you're bisexual, you might want three pictures altogether, one to represent yourself and one for each potential partner.

Now label the pictures with your preferred sexy terms for all the erotic parts of the body – vulva, penis, clitoris, testicles, vagina, anus, buttocks, breasts. If you have erotic terms or pet names for parts of the body other than these, like the mouth or the feet, label those too. The wealth of names for the genitals really obscures the fact that for many of us, erogenous zones extend from top to toe. If you have names for some of these places, good for you. Next add to your picture any words you find anti-erotic – put these in a circle with a line through it, like a "no smoking" sign. If you've done the exercise with a partner, compare your labeled pictures – or hide them for each other to find, or mail them to each other. Hang them up on the fridge or in your bedroom.

If you do either of these exercises with a partner, you'll find your erotic talk can become customized. Just remember, if you have more than one lover or change partners, you'll want to do the exercise again or in some other way ensure you've learned your new sweetheart's preferences and conveyed your own.

Look, now, at the words, which you'll find in Appendix 1: a whole string of (mostly) Anglo-Saxonisms - with a bit of Spanish and Yiddish thrown in - meant to spice up the Latin-derived language of biology textbooks and bring it down to earth. If your cultural roots aren't Anglo-Saxon or European, you probably know erotic words or phrases that differ from these. If I haven't listed all the words you know, add your own.

Imagine the colorful history behind each of the sex terms. You may have found some of them too funny to eroticize. Or perhaps you dislike many of them and find them too harsh or not sensual enough. If you don't like sexual street slang, you're not alone - and you can still talk explicitly and erotically about sex.

IF YOU DON'T LIKE FOUR-LETTER WORDS

You can learn erotic words in another language, like French, Italian, or Spanish. You may have to teach the terms to your partner, but on the positive side, you'll have a lexicon of words you like - and if you ever find yourself in Paris, Rome, or Barcelona, you'll be all set! One of my lovers liked the sound of French erotic talk so much - although in fact she didn't understand a word of French - that I once impelled her to tear my clothes off in the middle of the afternoon by reading aloud to her from a Sabatier kitchen knife brochure.

If traditional erotic language is threatening or distasteful to you, don't use it. Invent your own terms; many lovers have a secret language others don't share. If you feel you could more readily speak up if you had your own personal glossary, by all means begin to create it. Devising a private language with your lover can be a very intimate, as well as fun, thing to do. If you want ideas about erotic language creation, sample the charming way with words of author Nicholson Baker. His two novels, *Vox* and *The Fermata*, abound with sexy and fanciful turns of phrase for all the usual erogenous zones and deeds - and then some.

Some people give proper names to their own and their partner's sex parts - that's undoubtedly the derivation of "John Thomas," an archaic term for penis. Rumor has it that Elvis Presley named his penis "Little Elvis."

Or perhaps you'd prefer the elegant erotic language of another culture, like the archaic phrases from ancient Taoist China I've culled from Valentin Chu's fascinating book *The Yin-Yang Butterfly* and listed in Appendix 2. Erotic language like this affords sexuality a respect unknown in our slang, tainted as it is by the shame our own culture heaps upon its traditional dirty words. For many people that shame has provided the fuel for much erotic heat. Once we get past guilt and embarrassment, many of us enter the realm of pure sexual excitement, so don't knock the Anglo-Saxonisms till you've tried them. But whether or not they're for you, you might find the Taoist sex terms enlightening – and quite sexy.

The Taoists had names for things our puritanical culture has few or no names for, like the different depths of the vagina. Indian Tantric sex and Native American Quodoushka also view sex in a strikingly different way than Westerners tend to do, and each of these philosophies and practices comes with its own erotic language. We can learn more from other cultures than words. That humans have conceptualized sexuality in so many different ways in different times, places, and societies helps us put our own ideas and feelings about sex into a fresh perspective. To learn more about this, check out books about sex in other cultures, including works like Ford and Beach's classic *Patterns of Sexual Behavior* and Suzanne Frayser's *Varieties of Sexual Experience*.

Other terms from *The Yin-Yang Butterfly* describe Taoist lovemaking positions. It's a charming array that leaves our old standby "missionary position" in the dust.

To set out to become a consummate erotic talker, the most important thing is not the language you use, but the very fact that you have decided to learn to use language to arouse and to enhance your sexual adventures with your partners. The "cunts" and "cocks" are optional; your desire to add your voice to the erotic experience is the only requirement. Remember, even if you never use a single "dirty word," you can talk during sex and talk about sex.

Consider your options. If you just can't bring yourself to shout or even whisper "Fuck my pussy!" or "Suck my dick!" – or if these phrases simply leave you cold – what *can* you say? Maybe references to cinnabar fields and jade spoons aren't your style, either. If you let your sexual arousal into your voice, cries of "Ohh, yeah, do *that!*" and *"Please* put your mouth on me now!" can be devastatingly hot, even though you haven't used a single word considered dirty or even overtly erotic.

Adding Erotic Nuance

Cultivate an erotic tone of voice, or several. Your tone may be dependent on the role you typically take in sex or a persona you assume: perhaps it will be breathy, or urgent, or pleading, or demanding. If you develop an erotically severe, dominating tone, remember it won't get you far if your partner isn't turned on to you in that role; try to make sure the tone matches the way you feel and act when you have sex.

Pay attention to the voice you use when you talk during masturbation. It doesn't matter what you say – try repeating the phrase "Oh, yes" during masturbation, giving it every erotic inflection you can. Do any of these tones feel more erotic to you? If you find one that does, explore it some more – narrate a fantasy, talk to an imaginary partner, or say anything sexy that comes into your head. You want to find elements of hot talk that make you hotter, and masturbation is the very best time to do this – especially if you feel self-conscious experimenting this way with a partner.

Read erotic literature aloud, varying your tone with the characters. This can also help you tune into erotic archetypes and personas – with whom do you identify the most? Which part does it turn you on most to read?

Needless to say, if you can write sexy stories or scripts and read them, you'll have the advantage of having already tapped into your own erotic subconscious. When you read these stories aloud, you may get into character even more easily.

Whether or not you use very explicit words and phrases, how you say something will color your talk for you and your partner as much as what you say. Think about the many emotional colorations that come into your speech in the course of a day. Sometimes you're animated, sometimes low-key; sometimes people around you can tell from your tone of voice that you're tense, sometimes that you're happy, sometimes that you're feeling down. To begin training yourself to notice these variations in inflection, pay attention to the emotions expressed in other people's voices; pay attention to the emotion your own tone of voice expresses. Note when your changes of emotion show up vocally. Actors do this to make themselves more aware of their character's nuances and more convincing in their portrayal.

Check Appendix 3 for a list of words that convey a feeling or emotion that might be relevant to sex. Some of them will pertain only to certain kinds of play – several of the words, for example, describe feelings that may be common to S/M or dominant-submissive sex, but not as common to other kinds of lovemaking. Some may describe emotions that you recognize from your own fantasy life and erotic experiences. Mark these. Others will convey feelings you might prefer to leave out of your sexual encounters. Note these too. If some of the remaining words are "maybe" words for you – if you find yourself attracted to some words conditionally, rather than feeling strictly positive, negative, or neutral about them, mark them too. These are the emotional states you might feel comfortable experiencing with only a particularly trusted partner, only solo, only if you were very aroused, only if you were in a particular role.

This exercise can be done with a partner too, of course. Just as with the last word list, marking your preferred words, the words you don't like, and the words you might like gives you more information – about your own preferences and about your partner's. Add to the list if you wish.

Consider the way the two lists interrelate. You can read the list of sex terms aloud in a perfectly neutral tone of voice and probably not wildly arouse anyone, including yourself. But if you read the same words in a whispery, kittenish tone, or a forceful, dominant tone, or a seductive, rapturous tone, they will sound quite different – and hearing them will feel different.

Pick some of the sex words and read them using a variety of the feeling words. Choose those you find most erotically persuasive; try to infuse your material with the emotion. If reading a list of words doesn't give you enough to sink your theatrical teeth into, make them into sentences – or use the subset of dirty words from Appendix 1 called "Things to Say/Exclamations." You can also use a favorite passage from an erotic story or novel.

If you want to hear how your practice is proceeding, record yourself. Compare the sound of your material read neutrally with the effect of an added emotion.

When you watch erotic movies, especially porn, notice how often the actor's erotic effectiveness depends not on what s/he says, but how s/he says it. The difference between a poorly-delivered, clumsy line and a persuasive one is often the skill with which the actor conveys erotic emotion.

The more nuances of feeling you can convey in your erotic talk, the more versatile you will become. However, don't treat this like an acting class where you have to be able to convey all these different emotions in order to pass the final. The number one test here is: does it enhance your arousal and your sexual experience? The number two test: does it enhance your partner's arousal? You may have only three favorite dirty words and one tone of voice in which you like to utter them, but if those three words always get you hot, you're all set.

You can also convey nuance verbally by being more descriptive. Once you can utter one hot word, you're set to embroider it into phrases and sentences. If you say "Fuck" while having sex it will convey your turn-on in one way; if you say "Fuck me" you'll give a somewhat different impression; if you add specifics: "Fuck me slowly," "Fuck me hard," "Fuck me now," "Fuck me up against the wall," you'll begin to get control of the word's erotic power, able to convey what you want and how you want it. Similarly, when you load your sex talk with adjectives – "your hot, wet, dripping, hungry pussy" – and descriptive phrases, you weave a stronger erotic spell.

Shar and Jackie have customized their hot talk with detailed nuance and description. When Shar tells Jackie a story she takes a long time to build up to the climax. "She knows what color the walls are," says Shar. "She knows what the shoes sound like on the floor. She knows what the air smells like. She knows what the velvet feels like. One very simple story I told her recently was set in the '40s, on a train. In the story, Jackie hadn't touched a pussy in a long time, and she was about to touch mine. The wind was blowing my hair, my dress was falling open, I had on thigh-high stockings, and she reached up to touch my ass. Her hand slid up past my stockings and onto the fleshy thighs. I described that brief moment before she touched the pubic hair – she hadn't touched such nice, silky, moist pubic hair in so long. She felt the electricity from my pussy in her fingers. Just when her middle finger slipped between the silky pussy hairs into the crack of my cunt, where it was so wet that she could just slide back to my asshole... Bam! Jackie came."

In telling stories like this, Shar uses her rich imagination, pulling things out of thin air and making them into scenarios as she goes along. A beginner can plan his or her stories ahead of time; partners can have one story that always works, that they always return to. In sharing stories with your partner, learning to embellish simple erotic language with modifiers, and weaving these into sexy stories, remember to listen for your lover's response.

"The other day Jackie was reading a story to me," Shar says. "She actually changed a couple of sentences in the story because she knew what would get to me." That's a great way to get into the flow of erotic storytelling – just start customizing already-available material. Before long you'll find yourself creating hot scenarios from scratch.

If you have a hard time going from words to complete sentences, narration like this can help. Tell a story. Describe something – a sexual activity, a body part, the story's environment, the characters. You and your partner can practice with a game – start by making up a sentence using a hot word or phrase. Next your partner will say something to continue it. The next sentence is yours. You can use your flash cards or the "Dirty Words" card game to structure this, or decide the story's topic in advance. ("Let's describe a woman getting picked up in a bar. I'll go first: 'She looked like she wanted to fuck.' Your turn.")

TALKING IN ROLE

Don't forget to weave in your favorite erotic roles or personas. Consider which roles, characters, or personas tend to appear in your fantasy life; which characters you especially identify with when reading or watching porn; whether any role or character is especially sexy to you, and whether that character has a "natural" partner – seducer and virgin, dominant and submissive, prostitute and client.

Make a list of as many such characters, roles, and personas as you find erotically inspiring, even if you've never taken on the role before. What matters is that you think you would find it a turn-on to do so – even (or perhaps especially) if it's a little scary to imagine yourself in that role. Of course, if you do have a favorite role or persona you live in sometimes, put that on the list. I've included a few in Appendix 4 to get you started.

Now go back to the list of emotion words. Which words seem relevant to each role or character you've listed? For example, let's say you listed "Mommy" and "Virgin." One of the wonderful things about the erotic realm is that you can abandon logic and linearity within it – so you can be a mommy one day, a virgin the next. And you never have to give a moment of thought to whether this makes sense!

Your Mommy self will be motherly and possibly feminine – at least sometimes; she may be stern, loving, affectionate, unselfish, and/or tough. If one of her attributes is that she initiates, she will probably also be assertive and seductive. Your Virgin self, on the other hand, may be very shy, awkward, and even ambivalent. He or she may be nervous and frightened or brave and even mischievous. Either of them might be adventurous or cuddly.

Now you know how this erotic character might speak and behave. What will she or he say? Go back to the first list, the one of sex words, and give the character a vocabulary. How will the Mommy refer to penises, clitorises, vaginas? How will the Virgin? The Mommy may say things like "Do as I say!" or "Don't be afraid, darling." The Virgin might cry, "No! No!" or ask, "May I touch it?"

Two things, especially, will guide you in fleshing out your character's verbal personality. First, something about why you find a given character erotic will probably guide you to hot talk that is both appropriate to the character and sexy for you. The key to that "why" may be in the character's attributes and how you perceive the character's logical behavior; do you eroticize that s/he initiates or resists, is insatiable or responsive? Second, you may have become aware of this character's attraction for you via porn; if so, you may have already assimilated some of the language associated with it in the books you've read or movies you've seen.

Consider a third factor – does your partner eroticize a "matching" character?

Even if we go no further in our sex play than to talk in the voice of a character or persona, if we talk with a partner, it's important that s/he responds erotically to the persona we assume or character we portray. In negotiating for compatibility, all three aspects of talking dirty can be looked at separately. Does our partner find our preferred character erotically interesting? Does s/he respond erotically to the things we say when in role?

Does s/he respond erotically to the way we say them? All three aspects offer possibilities for erotic compatibility – or not. Talk frankly together about likes and dislikes, turn-ons and turn-offs.

A variation on the theme of talking hot with partners should be mentioned – with some partners, you may not want to talk at all, while with others you may find yourself waxing eloquently purple without giving it a second thought. We can put this down to interpersonal chemistry, to some degree; each twosome develops its own erotic personality, based on the unique things each partner brings to the relationship and the context in which the relationship happens. Add to this the erotic potential of the two people together, calling out elements of each others' sexuality neither has experienced before.

Sometimes partners respond so strongly to each other's erotic potential that it helps bring that potential to life. Bill, for example, found that he began to eroticize talking dirty within a relationship because his partner responded especially strongly to talk – which helped him turn on to talking in a way he previously hadn't.

Now you have the basics of hot talk: a fantasy, a character, erotic vocabulary, and tone or inflection. All you have to do now is figure out what you want to say. Invent your own erotic games using fantasy, roleplay and sexy language – and start talking!

€ 8 ※

I Like To Be Watched

There's no one set of behaviors, fantasies and desires that every sexual exhibitionist shares – each person will develop exhibitionistically in her or his own way. In this chapter you'll meet a variety of exhibitionists, hear a few of their experiences, get some of their insights and suggestions and some of my own. Some of these ideas will sound hot to you, some not. Remember what's most important here: you and your desires. Borrow what sounds good to you and leave the rest.

Remember, too, that erotic exhibitionism isn't meant to be the last word in your personal growth. It's possible to use sexual experimentation, and develop personas and roles, to avoid or distract yourself from your own issues – dealing with feelings of insecurity or low self-esteem, for example. If exploring exhibitionism leaves you feeling that there's still something missing in your life, you're probably right! Listen to that inner voice; do go deeper into yourself. This book's purpose is to inspire you into exploring new arenas for pleasure – it's no substitute for getting in touch with your feelings and your boundaries, being honest with yourself, and pursuing any other course of personal growth that may appeal to you. In fact, it ought to dovetail nicely with all these things.

YOUR INNER SHOW-OFF

Did you develop an interest in an alternate self or two during the discussion of roles and personas? Maybe you recognized one that has been part of your life for a while. So far I've emphasized the usefulness of developing eroticized roles or personas for sexual talk; sometimes it's easier to put words in the mouth of a character who's not quite you. Of course, you might find an inner character who loves to flaunt and tease – this self can really help you open up to exhibitionism, because part of her or his eroticism has to do with showing off. So if you have more than one persona or role that's sexual for you, ask yourself which one is the most outgoing.

Even if you have not discovered an alternate persona within, you can see whether you have moods during which you feel more brave and exhibitionistic. Regardless of whether you see this mood as the kernel of a persona, you can take advantage of the mood to guarantee you'll feel better about showing off than you do when you're in a more reserved frame of mind.

You can use erotic characters as a basis for pretending, imagining, fantasizing – in short, taking on a role that differs enough from your everyday personality that it allows you to act different. "Act out scenes from movies," Jackie recommends. "'You be Stella, I'll be Marlon Brando.'"

Characters and personas are relevant in another way, too. You can dress them up. When you do, you may find that either the clothing you put on or the persona or role you're dressing gives you access to a whole new level of pleasure in exhibitionism. You can dress in a more revealing fashion than usual and stay well within the bounds of propriety (unless you're an outrageous dresser already!) – remember, you don't have to go outside in your underwear to explore exhibitionism. Wear your ordinary street clothes without undergarments. Unbutton your shirt or blouse a little more. Try sheer fabrics or shorter skirts or tighter pants.

If you've thought of your erotic potential in a new way and identified some characters that attract you, you may have some different ideas now about what you'd like to wear. Dressing in role is a lot like talking in role – what resonates erotically? What makes sense? How will you feel sexiest? What elements help you feel that you fully express the role?

What you'll wear will depend not so much on how you see your baseline self, but on which persona or character you wish to express. In the case of a persona, which might have a real "mind of its own," what does the persona itself want to wear? Any erotic persona may have preferences about the way it wants to dress.

Even if you haven't developed clear-cut personas with names and distinctly separate personalities, you may notice that you feel different when you explore dressing erotically. In fact, dressing up can lead you to other personas. And remember that shyness, too, can simply be seen as the attribute of only one persona. "Right now I feel like my shy self," said Bayla when I asked her about exhibitionism. "But when I'm dressed a certain way, I'm not shy. I'm some other person that doesn't really have a name yet."

DRESSING – AND UNDRESSING – FOR SEXUAL SUCCESS

If you haven't experimented with clothing to get you in a sexy mood, consider playing dress-up. You can do it alone as well as with a partner; you can be as fanciful as you want. Second-hand stores are full of costume elements that you might usually only assemble for Hallowe'en, but why wait? Over time I've stocked my closet with costumes so that I can emerge looking like a bride, a Girl Scout, a boy, a turn-of-the-century belle, a pirate, a sailor, a *Folies Bergere* girl, a flapper, a '50s housewife, a dominatrix, a porn starlet, a butler, a hooker... and with each character I find erotic possibilities to explore. The very fact of dressing differently, and dressing for erotic purposes, brings in an element of visual excitement and interest that feeds directly into getting off on voyeurism and exhibitionism.

Clothes really can make the woman or the man in the realm of erotic fantasy – in fact, they can transform one into the other! You and your partner can try cross-dressing together. How does it affect your erotic play to find that "girls will be boys and boys will be girls"? You can try this kind of sex-play without cross-dressing, too – just give each other new names and talk to each other as if each of you is the other gender while you make love in your usual way. You might find the same sexual activity with that familiar partner feels startlingly new when you transform yourselves with this cross-gender fantasy.

Carolyn noticed her erotically outgoing tendencies through her love of clothes. The shoes and lingerie she bought got wilder, and "somewhere along the line I realized that I was wearing lingerie-type items as outerwear in public places." Her past shyness wound up on the heap with her discarded outfits.

Rita used to think of herself as unattractive and unable to compete with the women in the porn magazines her boyfriend read. I asked her how she got from her feelings of insecurity to her current erotically competent state. "I had to let go of certain hang-ups about my body – it was really a process of shedding self-hatred and the feeling of being insecure, unpowerful, unlovable, ugly. I took slow steps. I remember dragging one of my best friends down to a lingerie shop and buying an outrageous black lace thong teddy. She said, 'Oh my god, Rita, what are you doing?' I said, 'I look great in this, I'm going to buy it.'"

Another time Rita's purchase of a skimpy black leather mini-dress provoked a big fight with her conservative boyfriend, but she was determined: "If I don't ever buy myself a black strapless leather mini-dress," she thought, "I'm going to regret it for the rest of my life." She was definitely attuned to the erotic power of clothing and the ways it could affect her sense of self, even before she began getting support and positive feedback for dressing the way she wanted to.

Jamie doesn't usually dress up in a super-feminine way; she prefers to dress on the butch side. But once in a while she makes an exception, and the clothing change seems to have quite an effect: "I have a tight dress with a sweetheart neckline and a slit in the back. My date asked me, 'Are you wearing any panties under that thing?' I looked at her and said, 'I don't know. I'll check.' So I went off to the bathroom, came back with the panties in my hand, gave them to her, and said, 'No.' I didn't get them back for a while!"

Shar says exhibitionists thrive on appreciation. One night she put on go-go boots and her dad's old Yamaha muscle t-shirt from 1969. "I had done this for people before, and they would just be bored to tears," Shar says. Not this time – Jackie loved it. "Then she ratted her hair up and put on a tight negligee," says Jackie, "and did this whole other persona." Changing into outfit after outfit, Shar reveled in the attention.

The erotic appreciation of dress works both ways for Shar and Jackie. "One night Jackie had on baggy men's pants and suspenders and a v-necked white t-shirt with the sleeves rolled up. She looked dapper, but she also looked like the guy in 'Cat on a Hot Tin Roof' – like she should be sweating. And I said, 'Would you just stand on the bed and let me masturbate and stare at you?' I felt so nasty asking for that because I'm not normally a voyeur – it surprised me.

"But that just reminds me of something really hot – fashion. There's a lot to be said for cooking in high heels and a spandex dress." Jackie elaborates: "All of a sudden she got a bug up her ass and decided to go cook dinner in this tight thing pulled up, and her ass hangin' out, and five inch Frederick's of Hollywood shoes. Oh my god!" "And the next thing you know, she's fucking me up against the stove."

Sometimes it's not what you wear, it's how you take it off. Most of us associate stripping with wearing sexy undergarments, but Juliet runs a workshop on stripping, "How to Be a Tantalizing Tart," that emphasizes how you feel about yourself and your eroticism, not fancy lingerie.

Juliet started stripping after she entered the porn business in the '70s. Now she's in her sixties. She developed her workshop because of an experience she had helping another ex-porn star, Annie Sprinkle, with her workshop, "Sluts and Goddesses." Annie spontaneously suggested that Juliet show the women in the workshop how to do a striptease.

Juliet wasn't prepared for the request. "I was in a t-shirt!" she says. "I had very little makeup on. I had no music, I had no high heels or lingerie. The women in the workshop had already taken the best stuff to dress up in."

Even with nothing erotic to wear, Juliet gave it a shot. "This is really what I want to get across," she told her audience. "It's not what you have on or what your body is like, it's how you feel about yourself and your sexuality. All of you are young enough to be my daughters or my granddaughters. So you can't cop out because of your age, and you can't say you don't have anything to wear – look, I have nothing."

She borrowed a New Age music tape from Annie. With slow music playing, she proceeded to show her audience the moves. "Okay, you're in a t-shirt. Now here are a couple of ways to tease. You turn your back, and you lift the shirt a little bit. Show a little bit here – then move around and unzip your slacks a little. Turn around and slide your hand slowly down into your pants, play with your pussy... Lick your lips." Juliet showed them how to get out of pants gracefully: "Lie on the floor and pull them off. Pull them down to your mid-thigh, then reach down and pull off one leg, then the other."

Stripping is an erotic treat because you reveal your body in a tantalizing way, and you're in control of the pacing. Don't do it too fast. Most professional strippers' shows last for at least three songs – that's ten minutes or more. Pick music that's sexy for you. If you're concerned that your body isn't attractive enough, consider Juliet's advice: "It's a frame of mind. We women are our own worst enemies. We put ourselves down constantly, we think because we don't have a figure out of *Vogue* magazine that we're not pretty.

"If you're a heterosexual or bisexual woman, remember that it takes very little to turn men on. They will concentrate on what they like and forget the rest. Some men like breasts, some men like earlobes, some men like feet, some men like asses – big asses, medium asses, small asses, no asses... you never know. So the important thing is that you feel good about yourself – then the person you're doing it for will love it. Do it for you. Practice in front of the mirror. Try a few props, light candles, have fun.

"I've got five scars on my belly. I'm not going to pretend they're not there. But let's say that I know I have nice breasts and a nice ass, which I do. I'm going to accentuate or draw attention to what I feel really good about. I'll wear something that covers up any area that I don't feel so good about."

Nina Hartley, who became a professional stripper to explore her desire for exhibitionism, concurs. "In a performance situation people will believe what you show them. They can't read your mind. They don't know how scared you are. Just smile and look confident, and they will be blown away. They will be mesmerized by you because they want to be. Once I learned that the audience couldn't read my mind – couldn't see the fat fourteen-year-old because she was long gone – it gave me a lot of confidence."

Juliet has mostly stripped for men, but what she says about them is also true of women. Regardless of whether you're a woman or a man stripping for a female partner or audience, if you convey eroticism and confidence, you'll be a hit. In fact, you may have a special advantage – lots of women have never been the recipients of that kind of focused erotic attention. You may find your girlfriend as easy to whip into a voyeuristic frenzy as those gals who go to watch the Chippendales or the women-for-women shows the Burlezk troupe and Fairy Butch used to put on in San Francisco. If not, try a few words of encouragement, like "It will really turn me on to put on a show for you." So many women grow up never thinking that they'll find erotic entertainment geared to them that some don't know how to relax and enjoy it.

Men can strip, too. Juliet recommends that heterosexual women "take the initiative, because men are often very shy about this. Buy your boyfriend or husband some sexy briefs and say 'Here, honey, I want you to strip for me.'" No matter what your gender and that of your partner, each of you can explore the fun of providing erotic entertainment and consuming it; trade off with each other once in a while!

I can't teach you stripping, a highly visual art, via words on a page. Fortunately, there are several ways you can learn the moves. You can visit a strip show and study the people working there. If a Strip-o-Gram-type business exists in your area, perhaps one of their strippers would be interested in giving you private lessons, or would give a class if you get some of your friends together. If you live in a city with a Learning Annex or another non-traditional adult education series, you may be able to find a class. There are also a few video classes available. Sheila Kelley began her fitness classes, which she calls "The S Factor," after a role in the movie "Dancing at The Blue Iguana," for which she had to learn stripper moves; there are also pole dancing classes, Strip Aerobics, and other exercise modalities that borrow from sexy sex industry moves.

If you've just figured out how you want to dress up erotically, don't think that you have to immediately strip out of the clothes you just put on! Go ahead and have sex while wearing them. In fact, having sex with your clothes on can be so much fun that you don't even have to wear anything special or out-of-the-ordinary to appreciate its eroticism.

Erotic Environments, Public and Private

You don't have to stop at dressing up yourself and your partner. You may find that you feel more inspired if you also dress up your environment. Is your bedroom decorated in a sensuous way? Satin or soft flannel sheets on the bed are fine, but some people like to add ambience to the room itself. Accentuate the visual. Some Tantra practitioners favor gauzy drapes hanging around the bed; to clothe yourself to match, try sheer scarves or just lots of jewelry and nothing else. If you're into S/M, black drapes and chain might get you in the mood to put on your leathers. You can decorate with pictures you find sexy. And virtually any erotic atmosphere benefits from candlelight.

Juliet recommends getting out of the bedroom for your exhibitionistic escapades. You don't need to go out to the park and hide behind a tree, but getting frisky elsewhere in the house, if you usually restrict amorous goings-on to the bedroom, can free you up to explore your more outgoing, experimental side. Often we think of the bedroom as our only really private space, so that even if no one can see us in the more "public" rooms of the house, erotic play there feels more exposed and exhibitionistic. So does being sexual near windows and outside – again, even if no one can see. "If I want to masturbate and I can't get turned on, I'll take off all my clothes, open up the shades, and walk around the house for three seconds," says Shar. "It works like a charm."

"Make a whole ritual out of it," suggests Jackie. "I like to take a shower and take my time. Afterwards, even if I have a towel around my body, when I spread my legs that wide open, air-on-my-pussy feeling is really hot. Nobody has to be there. Nobody has to even be looking through the window. For me, being a little more shy, just the sheer fact of being completely bare is a thrill sometimes."

Perhaps you have fantasies of sex in the alley, after dark – but you don't want to risk being caught and you really don't want strangers to be able to see you. Do you have a garage? Even that much similarity of environment might be enough to get you going – especially if you and your partner have also been practicing talking dirty. You can spin out a nasty spoken fantasy together about all the outlaw bikers who are watching, even if your only actual witness is the WeedEater.

Your erotic creativity, the grown-up version of the creativity you expressed as a child through play, will help you construct environments that make you feel especially sexy or adventurous even as they protect your privacy and keep you out of hot water. Let your fantasies go wild and even the most mundane atmosphere can become charged with erotic tension. "Masturbate in the car while your lover drives," Shar suggests, "and talk really nasty. Just don't have an accident doing this. We were in a convertible when we went to Las Vegas, and I made sure I had a little skirt that the wind could blow up, and a shaved pussy. 'Honey, I'm so bored when you drive. I guess I'm just going to have to do this.'" Remember that I don't equate exhibitionism with public exposure, but then, the Nevada desert is full of empty stretches of road!

Your creativity will also help you find opportunities for exhibitionistic fun while you're in public. This can be a challenge; most of us don't want our sexy good time to annoy, offend, or frighten someone who doesn't anticipate stumbling onto a sex show. I do not recommend you engage in out-and-out sex in front of unconsenting people in a way that infringes on them – in short, in a way that they notice. You have a lot of public leeway, though, if you're careful.

Simply talking dirty together, quietly, can become a powerful exhibitionistic scene when done in public. For many people, needless to say, the dirtier the better. A special variation of this, one I've already mentioned, is the phone call made by one lover to the other at work or some other context in which s/he can't respond. Here the thrill comes partly from the incongruity of hearing very blue language in a "polite," non-sexualized setting; this can also have a hint of dominance and submission, since the person who can't let on that the call is overtly sexual is to some degree at the mercy of the dirty-talking partner.

I have only one caveat about public talk, based on something that actually happened to me. I was engaged in an incredibly nasty and very quiet conversation with Robert in a family-style Italian restaurant. We were careful to keep our voices down and sure no one could overhear us. As we left, however, we saw that the table next to us was full of people conversing in sign language. We'll never know if they also read lips, but I fancied they looked at us with special interest as we departed!

Related to quiet public talk is the "shared secret" – like Jamie's "discovery" that she wasn't wearing any panties. Slipping your underwear into your lover's pocket after a trip to the restroom, handing your partner an envelope containing an erotic book or drawing or a spicy letter while sitting in a restaurant, tucking a sex toy into purse, pocket or briefcase – all these acts add up to sexy promises that will hang between you until you get home or to another reasonably private destination.

Lingerie, or the lack of it, may be the most time-honored vehicle for this very common kind of secret exhibitionism. Going braless – or removing your bra mid-date – can give you a sexy, exposed feeling, especially if you usually wear a bra all the time. Here's one man's variation on the lingerie theme. Once in a while Robert reaches beneath his coat or returns from a trip to the restroom while we're in public and snaps his cock ring onto my wrist. Almost anyone who noticed this would see nothing more than a leather bracelet, but I know what it is – and can still feel the warmth of his cock and balls.

Carolyn and her lover Barb love to play semi-publicly. "I've done things like walk into a restaurant and whisper to my date that I have on crotchless panties under my skirt – and then watch her forget how to use her chopsticks! Then there was the bookstore that we wandered into one day when I had on a skirt and no underwear – we found a place in the store where I was actually right in the window looking out, but there were bookshelves that came up to my chest height. And she's on the floor looking for a book and running her hand up my skirt." "Because of course she had *told* me earlier that she had on no panties," Barb adds.

Skirts are ideally suited for public exhibitionism; if there's a long cloth on your restaurant table, you can get away with a lot. Not everybody wears skirts, but luckily, you can play footsie under the table with a partner wearing pants, and, especially with a long tablecloth, your foot can stray very high. (If your feet are especially sensitive, beware – your lover may retaliate.) If you're wearing a long or loose-fitting coat, your partner can gain enough access for more interesting public groping than you might otherwise be able to manage without committing a breach of propriety. And surely the old "coat-over-the-lap" routine has provided thrills since at least the advent of public transit – it's good for masturbation as well as playing with your partner.

The point with games like this, as Carolyn puts it, is "not necessarily doing things for public display, not flashing or doing something where there are non-consenting people watching, but doing things in a situation where there could be. There's just a hint of risk." If the element of risk - or just feeling very turned on in public - is especially hot for you, this is easy to emphasize through talk and fantasy. Of course, you may find venues where your observers consent enthusiastically to practically anything you want to show them.

Juliet was once engaged in an erotic photo shoot in her second floor bedroom, safe, she thought, from any onlookers. She was surprised to glance out the window and see a telephone lineman with his mouth hanging open - fortunately well-secured to his phone pole. Concerned that he might be offended, she waved to him - thus signaling him that it was okay if he looked, and alert to his response. When he grinned and waved back, she went on with her posing. In this case, everyone had a chance to consent - except maybe the phone company, who probably had to pay their lineman a bit of overtime that day!

As Juliet's story illustrates, you can stay alert to possibilities for exhibitionism in your everyday environment. Just remember to be equally alert to issues of consent - just because someone can see you doesn't mean they want to and have agreed to look - and your own personal safety.

GPenn says, of his polyamorous goings-on with his girlfriend Heather: "Showing off and our general sense of adventurousness inspired playing with covert public sex. Once she sat in my lap, on my cock, as her husband drove us across the Golden Gate bridge. We then sat in the car in the overlook parking lot (her skirt discreetly covering us), watching the tourists walk past. Probably the edgiest thing we did was standing there with heavy clothing concealing what we were doing as I held her from behind with my cock inside her - it just looked like we were standing with my arms around her looking at the ocean. A cop walked over to us from the parking lot. We got discreetly disengaged before the cop got too close; she said hello and continued on."

Hot scene, huh? A cop! A *lady* cop! Could it get any better than that? But GPenn's feelings about this kind of adventure are mixed, and not just because the lady cop might not have consented to his and Heather's discreet show. "A previous girlfriend of mine used to love sex in the car in a place where it was potentially risky to be discovered," he continues. "I always felt pushed by that, partly because of the gender reason. Heather has done it some too; the woman looks at it with glee, including my own fear about the situation, enjoying my nervousness, but part of my nervousness is feeling it would be perceived significantly differently for a woman to be discovered being sexual compared to a man; what might end up being exposed is different; she can pull down her skirt and hide herself and have less risk of getting an indecent exposure charge."

Given that more men than women have been busted for exhibitionism (and remember that this can be a serious legal charge, in some locales requiring registering as a sex offender), GPenn's worries may not be all in his head – and his points should be well-taken by anyone looking to go play (exhibitionistically) outside.

EXHIBITIONISM AS EMPOWERMENT

Non-exhibitionists often assume that being observed, especially by strangers, results in feeling, and actually being, vulnerable. They can't understand why anyone would allow this, much less go out of their way to set it up or attract it. Sexy or exhibitionistic clothing, erotic behavior in public or semi-public contexts, nudism or sex parties – any of these attractions for the exhibitionist seems potentially dangerous to them.

Yet in fact most exhibitionists I talked to, including people who had been, or still are, quite shy, talked about exhibitionism more in terms of feeling enlivened and empowered. They actually feel stronger, not more vulnerable. Why?

For one thing, many shy people have lived through years when they considered themselves not particularly attractive or interesting to others. They have not seen themselves as potentially capable of getting others' attention in a sexually powerful way. When this aspect of self-image changes through exhibitionistic garb or behavior, we often feel more attractive and erotically powerful simply because we're leaving ourselves open for a new kind of attention.

Also, it makes a difference to try something we'd thought ourselves incapable of doing. This can precipitate a change in our self-image and our feelings about ourselves even if no one responds to us. The important thing is breaking out of our habitual shyness and trying something new.

Finally, when we set out to explore exhibitionism because the idea of doing so turns us on, we access a very powerful source of pleasure and positive self-image: our own eroticism. Our culture, which often tries to separate sex from other parts of life, does not always acknowledge the importance of sexual satisfaction to self-esteem. This is odd, since so many people find it absolutely central.

Simply making it a priority to masturbate and give yourself pleasure – regardless of whether you add any of the exhibitionistic "extras" we've discussed in this book – can affect the way you relate to the world. Getting past the fear of being "kinky" or sexually unacceptable may have an even greater effect, and making sex play a priority with your partner – even setting aside scheduled time for it – can positively affect not only your feelings about your partner and your relationship, but your feelings about yourself. Too many people feel guilty if they think about taking more than a smidgen of time for themselves, especially to devote to something as "non-productive" as sex – you have to be willing to be selfish, if necessary, to prioritize pleasure in your life.

Bayla notices that when she dresses erotically or explores semi-public sex environments, she feels different about herself. "It feels extremely free. I feel better about my body than I ever do when I'm walking around in regular clothes." She also finds people respond to her differently: "In being exhibitionistic I've had more people say complimentary things about my body than I ever got in relationships. It's just wonderful. I wouldn't have gotten those compliments if I hadn't been an exhibitionist because I wouldn't have been in those situations. I've had people say, 'Your body is really beautiful.' I didn't realize how much I needed to hear that until someone said it. God knows how long I would have waited for a lover to say it. Now I feel like I'm so much more likely to pick a lover who would."

Candye Kane has thought a lot about this; she's a big woman who had to talk her way into her first erotic modeling job, insisting that she be given a chance to prove she'd be good at it. Exhibitionism has played a pivotal role in the development of her sexuality – and her positive self-image. "I do think your sexuality is deeply connected to the way you feel about yourself," she says, "and I think it's made me so much stronger to be able to be free sexually, not only professionally, but also in my own relationships. Repression keeps people from being themselves and going for what they really want. It's so exhilarating, I think, to have a desire and then act on it, and be free to go on – it fucks up so many people in our culture to carry around all this baggage, feeling ugly and weird and terrible about what they're thinking, not realizing that the guy or girl next to them might be thinking the same thing."

Exhibitionism provides the link between knowing that someone's attracted to me and really *feeling* desired. When a lover or potential partner responds to me when I'm being exhibitionistic, it feels like I've taken the awareness of their desire right into my body. It increases my arousal, and it also helps me feel more erotically present and sure of myself. When I'm showing off, I'm not just going through the motions, and when my partner responds to my exhibitionism, I know he or she isn't either.

Finally, the very fear even diehard exhibitionists sometimes still feel about exposing themselves to a new partner or in a new situation can in itself be arousing. Some of us actually get erotic energy from a case of nerves or a scary situation.

So far I've focused on how we feel about ourselves, and I maintain that's the most important reason to enjoy exhibitionism. I would be remiss, though, if I didn't acknowledge that a certain kind of sexual power often attracts us to exhibitionism. Whether it's a particular kind of attractiveness we exude, the affirmation we get for being sexy or sexual, being seen as proficient, or simply the effect our erotically outgoing presence has on others, the fact is that exhibitionistic people often notice that others begin to treat them with a sort of awe. Some have taken advantage of that response to make a career in the sex business. Others just revel in their erotic power off the job.

"You can do the least little thing that's exhibitionistic and people give you all this power," says Bayla, adding that not only does she feel that people treat her differently when she's feeling more exhibitionistic, she notices that she thinks of others differently if she's seen them showing off. She never pictures them home alone, without a date; she ascribes a certain sexual power to them if she's seen them behave or dress erotically in public.

Then there are the other power-related reasons to become exhibitionistic, like attention and money, that have nothing to do with enjoying one's sexual power per se. A woman who attended one of my "Exhibitionism for the Brazen" workshops told a tale of indulging in something I can only call "revenge exhibitionism." Her boyfriend had recently broken up with her, and she was mad. He worked outdoors, as a member of a road crew, so she arranged to drive past while he was at work, naked under her coat, and flash him. She didn't do it for her own erotic pleasure, but to make a powerful statement which I'll take the liberty of translating as, "I'll show that motherfucker what he dumped!" She seemed entirely pleased with herself as she recounted the story, so I'm sure she got ample pleasure from her act.

Particularly for women, being exhibitionistic has much to do with admitting that we're sexual – and that we want sex. It's about calling attention to ourselves sexually. Of course, we want it on our own terms and according to our own fantasies – an exhibitionistic presentation virtually never means we're sexually available to just anyone, and sometimes, especially publicly, it doesn't mean we're sexually available at all, only that we get off on being looked at. There are other ways for women to assert sexual desire, of course – read Susie Bright's remarks on what she calls "femmchismo" in the introduction to her anthology of women-authored erotic fiction, *Herotica*.

Overtly sexual women are stigmatized as sluts because of society's disapproval of independent female sexuality – and, as I've noted, society is not so supportive of many of men's sexual desires either. Many women and men have found they feel very powerful when they say no to sex-as-stigma and yes to their own erotic desire.

Hence, some of people's fear about exhibitionism and vulnerability may boil down to a fear of displaying their own desire and interest in sex. Jamie notes that when one embraces exhibitionism among people who appreciate it and are open and adventurous themselves, "Wanting does not make you vulnerable. Wanting makes you powerful. Going out dressed to the nines, with your tuxedo on, with your shirt on but nothing else, or all your froufrou stuff – it's saying 'I *want*, and that puts me in a position of power, not a position of no power, or less power.'"

Indeed, depending on whether you feel that sexual signaling indicates power or vulnerability may dictate your gut-level response to exhibitionism. This dichotomy underlies some of the feminist arguments about sexual show-offery discussed earlier. Is exhibitionism primarily for the benefit of the voyeur, or the person being looked at?

The sort of behavior I'm discussing has lots more to do with the motivations and pleasure of the exhibitionist her- or himself; the viewer's pleasure may be involved, but the pleasure of the one exhibiting is paramount. We can't simplify it too much, however. Often our motivations will be mixed and our exhibitionism conditional – we might not do something for free we'd do for pay, we might not do something for just anyone's eyes that we'd do for a lover.

Safety and Control: The Importance of Context

We can't always control the response and assumptions of the people who view us, so sometimes being exhibitionistic can get us into situations we find annoying. We may in fact have to set limits with others, or even limit ourselves more than we want to, because we don't want to attract particular kinds of attention: Rita's least favorite thing about exhibitionism is the stranger who approaches her, saying something like, "Nice breasts! Can I touch them?" This is very poor form, but we've all noticed how many folks around us are remiss in the social skills department; unfortunately, exhibitionists can attract those who assume we're sending a simple signal of availability, even when we're not.

Assess the potential risks of any public exhibitionism realistically. If your chosen context for exhibitionistic forays has you playing with or around strangers, how will you keep yourself safe? Never let your excitement about showing off get in the way of a sensible consideration of your own security. You can be safer masturbating openly at a sex party than you might be doing it in the bushes at the municipal park or dirty dancing with all your clothes on at a bar. Where public sex and nudity are acceptable, people are usually socialized better around issues of consent; where strangers gather to drink and drug, consent can fly out the window as fast as you can say "date rape." Keep these issues in mind as you determine what you want to do and where you want to do it. It's no wonder that many exhibitionistically-inclined people keep their play behind closed doors; my recommendation for those who want to take it out into the world is to team up with a friend or partner.

Stay conscious of these issues especially if you've supported your exhibitionistic inclinations by dissolving your inhibitions with alcohol or drugs. "I did a lot of joyous exhibitionism while I was still drinking," says Bayla. She was hardly alone – many people who stop using alcohol or drugs say they have to learn to be sexually outgoing all over again. If you sense that you sometimes drink and/or drug to give yourself the nerve to show off – or to have any kind of sex – please know that you can learn to have the same pleasure when you're sober. "I never felt guilty about things I did when I was drunk," Bayla adds, "but I do wish I had felt free enough to enjoy them sober. I'm finally learning to become that uninhibited now."

A concern that can stop us from any kind of sexual show-offery is the fear that, once we step across the invisible line that separates exhibitionists from non-exhibitionists, we won't be able to behave like an ordinary person again. Some people are afraid that they're going to be permanently tainted or damaged. We might worry that people will come up to us in public and treat us like the brazen slut they saw at the party last weekend, expecting we'll respond accordingly. To stand the best chance of avoiding this pitfall, clearly communicate expectations and limits at the outset: "I think it'd be fun to play with you tonight, but it may turn out to be a one-time fling;" "I love coming here and getting wild, but please don't expect this kind of familiarity if we run into each other somewhere else."

Julia, whose performance art frequently deals with sex, notes that sometimes she feels her friends tend to distance themselves from her exhibitionistic ways, probably because they feel a little uncomfortable with her public behavior. Though Julia is still very shy, she masturbates on stage as part of her show. "I'm always talking about sex," she says. "I'm always shocking people. I've been doing it all my life. I was the little first grader who said 'fuck' at school and got in trouble for it. It's really powerful."

I can relate to Julia's experience; one of my own exhibitionistic acts, not related directly to my own sexual arousal, is talking more openly and comfortably about sex than a lot of other peoples' comfort levels allow. Interestingly, I can feel more powerful and comfortable doing public sexual performance, whether verbal or physical, than I sometimes feel talking openly but non-erotically about sex to people who don't approve of direct sexual communication. I'm not talking dirty, but I am challenging them, and I'm also aware that at these times I feel more vulnerable; their negative judgment affects the way I feel.

Talking about sex more openly in these non-sexual contexts is actually related to getting more comfortable talking in intimate situations, so you might want to explore this further. You can spread a little friendly gossip about the love life of a movie star, talk about the sexual theme of a book you read or TV show you saw, talk about sex as an issue: "What do you think about that Surgeon General who got fired for talking about masturbation?" You can self-disclose: say something about your own sexuality in conversation, not necessarily very detailed or intimate, but something that acknowledges you're a sexual person. You can also encourage the person you're talking to to say something about themselves: ask questions about their opinions regarding a sex-related issue, ask them about their own sexuality. In general, talking about an issue or a third party will be potentially less threatening to your conversation partner; asking them personal questions may feel very threatening indeed. If you explore this, be sensitive to your friends' comfort levels and boundaries; it's probably not your intent to put them on the spot, and in general this is something to actively avoid with work friends because of legal regulations about sexual harassment.

Our comfort – even safety – in any kind of exhibitionistic situation has to do with context, as well as with support. In your own life, look at where your support comes from and might come from: a primary partner, casual partners, friends, a sex-positive or sex-oriented community. You may not take the need for support seriously until and unless you have an experience with others' negative judgments. Disregard for the need for support is most often found in people who have never thought of themselves as sexually different or divergent. It's a myth that heterosexual people don't need social support for their sexuality. They're still affected by erotophobia, and conservative heterosexual norms mandating monogamy, marriage and procreation don't leave much room for claiming the right to erotically experiment.

Julia notices another effect of exhibitionism that several others echo: feeling more aware of and connected to her body when she behaves exhibitionistically. Julia has been disabled since an accident when she was young, and she also finds that exhibitionism helps her fight others' assumptions that disabled people are asexual.

Jamie makes an important distinction between exhibitionism based on looks and that based on erotic behavior: "It's very important to me that people like what they see," she says, "but it's much more important that they like what they see me *doing* rather than what they see me *look like."*

"I associate exhibitionism with being kind of bad," muses Bayla. "I'm doing things nice girls aren't supposed to do. I don't feel out of control or uncomfortable - it feels fine, but it's something the shy person in me doesn't feel." (Of course, not everyone will feel bad or naughty about exploring exhibitionism.)

Bayla attended my "Exhibitionism for the Shy" workshop and felt very nervous about doing it; she almost skipped that night. "I had so much anxiety about it; that was my clue that I really needed to do it. When you feel that way, it's your cue that you probably need to do the thing you're nervous about, that there's something really wonderful to be gotten out of going through it." Also, she reassures those who think they're new to exhibitionism, "I'd like to remind people that if they played Spin the Bottle or any of those adolescent party games where the point was to be watched while you did things, they probably have been exhibitionistic. I think a lot of people forget that they've already had a sort of public sex."

Candye is sensitive to the problem of performance anxiety, too, and she also has words of encouragement. "Try not to be afraid of things. I think what holds people back, probably, is fear that it's going to label them somehow if they do something really different. Realize that it's just a momentary, wonderful plateau that you've reached, not a life-long commitment. It doesn't have to be a commitment, it can be just one fun thing that you did. It's like trying new food, really - experimenting a little bit shouldn't be a big deal."

I love Candye's food analogy - I often use it when speaking in public about sexual variation and people's differing erotic tastes. Trying a new cuisine does not require you to keep that restaurant in your repertoire, much less to go eat there every night from now on.

But to take this idea a step further, *are* you ready to go out for dinner? Read on.

☾   **9**   ✺

Practice Makes Perfect:
Some Hints for Finding Partners

Y ou can confine showing off, dressing erotically, and talking dirty to the privacy of your room, turning only yourself on with your exhibitionism. You don't even need a mirror – though it adds a lot to the fun and heat of autoerotic exhibitionism.

Sooner or later, though, you will probably want to explore these erotic games with a partner – or several. Where will you go? What will you do? The answers depend on you, your particular turn-ons, your relationship status, and a host of other variables. In this chapter we'll assume that you're single and looking for playmates, or that you and your partner are looking for like-minded friends with whom to have exhibitionistic adventures. If you're partnered, but not with an outgoing, appreciative, or experimental person, this may help you work up the motivation to discuss your desires with him or her or give you ideas for things you can do alone.

Keep It Safe

You may think few opportunities for exhibitionistic fun outside your own bedroom exist where you are. Perhaps you live in a small town or a conservative area of the country. Perhaps you are concerned about safety.

Whether you live in small-town America or a big crazy city, remember that your exhibitionistic forays can lead to trouble if you don't consider the issue of consent – who might object to seeing or hearing you? Neighbors who live and let live when they're not sure what you're up to can get very riled if they see you're having more fun than they think you ought to. Perhaps you heard about the case of a Florida couple whose irate neighbor videotaped them as they enjoyed a rollicking screw inside their own apartment – the snoop then had the nerve to alert the police because "children might have seen them." Of course the kids would have had to stand on a crate and peep through the blinds, just as the busybody had, to see the goings-on.

While you can do little besides close the drapes to protect yourself from being watched by disturbed individuals toting mini-cams, do try to give some clear-headed thought to your situation before you decide to go skinny-dipping by moonlight in your neighbor's pool. There are laws almost everywhere regulating permissible public exposure and behavior, and you will do yourself a favor, if these sorts of high-exposure games are your fantasy of choice, to familiarize yourself with the relevant statutes for your particular locale. Sad to say, some of the people around us don't agree that sexual exploration and pleasure are good. Remember, they have the problem, not you. But if you do have any sort of run-in like the Floridian couple had with their nosy neighbors, get a competent attorney to defend you on the basis of your right to privacy.

Ironically, the Florida scenario makes a great exhibitionistic fantasy. Just think! You're naked, up on the bathroom sink, rutting like an animal with your very own spouse. A nasty neighbor spies on you – and takes pictures! Then he drags you into court, to be tried by a jury for the crime of FUCKING! Just think about the great passionate speeches you could make in your own defense.

It's fun as a fantasy scenario, but not in real life. Remember, your responsibility as a sexually adventuresome adult is to minimize the risks you run in your erotic exploration – that means being aware of everything from safe sex to sex-related laws.

If we dwell on this too much, though, we really will keep the blinds shut tight. Of course, that's no reason to give up on exhibitionism

– as long as you have an enthusiastic voyeur with you in your private hideaway.

How do you find one?

FINDING PARTNERS

One way to locate a sexually compatible partner is to hope that this compatibility will come as part of the package when you meet someone new, attractive, and interesting. Sometimes, of course, it does. Alternatively, you can make it a primary, non-negotiable quality you look for in a new love. Other options besides pair-bonding may appeal to some; many sexually satisfied people have no regular love partner, but rather share affectionate sexual intimacy with friends. Still others delight in erotic adventuring with the primary and explicit aim of meeting sex partners, not life partners.

Consider your ideal situation. Perhaps you want a monogamous life-partner who doubles as the lover of your wildest fantasies. Perhaps you would prefer to remain non-monogamous with that love of your life. Perhaps you tend to favor non-intimate sex, reserving your long-term intimate bonds for friends. Perhaps your fantasy mate is nowhere to be seen, but you are happy to engage in friendly sex, romantic or not, until s/he comes along. Look at both fantasy and reality; if they don't match closely, break down the elements of each (hot sex, love, intimacy, touch, companionship, and anything else that's important to you). Which elements match most closely, and which least? What things can you change right now? What kind of goals can you create to change the others?

People get what they want in a partner most easily when they know what they want, so consider that first. People who know what they have to give are also more likely to get what they want. Are your desires realistic? Are you the sort of person who'd likely attract the kind of person you desire? If not, what can you do about it? What kind of people do you tend to attract? Are you so focused on the perfect, elusive partner that you ignore the wonderful people in your life right now?

Every commentator on relationships from Dear Abby to Happy Hooker Xaviera Hollander says the same thing: If you are pleasant, friendly, reasonably well-groomed, a good listener, and interesting to talk to, other people – potential mates, friends, and everyone else – will find you congenial; some will find you sexually attractive. Abby always tells the lovelorn to look for partners in the places they already frequent – clubs, volunteer organizations, and the like – and it's sound advice. To fine-tune this recommendation: if your interests are sexual, frequent places that have something to do with sexuality.

Once you are there, don't forget Abby's advice. It will still matter that you are pleasant, friendly, and so forth. Happily, though, if what interests you is sex, when you begin to talk about it in an atmosphere where sex is acceptable, the people you meet will probably treat you like a peer. (If you try this tack at church or at work, the spouse-hunting locations some less sex-savvy relationship advisors recommend, you may find you're being treated more like an untouchable.)

Okay, how do you find the other folks in your town who are interested in sex?

PLAYING THE PERSONALS

If your town doesn't have any groups that are organized around varying sexual interests or orientations, you can consider starting one yourself. This doesn't have to be anything fancy. Whom would you like to meet? People interested in sexual experimentation? Non-monogamy? S/M? Swinging? Exhibitionism? All of the above? If you live in a town large enough to have an alternative newspaper (these are usually weekly or monthly), consider taking out a classified ad. It can be as eye-catching or as subtle as you wish; even if it's very vague, the right people will probably find it. Look at other ads before you compose your own; how explicit can you be, given the ad policy of the paper? Gauge this by the other ads, as well as by asking the paper's ad department directly. Another resource available in many places is Craigslist; if your town doesn't have one, go online to see what else might be available to you, including local members or affiliates of national sex- or fetish-related organizations.

A woman friend of mine wanted to have sex with women, but she felt out of place in lesbian clubs, as some bisexuals do. She placed an ad under the headline "Bi-Curious?" Soon she had not only an ongoing social group where other women like herself could meet, but also plenty of partners.

If your living room isn't big enough for a mixer or you're looking for only one new friend, not a multitude, you can place an ad designed to attract individuals. For tips on how to proceed, have a look at existing personals, and at books about playing the personals; an online search will lead you to several. Remember that if you really desire a partner (or someone to join you in a fling) with whom you can get into talking dirty, or who likes to watch, you need to state it in the ad, if the paper will let you, so those non-voyeuristic, non-talkative people who otherwise like the sound of you will be less likely to respond. If a partner who does like these things responds, but you don't like him or her, you have no obligation to proceed with sexual experimentation or courtship with that person. Now that you know other people out there share your interests, you can look for someone who's right for you.

Personal ads have a venerable history. Among groups whose sexuality lies outside an era's social norm, ads have long been a method of seeking out people of like mind for friendship, sex, and love. I used to delight in reading gay men's personals; many men were so explicit about what they did and didn't want in a sex partner that I found it pleasantly shocking. I wondered why everybody else couldn't be that upfront.

Well, we can; we just have to decide what we want, resolve that getting what we want is important, and locate a print or online publication in which we can place explicit ads. If any aspect of eroticism is so important to you that you'd mourn its absence in a relationship, write it down! In the realm of personal ads, you're far more likely to get what you want if you tell your readers what it is. Nicola Ginzler, author of an article about personal ads, suggests some strategies as you begin planning your ad: "Writing things down, even if it's a total jumble, can really help you figure out what you want. Saying things out loud, even if there's no one around, can also help. And this is so obvious that I think I need to say it – say things that are true. Don't say things that aren't."

What if the personals in your local weekly are full of ads from people who only want to sip champagne by candlelight and walk on the beach?

What if your ad is so explicit that the paper won't take it? It may be time to turn to the sex papers and sex-finder websites.

Every region in the United States has these – they're often called "swingers" publications, though not all of them, strictly speaking, are. (Swinging usually refers to a heterosexual couples' scene. If you're single, gay, a bisexual male, or partnered with someone who doesn't want to accompany you in the swinging scene, you're not technically a swinger even though you may be interested in group sex or multiple partners.)

I'm using the term "publication" here, but you will find many more websites and online communities today than you will find print (or "dead-tree," as the tech-savvy sometimes say) magazines or newspapers.

The sex publications will sometimes focus on a particular sexual persuasion, like S/M, erotic crossdressing, or men with big cocks. Sometimes various sexualities will be all mixed up, or occupying their own sections, in one "general-interest" publication, although the dead-tree versions are getting ever more rare as the Internet takes over this area of partner-search. Some papers allow ads from professionals, some don't; some restrict ads about certain kinds of sexual interest, like male/male sex. If you don't see what you want, you may find it in a different publication or on another site, so keep looking. Often the ads are illustrated with pictures – either of the advertiser's face, body, or just genitals or ass. Others leave it all to the imagination.

These illustrations, by the way, may be heartening for those who don't think anyone would even want to look at a naked picture of them, much less want to meet once they saw it. Do you assume the folks who send photos are all picture-perfect? Not so! Perusing the sex ads you can see photos of people as they really are – not just the young, made-up, worked-out bodies you see in most porn, but folks who look a lot like you and your neighbors. Women and men who are older, bigger, skinnier than the Madison Avenue norm proudly let it all hang out, naked or lingerie-clad. (Sometimes it's the men in the lingerie!) The message they send is obvious and infectious: I want to play!

Where these papers still exist, you can usually find them in adult bookstores; even if a town is too small for its own sex paper, there may still be one that covers the region. If you don't find one, it's time to go online.

Virtual Play

Another way to "meet" friends who share your interests is through computer groups, bulletin boards (a.k.a. BBSs), and find-partner websites. Increasingly, computers provide hot, interesting options for connecting with like-minded others. You can engage in "computer swinging," in which people send others explicit video clips of themselves – a moving-picture version of the Polaroids their less technologically-oriented neighbors send in to the sex papers and enclose with their contact letters when they answer an ad.

Polaroids and video are yesterday's exhibitionist tools and toys, and the computer is today's and (now joined by many cell phones) tomorrow's. They allow you to have relationships with voyeurs without ever seeing them in the flesh – plenty of people send videos or photos of themselves to appreciative new "friends" they meet online or via sex papers. Some folks advertise for this alone, with no desire to meet their "partners" in the flesh.

Naturally, these toys fit just as well into ongoing exhibitionist-voyeur relationships. One of my workshop attendees told of sending explicit videos to her lover in another city, who returned a video of himself masturbating watching the video she'd sent him; today, if you prefer, you can leave the US Mail out of the picture. The next best thing to being there!

Before you commit your image to film or digital file, especially if you're going to send it to a stranger, consider the ramifications. Will you want to run for the Senate ten years from now? How will you feel if your children stumble across it some day? Are you exhibitionistic enough that, if your picture surfaces, you can face possible public opprobrium?

If so, I'll vote for you! If not, you're by no means alone: many exhibitionists deal with their concern about issues like these by concealing their identities in some way before they part with a picture or a disc. A friend of mine who used to send photos of himself to potential sex partners always cut part of the face away; his new friend could tell he was good-looking, but not exactly who he was. Some people leave their faces out of the picture, either obscuring their features by position, costume (such as a mask, a veil, or a hood), or simply aiming the camera below the neck. Photoshop and other web-based image editing programs allow you to simply or artistically alter pics of yourself so you can't be recognized. (They also allow you to fool other people about how you look in real life; please don't do that. Someone really does want to meet and watch you just the way you are.)

There is in fact a subset of the sex community that does all of its exhibitionism and play through the media of computers, phone sex, home-made porn videos, photos and hot letters. Some folks never meet their playmates in the flesh, even if they have enjoyed long-term connections with them. This form of sexual sharing has a number of advantages. It is physically safe and can be done in ways that safeguard your privacy; you can experiment with fantasies of things you wouldn't ordinarily do; you can remain anonymous, even in some cases let inner personas out to play that might not be believable in the flesh. Some people engage in such play without feeling they're being unfaithful to a partner (though I should note that not all of their in-the-flesh partners would agree). If you're so shy that the idea of meeting and getting to fourth base with a new partner is very daunting, using any of these methods may loosen you up substantially; when you're not face to face with a partner, some of the pressure is off.

Then again, you can't kiss your hard drive, or if you do, it won't kiss you back. After a technological courtship, you may decide you want to meet your on-line flame in the flesh. Take some advice from personal ad authorities. Especially if you have only exchanged a letter or phone call or two with your prospective play partner from cyberspace, arrange your first face-to-face meeting in a public, neutral location. You may not want the person you are meeting to know where you live; you may not even like them, once you are both in the same room. Everyone I've ever talked to about meeting through the personals or any similar method agrees: trust your intuition, and be realistic about both the advantages and the risks of this type of "blind dating."

The vast majority of people you will meet this way are honorable folks with motives very similar to yours – they want pleasant connections, fun sex, perhaps even a relationship. If you get a feeling you've encountered one of the few whose intentions are not good, though, just say you don't think it's going to work out, and leave. If you meet a new contact for a date, let someone know where you're going and what time you expect you'll be back. You can even arrange to check in at a certain time to let them know you're doing fine. And avoid mixing drugs and alcohol with your first meeting with a stranger. Give your intuition a head start. None of this is pleasant to think about, but it reinforces the importance of realistic thinking and not giving personal information (that would allow you to be located in real life) to an online play partner before you know it's safe and appropriate.

Support and Social Groups

If there are groups in your area that deal with some element of sex that interests you, get involved. Most such groups sponsor getting-to-know-you evenings where prospective new members can come meet each other and already-established group members; many of these groups are very happy to allow you to use a pseudonym if you want to retain your privacy. If you set foot in one of these introductory gatherings with lurid fantasies about group S/M or any other kind of wild sex, you may find yourself astonished at how tame it seems! When I say "get involved," I don't mean "Offer to fuck everybody there"; rather, volunteer your organizing or fundraising skills, offer to help set up for the next event, and generally make yourself known and welcome. This way you'll do in a different habitat what Abby suggests you do at church: you'll become one of the group. From there you can get to know likely partners.

Make sure you pick a group whose members are likely to share your interests. I once ran a college gay association, the only sexuality-related organization for over a hundred miles. We ran a campus office where gays, lesbians, and bisexuals could drop in and get information, support, and referrals. Sex was not the main focus of the group, though plenty of love affairs did get started there. However, we got many calls and visits from non-gay people who figured that because we espoused an alternative sexuality we would understand their own desires. Several transsexuals contacted us, as did some heterosexual people interested in S/M, a number of heterosexual male cross-dressers, and even one married couple whose full story we never did learn – I think they were experimenting with reversing roles. We welcomed all these people, but it was clear that their desires and needs for support weren't really being met by our organization, and I often remarked in frustration that if only one of those folks were willing to organize an S/M group, a transgender support group, or whatever, we would have someplace to refer the next one.

If your chief desire is to meet others with whom you can explore exhibitionism and hot talk, virtually any sex-related organization might accommodate you. But make sure you're compatible with the group's main interest. If you have no interest in S/M, don't go to an S/M group to find partners; even though the members of the group will probably look favorably on your sexual desires, you might not have any interest in theirs. If you're heterosexual, it doesn't make much sense to go to a gay and lesbian group to look for partners; likewise, if you're gay, you probably won't fit in with swingers, especially if you're male. These groups may, however, give you a referral to another organization. A few will offer support and advice so you can start an organization of your own.

A very few groups don't structure themselves according to particular sexual orientations or interests, but instead welcome everyone who identifies as sex-positive. In the '60s there was the Sexual Freedom League. In the 1970s, several cities around the country sprouted Sex Information hotline organizations; people got involved not only to do useful volunteer work, but to meet others who were comfortable with sex. Anti-censorship groups are often populated by people of various interests and orientations. Many S/M groups welcome members regardless of whether they're gay, straight, or bisexual. The '90s saw an upsurge of these sorts of mixed groups, and this trend continues, just as erotic art and literature has increasingly been presented in an "all-orientations-welcome" format, from grassroots 'zines, websites, and small literary ventures to more mainstream books and publications. If you are bisexual, "PoMoSexual," experimental, refuse to be pigeonholed, or simply appreciate and respect other people's sexual choices as well as your own, you will have increasing company.

This leads me to muse briefly on a topic that may seem to contradict what I said above, about not hanging around with incompatible groups. Given that there really is more support for sexual fluidity and curiosity today than there may have been in the past, don't decide too soon that you're too vanilla for the BDSM club, too straight for the campus gay alliance. If you're a supportive, sex-positive person with good boundaries, the scary leather master you meet at the S/M club might introduce you to his sister; the gay guy who welcomes you might actually be bisexual. Never assume – keep an open mind. This may even extend to your own sexual choices, but whether or not that's the case, remember that all of us who are interested in sexuality can be some kind of community for each other. This is still especially important in small towns – I'm sure that even now, somewhere a heterosexual cross-dresser is looking up the contact information for his nearest college's gay group. We have a world of community on the Internet – but close to home, we'll do well to extend a hand and watch each others' backs.

Start a sex salon, if you're not sure how else to attract interesting, sex-positive people into your life. Run an ad; or ask a few friends to ask a few friends. Meet in a neutral place – maybe you can locate a restaurant or a coffeehouse with a separate room you can occupy. You can discuss different topics, read stories together, even gather everyone together to watch Real Sex on HBO (or, better yet, because it's a better series, Toronto City TV's SexTV). Friendships will flower, trysts will be arranged, relationships will form – all in an atmosphere of support and comfort about sex. Who among us couldn't use a little more of that? A salon format bypasses any requirement for sexual activity – the idea is not to play nude Twister, but to talk about ideas, experiences, and feelings – so it can be accessible to everyone. One resource for such a group is *The Sexual Attitude Restructuring Guide*, which offers discussion topics and exercises aimed at helping group members become more comfortable with sex and aware of any lurking sexual prejudices they may have. Or get together to read and discuss a book like Sallie Tisdale's *Talk Dirty To Me: An Intimate Philosophy of Sex*. The way Sallie weaves together personal musings and thoughtful philosophy is perfect inspiration for group discussion. (A Reader's Group Guide is even available from her publisher.) Another great, and more recent, conversation-starter is *America Unzipped: In Search of Sex & Satisfaction*, published in 2008 by msnbc.com's sex columnist Brian Alexander. I've heard from book groups and salons reading my books *Real Live Nude Girl* and *PoMoSexuals*; in fact, any book mentioned in this one might be a good way to get conversation and connections flowing. If you want to recommend others, you can do it at the Resources website.

Finally, you can look for an appreciative voyeur anywhere you are by becoming a little more exhibitionistic in your public presentation and keeping an eye out for the people who respond favorably to you. Your neckline can plunge a bit, your skirt can creep up slightly, you can start wearing tighter pants, more noticeable fabrics, more makeup. When you meet someone you can hold their gaze a little longer than you used to. Talk a little more openly about sexuality or use more erotic language. Don't just flirt – show off.

You may not feel comfortable doing this everywhere, and in some places, such as work, it may even get you into hot water. There may be plenty of places in your life now where you could easily and safely incorporate your newly outgoing self, though, so look for them. And watch for who looks back.

Whether you already have an adventuresome friend or partner, have found one using my suggestions, or want to look elsewhere, your next step may be to find a venue where exhibitionistic play is appropriate and appreciated. Next we'll go where the exhibitionism is.

Go Where the Exhibitionism Is

What if you've found no groundswell of interest in sex in your hometown? Well, you could move; legions of people have left home specifically to pursue sexual happiness. But let's not start out so drastically. You can also go on vacation.

This may be the most time-honored strategy of all. Something about a holiday frees us from the day-to-day constraints of our everyday lives. Free time, relaxation, new sights, strangers, the absence of people we fear will judge us – all these factors combine to make vacation time one of the richest veins of sexual freedom and exploration we can mine. Add to this the fact that we can choose our destination, if we wish, with sex in mind, and that even the shyest of us sometimes finds that it's easier to talk to strangers than to our friends, family, and co-workers, and holiday becomes potential heaven.

BE PREPARED FOR PLEASURE

Consider what sorts of adventures you'd like to have. Will you be with an exhibitionistic or voyeuristic partner, or alone? Do you want to meet others, or just have an opportunity to be exhibitionistic somewhere far from home? Do you want to shop for sexy clothes and then find someplace to wear them? Are there alternative sexualities you'd like to explore?

There are certain places, including most big, cosmopolitan cities, where virtually every sexual interest can be explored, if you know where to go. No matter what your interest and destination, it will help immeasurably to do your homework before you pack your bags. Comb the Internet (and check our Resources website) for a list of travel guides that may be useful for the sex tourist. Whether you hope to meet someone when you get there or are traveling with your lover, you'll probably want to know about "sexreational" options ahead of time so you can plan. A well-prepared traveler usually has more fun, but when opportunity knocks, by all means answer the door!

In cities around the world, sexy locales often lack something – sometimes a great deal – in the way of safety. Stay aware of your surroundings and the people around you; consider your own security and that of your belongings. Keep your wits about you, and don't leave your drink unattended or allow a stranger to bring you one unless you can see its trip all the way from the bartender to you. Of course, some tourists don't need to wait for someone to drug them; please don't be one of them. If you indulge in drink or drugs, know your limits and stay well within them; there are professionals in sex tourist districts who specialize in identifying easy marks, and no mark is easier than somebody who's high as a kite. (Besides, do you really want to visit some erotic paradise and lose both exotic memories and brain cells because you over-indulged? Hangovers are no more fun when traveling than they are at home.)

You may want to befriend or engage a local who can show you around. If you find a guide you can trust, you will probably feel safer – and you may discover a more intimate side of your destination. This is especially true if you visit a country whose language you don't know; a bilingual local can help translate for you. But most seasoned travelers advise you do yourself and the locals a favor – learn at least a little of the language. I can't recommend a dictionary of sex terms that will cover every language, but there's at least one that covers Spanish, Italian, French, German, and Russian. If you're headed elsewhere, your best bet may be to quiz the locals.

Of course, it may be your plan to *play* with the locals. In many places this won't be hard to arrange; the next best thing to leaving home and having an affair is staying home and having a fling with someone who's just passing through. To the locals, you'll be a mysterious stranger. It's kind of inspiring, isn't it, to think that someone else might find *you* exotic? Meet locals by doing your homework – where do those who are interested in sex hang out? Of course, people who work in tourist trades often have flings with the people who are passing through, and you may need to search no farther than your hotel coffee shop to find a new playmate.

Nonetheless, a basic knowledge of the language will improve your chances of finding friendly locals. Much of the rest of the multi-lingual world scorns American travelers who don't even bother to learn how to say "please" and "thank you" in the tongue of the country they're visiting. Your access to the city behind the tourist guides may be dependent on this. You may have met your local friends before your arrival; look online for ads from like-minded people in other countries, and correspond with them before you meet.

To find the sexy places patronized by the locals, check online and any relevant sex guidebooks before you leave home and any local sex-related or alternative newspapers when you get there. Ask cab drivers and your hotel's concierge. Ask at sex-related shops.

Some sex places will be mostly geared towards tourists, like some of the "tropical paradise"-style resorts which cater to swingers, or the sex shows and shops in Amsterdam's Red Light District. These may not give you useful leads to the locals. However, don't underestimate them as locales for erotic vacation hijinks. It's true that most of the people you meet there will be on vacation too – but they, like you, seek adventure and playmates, and you might have more fun with the girl or boy next door if you run into them in Bangkok or Amsterdam than you'd ever have had back home. If you're up for a tourist-style sex vacation, you can find venues for very enjoyable ones.

Heterosexual partners may enjoy the ready-made sex holiday packages offered at couples-only places like Jamaica's Hedonism II and III. For one flat price, you can be transported to a lovely resort whose raison d'être, facilitating erotic pleasure, may have no parallel back home. Best of all, no one will object if you make love with the shades wide open or even down on the beach. For exhibitionistic couples, it probably doesn't get any closer to paradise than this – unless your doctor's told you to stay out of the sun!

Monogamy or Non? On Vacation (and at Home)

If you go on an erotic vacation with a partner, decide together ahead of time whether you will be sexual only with each other or whether you want to involve another person (or several) in your fun. For some couples, part of the excitement of exhibitionism includes finding scenarios in which one partner can play with someone else while the other partner watches, or exploring the many possibilities of group sex. If this idea is erotic for both of you, you can find suggestions for places to explore these fantasies at our Resources website, and you can probably locate plenty of people interested in joining you online. Some couples find themselves much more open to this kind of play while on vacation, knowing that their third party won't accompany them home to possibly complicate their domestic routine.

If, on the other hand, one partner wants to experience swinging, group sex, or threesomes but the other partner does not, pushing to do so anyway can badly mar the vacation as well as the relationship. If this is your situation, some of the suggestions in Chapter 13 may help, but many couples will need to learn to live with their differing desires and limits.

If one partner is willing but less than eager, start by giving him or her the power to set the limits of the play. To paraphrase a statement I once heard in a "Swinging 101" workshop, "The more enthusiastic member of a couple will get the couple into swinging (or other couple-based, non-monogamous play), but the less enthusiastic partner will keep them there." Basically, this means that if the less enthusiastic partner has fun and doesn't feel pushed, s/he's more likely to want to continue exploring this kind of play.

The swing community has noticed another prevalent dynamic in couples where one partner, more often than not the man, has more enthusiasm than the other. He has had terrific fantasies about freewheeling sex and plenty of it, and he finally convinces his initially reluctant partner to give swinging a try. When they get to the party, she has a great time and is in high demand, while he thinks the party's a dud – no one wants to fuck him! Before you pack up your sexy outfit and fistful of condoms, take some time to consider and negotiate how you will deal with the chagrin (and possibly anger) of the less popular partner if such a dismaying event happens to you.

Any couple considering threesomes or swinging will have to contend with its ramifications on their relationship, as well as the ways the actual experience does or doesn't match their fantasies. The experience may bring up jealousy and insecurity; it may unearth hidden power dynamics; it may be a total flop. It may also give a tremendous boost to the couple's sex life and ability to communicate together clearly about potentially difficult situations. The partners' trust levels and communication patterns will likely tip the balance.

Ditto for any foray into non-monogamy, whether you play together or separately. Deborah Anapol, proponent of "responsible non-monogamy," offers a very useful discussion of these issues in her book *Polyamory: The New Love Without Limits*. Anapol suggests that people have "relationship orientations" just as they have sexual orientations; some lean more naturally towards monogamy, others towards non-monogamy. "The mixed relationships," she says, "are the ones that get into trouble."

A most useful insight! As a bisexual, though, I know that people do not always fall at either end of the sexual orientation spectrum – far from it. So I would amend this observation; I think there exists a middle ground when it comes to monogamy vs. non-monogamy, too. Some of us will prefer one or the other lifestyle depending on our partner or any of many factors. I feel much more comfortable with non-monogamy when I can trust and communicate well with my primary partner; if there are impediments to communication or trust, it's too difficult to manage, and then I prefer monogamy. (Of course, if I can't trust my partner, there's no telling whether both of us really are monogamous!)

If both you and your partner enthusiastically espouse non-monogamy, there will be less to negotiate, but don't make the mistake of ignoring these issues altogether. A one-on-one relationship takes work – often delightful work, to be sure – and it stands to reason that the even transitory presence of anyone else in the intimate picture will take work too.

Today many organizations offer support and resources for people interested in exploring committed partnering in conjunction with a non-monogamous, often called polyamorous, lifestyle. "Polyamory," derived from "loving many," has come to be the term most used for what used to be called "open relationships," and many commentators use it without breaking down how it does or doesn't differ from other terms and definitions. If you and a partner want to open your relationship, or if you are looking for a partner who will be comfortable with this relationship configuration, you'll do well to carefully consider what you do and don't want and expect out of such a situation. Read up, talk to others, join a polyamory discussion group, and don't fail to read the best book on the subject: *The Ethical Slut* by Dossie Easton and Janet W. Hardy.

OPTIONS FOR GROUP PLAY

Locally or far from home, even the most monogamous couple can indulge in exhibitionism beyond their wildest dreams if they visit a sex club or a swing party. Some events, like San Francisco's mixed-orientation Masturbate-A-Thons and many S/M and fetish parties, also admit singles.

"Exhibitionism doesn't trigger my shyness if I do an explicit scene at a sex party," says GPenn about his adventures with his girlfriend Heather. "Being exhibitionistic is a way of sidestepping my shyness. It's much easier for me to show off with my girlfriend for an appreciative audience than to engage a stranger in conversation. I'm not directly interacting with the strangers, which is much less scary than talking to someone at the food table."

"For Heather, it's partly about creating permission for others to be wild and authentic and outrageous" when they attend parties together and engage in show-offy scenes. "It was a big jump for her to realize that she could do that, and she likes to do things in ways that give others permission to expand boundaries, to break down the restrictions they put on themselves regarding what's OK."

GPenn and Heather also love the feeling of being seen or witnessed when feeling really powerful or authentic sexually; it concentrates the experience for them in a way that powerfully emphasizes their sexual chemistry. "Being intense sexually, in a place where that would be appreciated, like at a sex or swing party as opposed to something really in public," is their preferred type of exhibitionism. "Not being into shocking or offending people, but finding a place where they will be envious or appreciative."

Gay and bisexual men have traditionally had more options than others for this sort of sex; even though the AIDS epidemic has resulted in the closure of public sex spaces like bathhouses in many cities, many remain open, often with a strong safe sex emphasis. I hope I don't need to remind you: no matter what your orientation, if you visit a place that has no safe sex regulations, go equipped with condoms and lube, and use them religiously. Then have a hot, safe time.

Exhibitionism, of course, can greatly enliven safe sex - in fact, it is safe sex. Some gay men's clubs capitalize on this - many cities around the globe, for instance, feature jack-off clubs for men, where much of the sex is visual. Male-on-male sexual culture has long included a strong component of voyeurism and exhibitionism; when straight women mourn (incorrectly, if you ask me, though I do know what they're getting at) that "the good-looking ones are all gay!" they acknowledge this culture of visual eroticism and the effects it tends to have on men who know they'll be looked at. In some neighborhoods in San Francisco, like the hilly area above Castro Street, men appear nightly at their picture windows to give jack-off shows to appreciative neighbors; I'm sure other cities with heavily gay neighborhoods also see this kind of action. Shar has a friend who engages in "kitchen-window exhibitionism": "He has a whole relationship, practically, with his neighbor. He polishes the silver naked and waits for the neighbor to come the window. Then they jack off."

Every city and many towns have parks and other public areas staked out by men who cruise there for sex partners, and this scene, too, tends to be highly exhibitionistic. To locate and explore these male-male sex environments, check out the Internet or any of the guidebooks published for gay men.

Lesbians have fewer public sex institutions by far. In a few locales women have taken the cue from their gay brothers and developed public sex clubs, though they're more likely to happen monthly than nightly. Perhaps in the future there will be more such places for adventurous women to visit. In the meantime, the lesbian S/M community hosts public and semi-public play parties, and lesbian and gay dance clubs provide exhibitionistic lesbians, bisexuals, and gay men a popular venue for scantily-clad dirty dancing. Some even feature go-go boys and girls - is this your dream job?

Gay/Lesbian/Bisexual/Transgender Pride celebrations, especially the ones held in big cities, also seem to bring the exhibitionists out of the woodwork. Folks who would never flash skin at work suddenly let it all show, and in the carnival-like atmosphere both skin and outrageous costumes stretch as far as the eye can see. Even at the 1993 March on Washington, a huge gathering with the serious political mission of drawing attention to sexual orientation issues, many excited marchers arrived with a show-offy, playful streak. In general, the larger the Queer Pride event, the greater the comfort level for exhibitionists, so if you live in a small city you may need to travel to a bigger one to take optimal advantage of sexual orientation-related show-offery.

I know plenty of heterosexuals who mourn the lack of such a celebration for everyone; in fact, the Gay Pride parades dating back to the early 1970s probably owe as much to the Sexual Freedom League's late-60s liberation marches as to the Stonewall Riots. Perhaps someday we will have all-inclusive marches again in which everyone can celebrate sexuality together. In the meantime, supportive heterosexuals who want to join the fun can look for a Straights for Gays or Family and Friends of Lesbians and Gays contingent in their local LGBT Pride celebration. And there's always Mardi Gras and, more recently, the Love Parade.

Sex clubs can come in any erotic flavor – they are either public spaces like San Francisco's safe sex club Eros, which caters to men (including transmen) and advertises openly in various gay publications, private groups which rely on a mailing list of interested persons and a rented hall, or semi-public venues which are accessible if you know where to look. Today, a few public sex environments exist which aim quite intentionally at opening their doors to everyone, regardless of sexual orientation. Radically inclusive clubs like these may grow more common as cultural biases against different sexualities break down; for now, they are relatively rare outposts where diverse people can share sexual space without worrying about homophobia, biphobia, or "heterophobia." I find them highly exciting – I don't think much of the practice of separating people on the basis of category, sexual or otherwise, and mixed parties definitely bring people together. They're a great, accepting environment for people who want to try new things or who simply cherish the reminder that we have a lot in common despite our differences.

They also have some difficulties. They can be upsetting to, and disrupted by, people who don't really feel comfortable with sexualities other than their own. Mixed parties also tend to accept single attendees, while most heterosexual clubs restrict attendance to couples. Mixed-orientation parties can't very well require men to attend accompanied by a woman. What about men who are there to play with other men? Event organizers don't want to set up a heterosexual bias, or any other kind.

Some parties have thus fallen prey to the problem the swingers made the "couples-only" rule to avoid: gatherings top-heavy with unattached heterosexual men. This is understandable; unpaired straight men are often the most eager potential consumers of this kind of sexual entertainment. Gay and bisexual men have their own sex venues. Coupled heterosexual men can go to swing parties with their partners. Women in general receive many more sexual invitations (a lot of them unwanted) than men do, and traditional female sexual socialization doesn't exactly lead women right to the sex club door. A very high male-to-female ratio is great if the women attending the party want lots of sexual attention, but it can frighten novice women – and frustrate the men.

No matter what kind of party you choose to attend, ask yourself some questions before you even get to the door. What do you want out of a sex party experience? What fears, attitudes, and behaviors might stand in your way? What can you do to affect the situation? Especially for people who want to find a place to practice exhibitionism, it helps to know and accept that other party guests may have different sexual agendas. If you want a hot, appropriate place to show off, parties may be just your ticket, but other people might assume you're there to fuck even if you're not. Be ready to turn down invitations, in a friendly way – if you make your intentions clear, most people you meet in this environment will gladly give you space to be the fabulous exhibitionist you know you can be. They'll appreciate you for it, too!

SWINGING

Heterosexual couples, as I've already mentioned, can always find a place to show off together at swingers' gatherings. Some parties will also welcome unattached women, although these women should expect to receive sexual invitations from other attendees. It's best to call ahead to find out whether you can come without a partner; don't just assume it's okay. Many parties, in fact, require that everyone call ahead. Often they require both members of a couple to call together, so the proprietor knows it's actually a couple and to get a sense that both members of the couple want to attend; they're trying to screen out the duos who arrive and leave one partner fuming on the couch all evening while the other one disappears into the playroom to get laid.

To learn more about swinging and to find out where the nearest swing club operates, contact NASCA (North American Swing Club Association), the national organization of these clubs. (You may also find unaffiliated clubs in your regional sex papers and, of course, online.) Their national conference, Lifestyles, is held annually – many couples schedule their vacations to coincide with this or one of many regional gatherings. These feature lectures and workshops, a large vendors' area where conferees can purchase everything from exotic lingerie to bondage gear, a line-up of parties, and a big Erotic Ball – a dance where exotic dress and dirty dancing rule. The Ball functions much like an off-premises swing party, and people often make play dates after meeting there. The Lifestyles conference presents a perfect opportunity to get your feet wet if you've considered making contact with the swing community, or even if you simply want to spend a long weekend with a bunch of friendly, sex-positive folks who appreciate exhibitionism.

You may not find a swing party house in your town, but you certainly will in your region. Swingers' clubs operate in all parts of the country. Some are "on-premises" – that means the play happens at the site where the party is held. Swing parties usually feature a buffet, a dance floor, and sometimes a hot tub as well as rooms where people can have sex in pairs or in a large group. In "off-premises" swinging, you and your partner meet another couple, or several, and adjourn to someone's home or to a hotel. Some clubs hold off-premises events at hotels just so the new friends won't have far to go to play.

There are also a few hotels and motels which serve as on-premises swingers' gathering places. Actually, not all of these places should be called swingers' clubs, since some are open to anyone. They can fall prey to the "many men, few women" problem discussed above, but they have a special charm for exhibitionists.

Consider the late and much-missed Edgewater West, a motel in Oakland, California, which served as such a venue through the 1980s and into the mid-1990s before closing. As at any other motel, you could rent a room for the night. Its glass patio door faced onto an enclosed courtyard. Any sort of play was fair game inside the room, and if you left the glass door open, people approach and in some cases asked to join you. When the glass door stayed shut, however, it signaled onlookers to watch but not invite themselves in – ideal for exhibitionists who sought an audience which didn't clamor for a piece of the action. It was a great venue for exhibitionistic couples and for singles wanting to feel peeping eyes on them while they masturbated or otherwise put on special shows. If you come upon other places like it, cherish them – and drop me a line!

There may be no swing house or adult motel in your town. Perhaps you'd prefer a different kind of sex club that doesn't exist where you are. You can throw your own party, if you have a place in which to do it. You'll need safe sex supplies (and guidelines covering when you expect them to be used), refreshments, washable coverings for the furniture, and some guests. If you don't have a bunch of wild and crazy friends, go back to the last chapter and review the suggestions for finding like-minded people – alternatively, you can ask just a couple of friends to ask friends to ask friends.

If you're going to try this, I recommend you make at least one visit to a sex club to get an idea about what to expect. Decide how you want your party to progress. Do you want to structure ice-breaker games? How will you decorate? How many guests do you want? Will you focus on creating exhibitionistic environments, spaces where a couple of people can have sex while others watch? Think about your goals for the party and then consider how to facilitate them.

Having a party involves work for the host. Get some help. If you have a co-host, you can trade off as the responsible ones in a room full of people having fun. Otherwise your chances for play and exhibitionism will be few – you may be forced to watch others on the fly, as you run for the toilet plunger or dash out for more paper cups and ice.

ALL DRESSED UP WITH SOMEPLACE TO GO

The Lifestyles Ball is not the only event of its kind. San Francisco holds the Exotic-Erotic Ball twice a year, near Hallowe'en and on New Year's Eve. Many urban areas now hold annual (or more frequent) events which bring out the fetish communities and others who love to "dress for pleasure." The most venerable such events are in London: both Night of the Senses (formerly known as the Sex Maniac's Ball) and The Rubber Ball feature various outrageous acts and give guests the opportunity to wear the most fantastic erotic costume they can devise. And don't forget Carnival – you can travel to the one in Rio de Janeiro, or visit its biggest rival in the United States, Mardi Gras.

These sorts of events are tailor-made for exhibitionists who yearn for a place to strut their stuff. You won't be the only exotically-dressed one in the crowd; if you can exhibit yourself publicly anywhere, you can do it here, with scores (even hundreds) of fellow show-offs having a grand time. If you're looking to meet an exhibitionist, you won't find more of them in one place – though the atmosphere can be a little too wild for quiet "getting to know you"-type chat!

An alternative to traveling to a Ball may lie closer to home: Hallowe'en. When else do we have carte blanche in the dressing-up department? On this night your inner exhibitionist will have a lot of company.

Hallowe'en is also among the best times to introduce an other-gendered persona to the world – or just to cross-dress for fun. If you yearn to cross-dress, you'll never find a more acceptable time – though you can certainly find year-round venues where you'll fit right in, if you're willing to travel to reach them. There are cross-dressing support organizations, including one that sponsors an annual get-together in Provincetown, Fantasia Fair, that attracts people from all over the country. Or contact Veronica Vera's School for Boys Who Want to Be Girls in New York City.

Some male cross-dressers, called fetish dressers, do not dress to pass as women – they simply wear lingerie or other "female" garb for sexual arousal. As my friend Steve says, "They're not *women's* clothes – they're *mine!*" Many of these men never leave the house while cross-dressed, but I have heard a distressing story or two about fetish-dressing men's attempts to get support at gatherings of "ordinary" cross-dressers, who sometimes make the fetish dresser feel unwelcome. If your cross-dressing fits the fetish dresser pattern, you may have more luck in the S/M and fetish communities, playing with a supportive partner, or even at an erotic ball.

Female cross-dressers have fewer organized options for getting together with others, though some lesbian communities and gender communities make a place for them. One very sex-positive option for women of any orientation is a workshop called "Drag King for a Night," in which all the participants dress as men and then go out on the town together. Naturally, this is another kind of play that you can do with an enthusiastic partner or friend. Drag kinging has become increasingly popular over the past decade and I have run into clubs featuring these performances, and artists teaching cross-dressing and "king" skills for women, all over the United States.

You don't need a special event or a support group to explore very subtle forms of cross-dressing that others aren't likely to find out of the ordinary – men can wear "feminine" fabrics, blousier shirts, lace under their suits or workshirts; women can wear tailored clothes, men's clothes, and fabrics that are seen as masculine. In some cases this may feel erotically, exhibitionistically charged; in other cases it may feel natural and even necessary to allow one's own sense of gender some expression.

Nude beaches and clothes-free resorts (sometimes described by the term "naturist") may prove ideal locations for quiet exhibitionism – these places are great for savoring the feeling of going naked and enjoying the company, but most naturist groups frown on sexual activity. If you can't distinguish nudity from overt sex, perhaps you'd better steer clear of these. Of course everyone, regardless of gender or orientation, can enjoy naturist pleasures, though some places cater to one or another sexual orientation.

PROFESSIONAL VOYEURISM AND EXHIBITIONISM

No discussion of how to find partners and contexts for exhibitionism would be complete without mentioning the sex industry.

First, of course, you can simply pay someone to be your partner in whatever exhibitionistic games you'd like to play. If you want to have sex with the person, hire a prostitute – also known as an escort, a call girl (or boy), or sometimes (especially among males) a model. If you don't want to get physically involved with the person, but would like to have an exhibitionistic companion for some event, you can also look for an erotic model or exotic dancer who sees individual clients. In all cases, when you contact a sex professional, don't assume paying a fee means they'll do anything you want, either sex-wise or exhibitionism-wise – especially in public. In particular, negotiate public scenes in advance. Even if you're not too concerned about being caught, your sex pro probably is – and remember, too, that hiring a person to have sex with you is illegal in most locales in the U.S., so proceed accordingly and cautiously.

If you haven't engaged the services of a sex professional before, you may wonder how to go about it. If the word "prostitute" conjures up for you images of too-thin women hanging around on street corners in bad parts of town, let me hasten to amend that incomplete picture. Many – in fact, probably most – prostitutes work in fairly middle-class surroundings. Some work in brothels (Nevada has the most openly accessible of these, and the country's only legal ones), some in massage parlors. (Not all massage parlors offer sexual services, so politely enquire and negotiate.) Many work for escort services, which often advertise in the phone book. Many more work independently and advertise their services in sex papers and even the classified ads in "straight" newspapers – and, of course, online. You can often tell whether a professional or a frisky amateur wrote the ad by noting the pro's use of code words which subtly connote money or finances, like "generosity," "champagne taste," "exclusivity." Sometimes you will find pros' ads in a separate section. These days many, if not most, sex professionals have found their way to the Internet, and special sites exist to help you find them; plus many well-established pros have their own sites.

Your professional will probably not discuss sex acts with you on the phone or via email – in this profession, discretion is very important – but if you have particular exhibitionistic scenarios you'd like to explore, she or he might talk about the not-specifically-sexual elements of these. S/he will reserve the right to say no to you, and you have the same right – if something about your telephone interaction with him or her tells you that you won't get along, follow your intuition. If you're going to pay for a partner to join you in an erotic scenario, you want to find someone you can enjoy. Not every professional will be ready to depart from the suck-and-fuck routine they get the majority of their calls for, and neither will every one be your type.

To get the most out of your time with a sex professional, treat him or her with the same respect you'd offer any other sex partner. Communicate clearly about your desires. You may find this process is easier with a pro than it's ever been with other partners – s/he does it for a living, and besides that, doesn't take personally what you say. If s/he doesn't want to do something you'd like, don't push it. Your professional partner may be willing to negotiate with you about a variety of things, including the amount of time the two of you will spend together, the fee, and what you'll do, but don't argue with him or her. It's also very rude to get grouchy about the fee. Paying for sex provides you an opportunity to have fun with a partner with clear boundaries and, probably, some expertise – if you can't feel comfortable about mixing sex with a professional transaction, don't do it.

It might be worth noting in so many words that many of these suggestions – staying polite, not pushing it – are also basics for the way you'll successfully negotiate with a stranger you've just met on Craigslist or in an online forum. Whether or not you're paying to play, you catch way more flies with honey than with vinegar.

You can patronize the sex industry in several other ways besides going one-on-one with a prostitute. If you love erotic talk, try one of the scores of phone sex lines that are set up to cater to practically any fantasy you can devise. You'll find their numbers in sex papers as well as national sex magazines both straight and gay, and also online. Not all phone sex workers are created equal – shop around until you find someone whose vocabulary and fantasy-spinning ability match your desires.

Combine hot talk with voyeurism and exhibitionism at the peep show, the places that advertise "Talk to a real live nude girl!" Here, in private, one-on-one booths, you can talk dirty, show off while you masturbate, watch her masturbate – or even, in some peep shows, watch two women have sex together. The latter sort of show is available at some strip clubs, too, depending on the locale, but these are more geared to voyeurs. If you want to show off too, you might appreciate a little privacy so your professional voyeur can concentrate on you. She may well appreciate the change of pace – you're showing off for her! There are also clubs that feature peep show booths (or stage shows) which cater to men who want to watch other men. The jack-off show is the staple of such businesses.

Not all peep show workers will give you what you want for your dollar. Some have a great time at work while others just collect the rent money. Look for someone who responds to you in a genuine, friendly way, and who really seems pleased that you want to put on a show for her or him, or is enthusiastic about fantasy talk. When I worked at the peep show I loved getting visits from exhibitionists and people with interesting fantasies – I had some incredibly hot sexual experiences with strangers. So I know that for some people, this form of sex-for-pay can create genuine heat – on both sides of the glass.

Most of the sex workers I know get a real kick out of being visited by couples. Many prostitutes, peep show workers, and exotic dancers are bisexual and can easily connect erotically with both women and men. When I worked in the peeps I was once visited by a young midwestern couple on their honeymoon – isn't that sweet? They'd come all the way to San Francisco to have adventures, and have them they did. They had their entire honeymoon with me in about nine minutes – they sucked, they fucked, they had brought a dildo along – it was marvelous! And it only cost them fifteen bucks. These two looked ordinary as Midwestern apple pie, but I'm sure they're hell on wheels wherever they live. I only wish I knew how they'd met – I'd recommend it to you.

WHEN WOMEN PAY FOR PLAY

I want to have a special word with women on the topic of patronizing sex professionals. I had a few visits from individual women when I worked in the peep show, but not many, and I know of a few women who've paid for sex – though almost all of them had once been sex workers themselves. I guess to them the idea was not as unthinkably foreign as it would be to many women.

It's true that as women we are not brought up to think that we can pay for sex. In fact, many of us are not taught to think that we can ask for what we want sexually at all. But why not? To take our sexual power we have to think in terms of what makes us happy, and we have to ask for it. How else can we create a world where we can expect erotic satisfaction? There exists a large industry which provides men with sexual entertainment; where is ours? True, many of us are not well-to-do enough to think about spending money on sexual entertainment, at least not as a regular option – nor are many men. But most of us either find nothing that interests us in the realm of the sexually commodified, or we shy away from it for other reasons.

I strongly encourage all women to at least consider what, if anything, they'd be willing to pay for – if they had the money, if they knew it would be a safe situation, if all their other concerns were addressed. Would you want no-strings-attached sensual and sexual attention? A non-judgmental partner with whom to try sexual behaviors you haven't tried before? Hot-as-fire phone sex peppered with words no one else will say? Dancing girls or boys to amuse and arouse you? A sexual expert who can take you to new heights? A "girlfriend (or boyfriend) experience" with someone whose intimacy skills are so well-honed that being together feels like unconditional love? Or a nasty, clandestine quickie?

These are the desires that motivate male customers to seek out gratification and entertainment from sex professionals. Some people claim that women's sexual desires differ greatly from men's, but I'm not so sure that's true, at least in this respect. Face it – most of us haven't had a chance to sample these sorts of amusements. How do we know whether we like things that have been largely inaccessible?

You may decide from your consideration of these issues that you'd like to try paying for some sort of sexual entertainment. If you do, you'll still be a rarity – a female patron in a field that overwhelmingly serves males. If you'd like to visit a strip club, a peep show, or some similar public venue, call ahead. Tell the management you'd like to visit, and ask whether they have security on the premises so you can feel comfortable. You can also invite a few women friends to go along – or even a group of both women and men. Juliet gives guided tours of sex shows for women only; because she's a former porn star, she's comfortable in strip clubs, and she wants to extend that comfort to other women who are curious about the business. If you visit San Francisco, you can engage the services of her business, Innovative Productions.

When you get to your destination, let the women working there know that you want to play. In a peep show, you and the peep show worker will be able to see each other. You'll have enough privacy to masturbate or do any sort of solo sex play you can devise. There's just enough room in these booths to bring along a lover, if you want. Strip clubs will feature a stage show. Bring some money for tips. Not only will you be taken much more seriously as a customer if you tip, and the women will feel more comfortable with you, remember that in many such clubs, tips comprise the strippers' only income. Many strip clubs also offer table dances or lap dances – when you call ahead, ask what the club offers and get some idea about standard tipping rates for these shows. In a table dance you watch the dancer up close – she comes to your table and either stations herself next to it or, sometimes, climbs on top of it. Lap dancing involves the dancer sitting on your lap or straddling you as you sit in your chair – she may wiggle and gyrate, chat with you, and sometimes you can touch her. Ask her to tell you what's allowed and appropriate in the theatre you're visiting. In most places you'll be approached with the question "Would you like some company?" if the dancer is interested in lap dancing or table dancing for you. Expect to tip for this.

Remember that many women who do this kind of work have to put up with the judgment and opprobrium of others, especially other women. If you can't be friendly and supportive, better stay out of the clubs.

A trip to a strip club can be interesting and useful even if you're heterosexual and have no erotic interest in the dancers. There may not be a club in your area that regularly features male dancers. Keep a lookout for visits from the Chippendales and other male dance troupes that perform for women, or get some of your women friends together and hire a private dancer for a party. Some escort agencies and many "Strip-O-Gram"-type companies feature sexy guys who'll visit you at home or at the office. Erotic boutiques can often provide a referral to a male stripper or two.

Many large cities have gay men's strip clubs, and here you could see a show complete with the raunch that's been sanitized out of the "ladies only" shows like the Chippendales. However, many of these places will not exactly welcome you with open arms. Try calling the management to ask whether you can visit. Perhaps you can convince them to feature a bisexual night. Or just maybe your male persona is very convincing!

To conclude this array of suggestions for singles and couples: use your imagination. Venues and partners for exhibitionistic exploration will seldom appear out of thin air – but when you start looking around with an eye to who might be interested and where it might be fun and appropriate to play, don't be surprised if your world fills with possibilities. And if not? Plan a vacation!

One more thing. You may truly have no access to most of the fun and games we've discussed here. Perhaps you haven't enough money to travel or visit professionals, or your partner won't consent to your solo explorations and doesn't want to join you... whatever. There may be factors unique to your situation that you can change, but if not, remember that you can play anywhere, in any way, with anyone, in your fantasies. No matter what situation prevents you from making these reality, in the powerful arena of your own mind you can always be the wildest exhibitionist in the whole world.

Travel books aren't written only for those who travel, you know. Maybe you're an armchair tourist in the sexual realm, but make the most of it. Let those dreams of making love at dawn in the piazza bring you all the pleasure they can. Let your imagination run wild. Who knows – maybe you'll win the lottery!

☾ **11** ☀

Techno-Exhibitionism:
Showing Off By Bits and Bytes

I have to admit it to you – I'm a little traumatized that the era of the Polaroid is over. There it is, one of my earliest entrees to exhibitionism, going the way of the dodo – its functions completely overtaken by digital cameras. I was actually a late convert to Polaroid exhibitionism – the earliest naked pictures anyone ever took of me were on standard film and needed to be developed. Later I realized how great Polaroids were for erotic show-offery: no need to wait for the image (beyond those enticing few seconds while the film developed before your eyes), no need to worry if the people where you dropped the film off would recognize you without your clothes. Now, digital has us covered as we bare all, and has the advantage of being instantly uploadable, so we can not only thrill right away to our spicy photo, everyone else can, too.

So just as the Polaroid proved to be an ideal format for certain types of sex photography, improving on the film camera, which itself went through generations of improvement from its earliest incarnation to the format we see today, which in turn superseded the need for an erotic image to be painted or drawn – the technology of sex and exhibitionism marches on. We can only imagine what new machines and methods tomorrow will bring.

Today there is little doubt that the computer, dealing in digital images of every kind, perches at the top of the technological heap. You can certainly be an exhibitionist without one, just as you can show off very privately and never before a crowd. But increasingly, the ease of digital image-making and online sharing – publication, really – means that show-offy people naturally turn electronic when they want to reach out and touch someone with their exhibitionism.

"In my opinion, the Internet is the single most dramatic change in the world of exhibitionism," says *America Unzipped* author Brian Alexander – and I couldn't agree more. "Talk about permission-giving! The ability to sit at home, produce images – still or moving – of oneself, and then send them speeding through the digital world to millions and millions of others has freed many people who would otherwise never carry out their exhibitionist fantasies. Voyeurweb, Real Voyeur, Watchers Web, YouPorn (and these are just a few sites in English) attract millions of visitors and thousands of contributors. On YouPorn, people from all over the world upload their own mini porn movies. Red Clouds is another site that's all about user participation. The goal for many is to receive the written sexual fantasies of the viewers in return. 'Tell me what you want to do to me!' many posters request.

"This is truly the democratization of erotica. Everyone can literally be their own porn star."

"Who knew there were so many exhibitionists in the world until MySpace came along?" says pro blogger, podcaster, author, and reporter Violet Blue. "And Facebook, and all the other social networking sites where users can set up free profiles. While not meant for sexual use, even just having to pick a gender suddenly has people using these new tools to define themselves (especially sexually) in ways we've never seen before in history. And they're having a lot of fun with it. People are using sites like MySpace and Flickr for exhibitionism, and often discovering what they consider their 'true' sexual selves in doing so, even if through trial and error. Especially shy people, outsiders, etc. (and not just fetishists). Alone in the privacy of their own rooms they can try on new personas, take sexy pictures of themselves and upload them to public sites for praise – and no one need know who they really are. It's very sexually validating, and I think it's giving people tools to carry that sexual confidence and newfound sexual self-definition into real life. Online exhibitionism is not just a great way to have fun, get off and feel good about yourself, but also to flirt with a lover or take a relationship to a new level. I'm talking about sex blogging, modeling, having a racy photostream on a place like Flickr, making social profiles on community sites like Tribe.net (which expressly encourages sexual communities) or even MySpace and Facebook." And Violet should know – she has online homes established in all these places and more and is one of the most active of all Netizens (that is, citizens of the stateless space that is the Internet).

Virtual Reality

Digitally-enabled exhibitionism has, in fact, become so common, at least in techno-savvy circles, that teens have to be reminded that an image of a naked 17-year-old is legally considered kiddie porn even if they themselves shot and posted the picture, and there are countless blogs in which citizens tell all, and I mean all, the details of their sex lives and relationships. You can't pick up a paper these days (and many of us don't pick them up any more; we read them online) without hearing about another person who, thanks to the know-all and see-all magic of the Internet, has lost a job because of an indiscreet posting somewhere or who has had a private picture or movie get out that was not intended to be seen – certainly not by their dad, their boss, their spouse or their kid. From conservative Dr. Laura's naked pix to American Idol contestant Antonella Barba's Internet pin-ups all the way to Mark Foley's spicy (and indiscreet) emails to ex-Senate pages, virtual reality can become all too real when someone has something to hide.

Does this mean I don't think you should show off online? Of course not! Your cat might be the next big thing on YouTube , and you on PornoTube, and who am I to stand in your way? But I do want to make sure you've thought through the implications of virtual exhibitionism, because throughout this book I've counseled you to strike your own comfortable balance between exposure and privacy, and to continue to do so in the age of the Internet means taking a hard look at the way so many of us have come to use the Web.

Just as phone sex in the '50s or '60s might have been riskier business, privacy-wise, than it came to be in the '80s and '90s – because Mrs. Appleby up the road could always be counted upon to quietly pick up the phone and listen in on the party line – the glowing screen before you is a technological link to the world outside that you cannot completely control. Confiding your latest adventures to your blog may seem as private and personal as telling them to your old red diary with the little lock and gold key. But using the Internet as a diary is like keeping a locked book in a room full of people who can see through walls. That's why blogger and author Audacia Ray, whose *Naked On the Internet* is the most up-to-date analysis on online friskiness, warns, "Think about the person you never want to discover you – and assume it will be *when*, not if."

That's right – your dad. Your boss. Your beloved old first-grade teacher. Your rabbi. The cop on the beat. Not only the hottie from your Anthro 101 class, but the stalker from Advanced Math. You won't be able to completely control this, and you'll think at your peril, "Oh, Dad would never go online to look at naked pictures." Yes, he would – and if you look hard enough, it's perfectly possible you'll find some of him and Mom. So really, really think this through before you start your uploading frenzy (or your extra-credit Anthro 101 Walk on the Wild Side blog), or your very own College Cutie site. Pick a clever pseudonym or be prepared to talk about your extracurricular life at all future job interviews; practice your camera angles well, or expect your cousin to blab to your grandma that you have an explicit Flickr stream. In fact, Audacia warns specifically that, not only should you always use password-protected space online, you should also avoid friending your co-workers on Myspace, Facebook, or other social-networking sites; the work life-private-life boundary is too easily permeated in a social networking context unless it's one, like LinkedIn, that is specifically meant to enhance working-world connections and doesn't involve personal-life disclosure.

"Maintaining anonymity is a lot harder than people think, especially if your pictures or blog or profile become popular," says indubitably popular sex personality Violet Blue. "If people want to stay anonymous, they should look at their profile or pics from the outside and ask, would my friends know that was me?"

Not only that, people – your online stardom could translate to much more. "It's also important to emphasize that people should assume that whatever gets put online becomes part of a permanent digital archive," says

Audacia. "Even if you personally delete things you put online – whether words, images, or an entire website – it will be archived, whether by an avid fan or by Archive.org. To demonstrate, go to Archive.org and type in the URL of a dead site to the 'wayback machine' and you'll get to see the content and design of the site as it once was. If you upload 'content,' a general word that means images, audio files, video, words, or profile information, onto a website you don't own, like a social networking profile (MySpace, Facebook, etc.) or user generated content site like YouTube, make sure to read the user agreement – many of them say that by uploading your stuff you agree to an infinite licensing agreement with them. That means they can keep your content on their servers even after you've deleted it from your personal profile, and they may be able to reuse it for whatever purpose. A good example is that YouTube could make 'Best of YouTube' dvds and include your videos without paying or even telling you that they're using them." Yep, there you are on "Best of YouTube Sex Bloopers": now on sale at your local WalMart, as well as the one where your grandma shops.

Are you taking this seriously yet? I hope so, because the capacity of the Internet to change your life is very, very great. "The downside to all this showing off should be obvious," says Brian Alexander, author of *America Unzipped*. "Though the Internet can provide lots of anonymity, it is far from foolproof – as a few local politicians, wives of county sheriffs, and job seekers have learned to their dismay. And you never really know exactly what you are going to get when you launch yourself into the digital universe. Though one might think the digital realm is free of the judgments one finds in the real world, it's not. So the overweight, the-less-than-perfectly-complected, the old, can often face the same meanness they may encounter anyplace else. Such sites are also notorious places for lurking computer viruses. There is simply no sexual paradise on this planet, not even the Internet."

Harm Reduction for Netizens

Aww! Brian, what a buzzkill! There is some good news to be had, though don't let it get in the way of your thoughtful planning. Here our experts help you stay as safe as possible from the privacy-munching aspects of the Internet.

"Blogs can be restricted from search engines," says Audacia, "but remember, if you share your blog with anyone else and they link to it, your privacy planning can be overridden, because now it can be found. Livejournal and other similar blog-posting locations can be filtered so as to allow access only to the people you choose. But still, someone can cut and paste from it and post it elsewhere. Even if a picture is protected from cut-and-paste, you can still capture it with a screen shot."

Violet adds: "I think the strongest issue is maintaining privacy: I mean, everyone knows not to give their address out to strangers, but not everyone knows that when they sign up for any site they need to comb through every setting to make sure their contact information (and real name, if applicable) stays private. Many people also don't know to use 'dummy' email addresses – meaning, not their everyday or (shudder) their work email addys.

"Anyone can make a WordPress or Blogger blog, Tribe.net profile, Fotki and Flickr photo account – they'll be around for a while and are great for starting out, are free, and signup is a snap. Flickr has really incredible tools for maintaining privacy and who can and can't see your profile, and you can block people who bother or offend. You can set up a stream and only grant one person access – or 100 people, or everyone (as long as you make your photo settings appropriate, R-rated, etc). Fotki is a photo-sharing site that's less restrictive with content guidelines than Flickr; I have accounts at both. The X rated stuff goes on Fotki where they allow me to set up an age check page, and the R-rated goes on Flickr with 'moderate' or 'restricted' safe search settings, so no one sees anything they don't want to by accident (and that way people see me who want to, and I don't risk account deletion by respecting the site's terms of use)."

Violet's point reminds us of an issue that we've discussed outside the context of the online world: consent, and the question of whether others choose to see us without our knickers. It may seem, especially to the sexually frisky, that all the online world's a sexually explicit stage, but regardless of how much of the Internet is given over to X-rated material, some people really do just want to search for people who hook rugs, not ones who'll have sex on a rug for cash. In the Wild-West world of the Net there is plenty of sexualized space, so if that's what you want, use it, and don't try to establish a virtual nude beachhead where nudity and explicit play are not wanted. That's one of the things for which the Internet remains under attack by social conservatives; we have better things to do than help them make their arguments against an open online world.

Playful Bent advertises itself as "an erotic and playful adult social network." Because it's based around sexuality, it doesn't have the limitations on content some social networking sites do. "Its focus is voyeurism and exhibitionistic sharing," says Audacia. "Create a login and profile, because you can't see other content unless you contribute too. It encourages engagement, not just quiet voyeurism" – sometimes known in the virtual world as "lurking," and not viewed kindly by all Netizens. "Facebook and Myspace disallow explicit content, but there are no guidelines that would help a poster know what they shouldn't include – Facebook picked on a breast-feeding activist. MySpace deletes if there's a hint of sex – mostly images, but this can trickle down to text and links." These sites may be far more fraught than the more explicit ones because kids so often have profiles there; remember that your harmless fun might look a lot like child endangerment to a concerned parent, so use a little sensitivity in deciding how to use the forums that do not restrict access to adults.

And more about using Flickr: "It allows explicit content, with filters to ensure viewers are over 18. In addition they have a 'safe search' filter, so even if you say you are an adult, you can still limit the kind of content that will be visible to you in random image searches. Not all adults want to see adult content randomly, when they aren't specifically looking for that. You can easily turn the safe search on and off."

I may as well say right here that by the time this book makes it into your hands, some of this information may have changed – and now that it's in book form it will be petrified in a soooo-20th-century way. Needless to say, continue to explore the Net for its new as well as established sites for erotic play. In this hydra-headed medium, if one goes away, many others are likely to spring up to take its place.

AN ARMY OF EX-LOVERS CANNOT FAIL, BUT THEY SURE CAN INVADE EACH OTHERS' PRIVACY

Audacia got involved with sex on the Net as a frank and explicit blogger, throwing caution to the winds and disclosing pretty much everything –

hence her thoughtful words to the wise now. "I know about these mistakes because I just jumped in; I did not think things through," she says. "Do you really want to chronicle everything about your sex life? That's one way to be an exhibitionist, even if you don't want to be depicted in images. But if you disclose everything," say, via a blog, "your sex history is online, and now it will be researchable by others. People can think online exhibitionism is a private act - and that's crazy. The act of producing writings, pictures or other images is intimate and private, but the content is no longer that once it's online. For instance, I blogged about the best way to make me come." You can see that this approach might have pluses as well as minuses - who hasn't wanted a new lover who comes with an instruction manual? - until, you guessed it, her family tuned in. "My parents read my blog, and when I complained, my dad said, 'I *am* the public.'"

Dad was right - but Dad wasn't the only person in Audacia's life who might have wanted a vote about what she disclosed. "People write about their sex partners on blogs - it's a more intimate 'violation' when pictures are involved, if there hasn't been explicit consent given for that person's intimate information or image to be posted online. But people make excuses when it's just writing, whether or not you can recognize them or their partners." Not all of Audacia's intimates were equally sanguine when their moist laundry appeared on her blog for all to read. It used to be that only those of us who wished to publish autobiographical stories or memoirs needed to consider the question of how much we could ethically reveal about another person, especially a lover - for instance, when I told you about Natalie in Chapter One, I phoned and asked her permission and invited her to choose her own pseudonym. (She named herself after the 1920s Paris lesbian Lotharia Natalie Barney, if you're curious. It reminded me of the reasons I fell in love with her in the first place!) But when I write about a real person, I always think hard about how seeing my writing would affect them emotionally, and how acquaintances who recognized their character despite the name-change might treat them socially.

This degree of caution seems a little quaint today, given the volumes of current- and ex-lover disclosure to be found on the Internet. But the Web is a publishing format, and it isn't one with any editors, or a sensible attorney writing cautionary questions on the manuscripts. Just as you might, without meaning to, over-disclose so as to affect your future job options, comfort level at Thanksgiving dinner, and air of trustworthiness vis-à-vis the dating pool, you can do the same to anyone about whom you write. So be careful and thoughtful, even if you're not in love with them anymore. You'd want your exes to have the same degree of respect for you, and this is a very good place to exercise the Golden Rule.

Audacia, the voice of experience, puts it succinctly: "Respect people you're writing about. Partner sex is a collective experience – negotiate!"

And lest I've been too subtle, I'll put it another way: Never, never post explicit material about an identifiable person online without their explicit permission. Even (sigh) if you've got a new stash of kinky pix of Dr. Laura.

Look at Me, World! (But Don't Be Mean)

I do not mean to put you off online exhibitionism, honestly. Sex and showing off on the Internet are big thrills to so many people, I feel like a bit of a fuddy-duddy (and not just a Luddite) when I write about this. If you're new to it all, take Audacia's advice first and go look around to see what's there. "Begin as a voyeur. This gives you a good idea of what's out there, and it's fun research to do!"

Remember when, a zillion chapters ago, I suggested that nouveau exhibitionists go out and practice erotic looking? Well, you don't have to track down a friendly strip club any more (though I continue to hold a soft spot for those places, stocked with live human beings from whom you can sometimes get something the Internet hasn't yet successfully developed: a lap dance). Now if you want to find a live sex venue you will probably go online to do it, and you'll most likely be able to find online reviews of the place before you decide to go out and hail a cab. And if it's raining and you don't want to go out, or there's no strip club in your town, or you'd really rather see big lady wrestlers sitting on writhing fellas' faces – or pretty much anything else in the wide sexual world – you can find it, that's right, online.

And if you decide that it should be *your* panty-clad ass on the screen with your boyfriend flailing happily under you, if you have the technology on hand, pretty soon you'll have joined the throng, and if it's a busy night on the fem-dom panty smothering site, you'll hear from your new fans before you have a chance to go brew a cup of ginseng tea.

But now we must think back to Brian's warning about how judgmental Internet voyeurs can be. The new or shy online exhibitionist will almost certainly have to contend with this at least a few times, and maybe constantly, for even as your fan base grows, someone will show up to piss on your party: "Though one might think the digital realm is free of the judgments one finds in the real world, it's not. So the overweight, the-less-than-perfectly complected, the old, can often face the same meanness they may encounter any place else." I'll hasten to say, and I think Brian will agree here, that these regular-Joe-and-Jane exhibitionists will *not* just get criticism – they'll also feel the love. In fact, one of the most thrilling and compelling aspects of Internet exhibitionism is that the shyest, plainest person will find people who'll tell them how hot they are. But everyone's opinion is likely to be worn on the sleeve – when it gets especially harsh it's called "flaming" – and you can't let the bigmouths, egomaniacs, and wet blankets stop you from showing off.

"Another speedbump to online exhibitionism and all its many rewards is the inevitable negative comments everyone gets from jerks known as 'trolls,'" says Violet. "For everyone even remotely sexualized, there's a troll who'll pop up and say something mean or cruel, and it's just part of the online world. You don't need a thick skin, but remember that they just do it because they can, not because it's true, and no you're not fat, and the next person commenting after that guy who just called you ugly will be saying how hot you are – or the next comment might be about a funny cat video they just watched. Don't acknowledge meanies, know that they're always going to be around, and get on with the fun!"

Really it just makes me wish that all the trolls and meanies and flamers had their own site where they'd show off themselves – it'd be bound to be a big favorite, don't you think? But Violet's right: let it roll off your back. The Internet's charm and power is the way it lets people communicate with vast or far-flung numbers of people almost instantly, and that is also one of its greatest failings. Some people just weren't raised right – but that isn't your problem unless you hang your self-esteem on the comments of people whose fetish is trying to tear it down. Just like in grade school, don't let the meanies win.

The Democratization of Erotica

It's even the Republicanization of erotica, really; everybody seems to be getting into the act. Brian is right – the Net is the biggest thing ever to happen to exhibitionism, bigger even than Velcro fasteners. In the old, old days (like when I first wrote *Exhibitionism for the Shy*), many would-be exhibitionists really had to take a walk on the wild side to get to the places where showing off and erotic garb were appropriate. You couldn't find the swing club without going to the porn store to buy a swinger's magazine. You couldn't try out at a strip club (or watch the show) in most cities without going to a semi- (or *very*) seedy neighborhood. These were the natural habitats of many people, but still erected a barrier of sorts for the shy newbie, especially women who wanted to explore without a partner. Today, it's all available online. You can buy your sexy clothes via Internet sites, dance around in them at home, and develop fans in Omaha and Boise and Guam who all clamor to watch you masturbate. And aside from the "think it through" cautions I hope I've succeeded in getting you to contemplate, the main thing slowing your rush into E-exhibitionism may be lack of bandwidth, especially if you live in the heartland and wish your naked pix would upload faster.

Online exhibitionism, like old-school showing off based in erotic communities of swingers, fetishists, and sex tourists, continues to flourish where people come together virtually in Net-based communities of interest. So if something especially intrigues you erotically, you can not only find (and, if you want, generate) porn based on it, you can also find friends, affiliates, and lovers, not to mention people to visit when you want to go on vacation.

"Don," whom Brian Alexander profiles in *America Unzipped*, bypasses the social networking sites in favor of "groups" which can be found on Yahoo or Adult Friend Finder or iFriends. "He uses his web cam to have virtual sex with any interested party," says Brian, "usually women, but sometimes men. For Don, exhibiting himself on a web camera for the entertainment of others, and often for mutual masturbation scenes with one or more people who could be thousands of miles away on their own web cams, has become a significant part of his overall sex life. Since he travels, he is also able to meet some of the people with whom he 'cams' for real world encounters.

"This sort of thing has become so popular that it can sometimes seem as if the Internet is one big pickup spot," Brian continues. "It isn't, but not much looking is required to find somebody who wants to see your genitals. Craigslist, for example, has become a place to find a job, a used washing machine, or an 'intimate encounter' that often begins with the exhibitionistic exchange of photos."

It's a marketplace of goods, of ideas, and also of images, the Internet – and in each of these markets it changes the culture. Flea markets have lost ground to eBay; the "blogosphere" is now a political powerhouse, helping to elevate candidates and shape candidacies; and if you want something, *anything* sexual, you can find it on the Internet.

It may seem a bit impersonal; it's certainly a new way of learning to interact with others, in non-sexual as well as sexual contexts. But consider what Audacia has to say: "People see me as very a brave, outgoing, not-shy person. That was *so* not me several years ago – I figured this out, how to be outgoing and open, by using the Internet. I had not even figured out relationships, dating, communication skills – I didn't know how to talk to people at all, but I knew how to write. I had experiences I'd never have had if I had stuck to meeting people in person. People would hit on me in person and I wouldn't even know it! The Internet can be really helpful in terms of gaining skills and confidence. You can filter, and if people have a weird reaction to you there, it can feel less personal."

It's a brave new world on the Internet, but the beautiful irony is, it's full of the people we pass in the grocery store or ride the train to work with, people in the next town over, and people all across the world. They may all have clever, unrecognizable screen names; many have newly-fledged personas (and often not just one; if there was ever a venue to allow for Bill Henkin and Sybil Holiday's "multiple personality *order*," it's this one). But they're our neighbors, they're bustin' loose, and every day more people will join them... maybe even you.

Let's give Brian the last word here: "Still, I find something heartwarming (yes, I mean heartwarming) in the uploads of the men who title their series of pictures 'My 60-Year-Old Hot Wife!!!' And then, when you click on the thumbnail pictures, there is a sixty-year-old woman looking about like a sixty-year-old woman looks, wearing her corset or her diaphanous nightie or just sitting naked in the recliner wearing a smile and cupping her breasts in her hands telling the world she's still got it. In an ideal universe, none of us would have to declare such a thing; we'd hear it all the time – or never need to hear it in the first place – but this is not an ideal universe and who doesn't want to be told they're hot?"

Log on, stay safe, and feel the love.

When Showing Off Is Your Job

J oin me for a moment behind the scenes at the peep show, where the dressing room was filled with more-or-less ordinary-looking women making themselves up and assuming their sex-show personas, complete with wildly creative, campy stage names. The time between walking in the door in our street clothes and sashaying onto the stage in wigs, high heels, and skimpy outfits became an almost ritualistic time in which we transformed ourselves from Carol and Mary and Amy and Susan into Minx and Shiva and Vixen and Tigress.

I'd had just enough experience with exhibitionism in my private life to guess I'd enjoy doing it for a living, but not until I started work at the peeps did I really learn how much I loved to show off. I had never been so orgasmic in my life as when I spent four hours a day masturbating in front of strangers. I no longer had a single doubt that being looked at could take my sexual pleasure to new heights, or that exhibitionism was such an important part of my sexuality.

WHO LIKES SEX WORK – AND WHY?

We hear a lot of conjecture about what makes sex workers tick, but too rarely do these theories take into account what the women and men who do the work find hot or exciting. The real experts are the strippers, peep show workers, phone fantasy operators, erotic models, and porn stars who make a living talking dirty and showing off. We can get plenty of useful information from them even if we'd never consider doing these things for money.

Not all sex workers love what they do. And in a society that deprecates people for sexual difference and paints a picture of sex workers as debased and exploited, there's a lot for even the happiest sex worker not to like. That said, though, several factors make a difference in the way sex workers feel about their jobs.

First, it matters that they feel positive about sexuality – both their own and their customers'. Some see their participation in the sex industry as a positive rebellion against conservative or anti-sex social norms. Second, they usually possess the ability to see their work as work. Third, they usually have a support system of friends and other sex workers with whom they can be open, not having to hide or apologize for who they are and what they do.

Finally, it matters that on some level they get off on what they do – they are exhibitionistic. Like I did, they may enjoy it on an explicitly sexual level. They may love the theater and spectacle of creating a sexual persona – or several. Like Lily Burana, who quips that "being a stripper is kind of like figure skating at the Olympics of Sex Work," they may be proud of their skill. And some find excitement in crossing a line, being "bad girls" (or boys).

Some sex workers appreciate the connections they have with their customers – the pleasant customers, anyway. Whether they experience these associations as erotic, friendly, intimate, or playful, they know they are performing a very personal sort of entertainment and/or service, and they like doing so. Other sex workers see their customers mainly as a source of income, with whom they rarely or never share an intimate or warm moment.

WHAT DOES THIS HAVE TO DO WITH YOU?

Perhaps you've even thought about being a sex worker. Certainly it's a common fantasy. While we don't all have the physical attributes to make it in a field where youth and good looks usually command the highest rewards, all you need for phone sex are a reasonably sexy voice and a creatively dirty mind. And people who think that only the young and conventionally good-looking can make it playing for pay often don't understand the nuances of the sex biz; plenty of older, more regular looking people, as it turns out, have what it takes. If as you read you find yourself thinking, "Oh, I could do that," this chapter may help you decide whether you want to keep it in the realm of fantasy.

I absolutely do not suggest that everyone who occasionally thinks it would be fun to get a job in the sex biz do so in order to polish their exhibitionistic skills and have access to exhibitionistic thrills. On the contrary – you could very well spoil a great fantasy by turning it into work. For our purposes, I'd rather focus on the experiences and insights of professional show-offs and consider how we can integrate some of their know-how into our private lives.

I have another reason for introducing you to my sex worker friends. It's easy to believe, if we've never done sex work or talked to people who do, that strippers and porn models and other sex workers have nothing in common with us. Even if we don't subscribe to the myth that they're all downtrodden and helpless, we probably assume they have physical attributes and looks we don't have; besides, we could never measure up to whatever ineffable sexual confidence they possess.

So, do you still feel shy? Do you assume that some uncrossable gulf separates you from the world's most outrageous professional show-offs? Do you believe deep down that exhibitionists are born, not made?

Think again. Many pros look downright average – even nerdy or mousy – on their days off. You'd never be able to pick them out of a crowd. And many sex professionals started out introverted, sexually fearful or reticent, without sexy self-images. Just like you, they had to build an outgoing erotic persona from the ground up. Nina Hartley wore baggy clothes and felt guilty and embarrassed about her desire to be looked at. Candye Kane, today a blues singer who got her start in front of an erotic photographer's camera, was affected all her life by being fat. "I was a big dork. I had thick glasses. My mother bought all my clothes for me: I wore horrifying polyester pantsuits and Avon jewelry to high school."

Former stripper (and author of the memoir *Strip City)* Lily Burana grew up sensitive to peer pressure, "bookish, not considered attractive, made fun of a lot, all that classic stuff." Annie Sprinkle, who got Jesse Helms in an uproar when she showed the whole world her cervix in her show "Post Porn Modernist," says she was an "excruciatingly shy" child who once lied to get out of going to a Beatles concert. Even though she was wild about the Beatles, she feared she'd humiliate herself because she wouldn't scream right.

In fact, most of the sex professionals I interviewed for this book shared my experience of having once been shy or intensely self-conscious. So how did they manage to get in front of the camera or on the strippers' runway?

I've met a few sex workers who had always wanted to be strippers or prostitutes when they were growing up, but I doubt that fantasy runs the risk of edging out nursing, fire-fighting, inventing computer games, or running for President as a grade-school kid's ambition. Many just happened into their adult industry careers – like Candye Kane and Juliet Anderson, they saw an ad at a time when they needed money. Others decided as adults they wanted to give the business a try and sought it out. Jeanna Fine had survived a nasty breakup with a boyfriend who thought her sexual fantasies, when she finally worked up the nerve to share them, were too far out. After experiencing the denigration of her desires by someone she'd cared about, her emotional reaction as she read for her first porn part was a defiant "Oh, yeah? How do you like *this?*" Rita got similar emotional fuel from a partner's negative response to her exhibitionistic tendencies – she explored in a peep show what she'd received no support for at home.

Some pros – like me, Nina Hartley, and Rita – got into the business to explore fantasies of exhibitionism. I also went to the peep show to increase my comfort with talking dirty. Others seek an environment where they can explore erotic personas. Jamie decided to apprentice in a professional dominant/submissive house because she was exploring these forms of sexuality in her private life.

PROFESSIONAL PERSONAS

Professional exhibitionists find the business rewards them for being publicly sexual and for developing outgoing, sometimes outrageous, erotic personas. This kind of supportive context is hardly the cultural norm. "There isn't a whole lot of opportunity to be sexually brazen in this culture," notes Lily.

"For as much emphasis as is put on the individual, we certainly don't seem to be very individuated when it comes to having a sexual personality. Sex work forces you to do that. That's part of your job description, even if it's changing personalities every different set or for every new customer. It gives you an incredible opportunity to explore sexuality in depth."

Some sex workers develop a very different working persona from their off-the-job selves. Often these "new selves" are idealized, sexy, wild versions of themselves that bypass everyday shyness or reticence. Even if they started out playing a role, over time the chutzpah of the professional sexual self can rub off on them. The gap between the person and the persona shrinks, as Sybil described in Chapter 6. What started out as an improvised character turns out to have real influence on the actor.

"So much of what makes sex compelling is theater," says Lily. "Out of their clothing and makeup, most porn stars and supermodels don't have supermodel potential. A lot of it is creating a persona that makes you feel strong, that you feel is magnetic. That's worked for me. It's not something I was born with."

Jeanna Fine developed her character, whom she calls "the Diva," partly from spending time with drag queens. "When I saw how fun and fabulous and flamboyant the underground gay scene is, I thought, 'That's where I want to go with this,'" she says. "Because life is a cabaret when you're onstage. When I put on the false eyelashes and the dominatrix boots and my costume, the overdrawn lips and full drag queen makeup, I become this freak. I instantly find the character. In the dressing room I'm watching this transformation going, 'Oh, yeah. Oh, here she comes. Oh, god – *there she is!*' I couldn't possibly be as outgoing, or eccentric, or sexual, in my jeans and sweaters."

While that may be so, Jeanna Fine's sexual presence has had a substantial influence on the private life of the woman who created her. Through the character, she has had a chance to explore her fantasies and develop sexually, and she says, "I think Jeanna Fine helped me an awful lot in developing my self-confidence and becoming the person I am now."

Nina Hartley, too, recognizes this process. "It was a long-held fantasy of mine to be Nina," she says. "Ever since I was eleven or twelve I wanted to be sexually confident. I wanted to be sexually competent. Everything I've done in between then and now has been directed toward those goals of confidence and competence. In the beginning it was a mask I put on, but as I've matured, the mask fits better and better. There's less wobble, it's not so separate from me anymore." Nina, the most outspoken self-identified exhibitionist in the adult industry, emphasizes that the material for her performer self lay within the nervous girl she used to be: "Nina's not a completely different persona. It would be too stressful for me to act for ten years in a way that wasn't also in concurrence with my basic beliefs. They don't pay me enough to live a falsehood."

If you have ever seen Annie Sprinkle's show "Post Porn Modernist" or read her book of the same name, you know that Annie evolved to protect shy little Ellen Steinberg, the girl she used to be, as she grew up and began to have the sorts of adventures that most shy little girls never even dream of. Annie was aided in developing this persona by her own erotic pleasure. "As soon as sex was involved I always found I wasn't shy. Sex wasn't something I was shy about. I was shy about having dinner with people, or remembering my lines." Her movie *Deep Inside Annie Sprinkle* plays with exhibitionistic themes; you can certainly see her turn-on at showing off – and her shyness evaporate – in a masturbation scene during which she talks to the camera, and her implied voyeuristic audience, the whole time. This scene is also terrific inspiration for dirty talkers.

Annie's persona development didn't stop there, and today she has become Anya, who identifies with the spiritual the way Annie does with the carnal. She unites these two sides of herself in her performance and in her workshop "Sluts and Goddesses." She is not the only sex worker, though, who explores and identifies with the goddess archetype. Nina and Jeanna both talk about powerful goddess-like aspects of their erotic personas, and many sex workers look to ancient role models like temple dancers and sacred prostitutes to offset the disdain with which our culture looks upon their work. "You're a goddess inside," Jeanna tells rookie porn actresses. "You are. You're a diva. Look what you're doing, it's nasty, it's terrific! *Feel* that!"

Annie told me that when sex workers come to "Sluts and Goddesses" they get respect of a kind they may never have had. "The strippers are always so natural, it's such an inspiration for other women to see them," says

Annie. "They get to see their gifts and the power they have. They get to see very clearly how really special they are."

When Sex Is Work

There's an exciting up side to the sexual exploration the sex business offers its workers, and there are few places a person – especially a woman – is so rewarded for developing a powerfully erotic public image. But this type of sexual entertainment is nevertheless not just an adventure, it's a job.

Sometimes the money gives a context for the behavior. Sex work gave me a reason to overcome my old limitations on being sexually outgoing. It mandated that I be as forward as I could be – and gave me an excuse for doing so that helped me bypass my reticence. Jamie mentioned she tried things when working she probably wouldn't have done in her private life. "It's like someone asking you to be in a play, plus you get paid for it," she says. Other times, getting money can contribute to a feeling of dissociation or confusion – even guilt or shame, if the sex worker has underlying feelings that what he or she is doing isn't right.

"Part of what makes the work hard is that it's so undervalued," Lily muses. "It's such an integral part of this culture but we value sex so very little – in any other form than procreation and the expression of love between two married straight people – that when you service the sexual needs of this culture for money you're devalued as a human being. That is a pathetically profound statement about how mixed up we are about sex."

The exchange of money can also bring out an unpleasant side to some of the customers. Lily tells about a time when a customer, resentful about tipping her, said, "Why don't you get a *real* job?" "That's the way a lot of these guys think," says Lily. "It's not even real work." Another time a customer said, "You know, my girlfriend is ten times prettier than you are." "I just looked at him and said, 'Then why are you *here?*'"

Lily's anecdotes aren't at all unusual. The sex business is a hot spot in what has been called "the war of the sexes," a place where yearning can be assuaged, but can also transmute into bad manners or even hostility. Ironically, women like Lily display expertise and a willingness to be openly sexual that their customers often can't find at home. "Why are you here," indeed? Because his partner wouldn't be caught dead letting him watch her masturbate, that's why. Instead of valuing Lily more highly because she would, the man vented disappointment that had nothing to do with her.

Lily is philosophical. "Everybody has their agenda. You cannot take the bad comments or the bad days personally. Sex is so personal that often what somebody is going off about has nothing to do with you. They don't know you. They only know what they perceive of you. That's a very important thing to remember, especially when you're starting. You're not responsible for what that person thinks of you."

I've met boorish customers too, but there's a flip side. I've also talked to plenty of men who were not defensive, who brought some degree of vulnerability to our interaction. I've heard, "If only my partner could do what you do. If only my partner was as outgoing as you. If only my partner was as proud of her sexuality as you are. If only my partner would talk to me the way you can."

Nina Hartley is one of the industry's biggest stars; she knows she has her audience's attention and, more than most sex workers can ever count on, respect. She uses it to inspire and educate, as well as to arouse. "I've always, from the very beginning, been conscious and conscientious about being a role model – how to be a positively sexy, lustful woman without succumbing to the whore/madonna sin thing, or wallowing in low self-esteem, the 'Please, please give me attention, I'll do anything for you' thing. I can model how to transcend that and get what you need without being pathetic or a bitch. I try to model a healthy sexual attitude to the dancers in the clubs and also to the customers in the clubs."

Not all sex workers have an easy time transitioning between home and work. Lily says, "There's a certain amount of occupational bleed-through. You come home from work, you don't always turn back into your real self. Also, you burn out. Your relationships can suffer because you're emotionally inaccessible – you only have so much intimacy and so much sexual energy to go around. You can't keep manufacturing it like it's a bottomless well – it's not." Many of the people I talked to stressed the need for an understanding and supportive partner. Too many sex workers have to deal with the projections of their customers and fans all day, then come home to a different set of issues projected by a partner who feels negative about their work.

Customers do project their own sexual issues and desires onto sex workers, which can be a complicated and difficult part of the job. Successful professional exhibitionists relish the attention they get in this process but don't make the mistake of taking it too personally. "Fans don't find out that we get our period," says Jeanna, "have a headache, run out of gas, wash dishes, or make grilled cheese sandwiches – they don't *want* to know that! That ends the separation between fantasy and reality." Sex workers must be willing to understand the degree to which the role they play generates fans' and customers' adulation and attention. The chemistry between the women and men they really are and the image they project is responsible for their success. In a way they are acting, but at the same time they are more than actors. That erotic chemistry – to which, if they're exhibitionistic, they're highly responsive – provides the charge on which both they and their customers feed.

Like an exhibitionist who delves into her or his erotic personas at home, a sex worker brings part of himself or herself to the role to make it really convincing, and a special, deep part of their sexuality must feed this chemistry if it's going to be erotically pleasurable for him or her. As any stage actor knows, there's got to be a certain amount of chemistry between you and the audience to make you feel you've really done a good job. In front of the camera, exhibitionistic porn models and actors have that kind of relationship with the camera itself; the audience isn't seen, but it's present anyway.

"I'm a heat-of-the-moment person, that's what I thrive on," says escort and stripper Elizabeth. She tried exotic dancing because she thought it might be a good fit with that part of her personality and was hooked. "The rush of it, you're up there, people's eyes are on you. You *have* to move, just try to do it nicely! It was more than having an audience and thinking about their reaction, it was the whole experience of being watched, tapping into being intuitive about your movement, primal in your connection to your body – it really turns me on."

What happens when sex workers identify too closely with their public role? Nina sees this happen to some adult film performers; especially if they haven't come to the business from a clear or sex-positive place, she worries that many "have internalized the culture's values around sex and desire and non-traditional behavior. While they may feel compelled or drawn to this kind of work, for the money or the fun or being treated like a star, they are also very uncomfortable with it and don't know how to integrate it into their lives very well. Most of the people in the business do have exhibitionistic fantasies and desires, but the level of self-awareness and consciousness is very low."

OSTRACISM AND PRIDE

"People come to sex workers for permission – to look, to submit, to fuck the way they want to fuck – because the constraints of propriety placed on people in this society are so rigid," Lily thinks. This sense of permission to watch and enjoy, to have a basic level of comfort about our own sexual desire, is really no different for those of us who only cross the thresholds of our own bedrooms. Many – in fact, probably most – sex workers feel they perform a legitimate service, even if the culture's guardians of morality don't agree. Many also talked about the sex business' limitations, and one of the most significant of these has to do with who gains access to its world of sexual entertainment and pleasure. Besides obvious economic constraints that affect some male and many potential female customers, women can't even comfortably cross the threshold of many sex establishments.

In short, not only do women risk social ostracism when they cross the line and become sex workers, they also risk it when they are customers. Female sex workers often like their jobs because their sexuality is expected to be suppressed elsewhere in public life; at work they're appreciated for being extremely sexual. Women who reject the social agreement that females are supposed to be unsexed, except in the bedroom, may feel adamant about this; they're also the ones who notice how lopsided the industry's customer base is. Many predict this imbalance will change as women become more economically powerful and in touch with their own sexual desires. In fact, it is likely one of the elements powering the past decade's rise of New Burlesque performances, which have a huge female fan base partly because, while often as erotic and explicit as much exotic dance, it's also campy, theatrical, and frequently removed from the sex industry venues you'd have to visit to see a stripper.

Sex workers who are proud of what they do don't hesitate to rake sex-negativity over the coals, blaming it for many of the business's problems: "I'd like to see sex workers recognized as a legitimate work force and the sex industry as a legitimate industry that fills a need in this society," says Lily, "on the same scale as restaurants. You have Burger King, upscale restaurants, places catering to every appetite from every culture. Anybody can go to any restaurant, according to their appetite and their budget. I'd like to see the sex industry viewed the same way.

"In all industries there is regulation, workers are cared for – except in the sex industry. The very nature of sex work supposedly defiles you as a human being. There is no other industry where work is considered morally reprehensible. Even something like insider trading or nuclear physics does not incur the same moral wrath."

Well, let's say you know you're not cut out to be an inside trader, but you might be willing to cross other social lines. Exhibitionistic people have the most fun with sex work, and the ability to create a larger-than-life persona can really help. "For a long time I felt like I was too big, too loud, too strong, too brassy and too blonde," says Lily. "I was not enough by virtue of being too much. This is a place where you can't possibly be too much: your hair can't be too big or too long, your tits can't be too big, your nails can't be too long. Even if you're dainty and feminine, you can't be too much of that either. If you're going to fill that theater, you've got to really create a persona, even if it's the Girl Next Door."

Oddly enough, there is a real hierarchy within the sex industry, with its own version of prudishness and projection that parallels the way sex workers often feel when confronted with their "straight" sisters. Topless dancers may decry those who get naked; the nastiest dancer might say, "At least I'm not a whore." Elizabeth, an escort who gets most of her business online (and who started in the business as a stripper) notices an interesting lack of exhibitionism in some sex workers' Internet ads: "Online, there's a class distinction between girls who show their faces and those who don't – it's making me crazy, because what's the point? I'm an exhibitionist and the whole point is that I can post naked pictures of myself – that's so much fun and the whole point of it to me! I want to be naked on my website! Why is there this value associated with it? It says something about your spirit, I think!" Some of the women, she notes, don't even show their bodies, as if this would put them in a trashy category, not a classy one.

Sometimes this isn't because the women want to set themselves apart. "Some places have different rules about how you can advertise," Elizabeth explains. "With some girls, their sites are more like porn, and for others, more like 'what I'd look like at dinner at The Top of the Mark.' With all the competition, people have been promoting these ideas that the more pure, i.e. not sexual, you are, the more valuable your services. But I'm going to prove them wrong – I think the naughty can charge more too! I understand it's about the mind game you're playing with your client, but I have more allegiance to the pleasure I get out of being an exhibitionist than to capitalism."

Wild-child Elizabeth is a perfect example of Lily's insight about what makes for a happy, successful sex worker: More important than anything besides a positive view of sexuality is a willingness to be rebellious. "People who know there's more than biology or God Says So, people who understand that rebellion can be a real asset" might have what it takes to enjoy sex work, says Lily. "There's a certain amount of anonymity and a lawlessness about sex work that frees you up to do so many things outside your image of yourself. It's the part of sexuality that Dworkin and Steinem and the powers that be can't deal with. It's not correct, it's not easy to pigeonhole and it's not necessarily very pretty to look at. It's *real*. Part of my sexuality really responds to that lawlessness."

You have to be willing to see sex commodified – many people who would otherwise be terrific sex workers feel uncomfortable about the money exchange. If you can feel good about sex and simultaneously about the marketplace, two of sex workers' biggest demons can be kept at bay. Lily recommends this choice of career only to "someone who understands, or wants to experience first hand, that sex is not a commodity whose value is retained by maintaining sole possession of it. No matter how many people smell a rose, it still smells good. You can become enriched by sharing it with other people and you in no way become diminished."

Many sex workers, though, perhaps the majority, are not out to explore sexuality or strike a blow against sex-negative culture. They're simply trying to pay the rent. "I didn't know what else to do and I was really surprised that

I enjoyed it as much as I did," Jamie says. Especially for these people, Lily recommends pragmatism - never forget that you're doing a job. "Anything bad that happens in the course of that job is the result of an occupational hazard - keep that in context and have enough of a good relationship with yourself that if you dread going to work you will stop."

There's another aspect to the "lawlessness" Lily and many others respond to - you can't always control what you experience emotionally, especially when your own sexuality is involved with the work you do. "You can learn things about yourself doing sex work that you may not necessarily be ready to know," Lily says. "Because sex is such an incredible way to educate, and it's your job to be sexual, it reveals so much. The first time I ever had an orgasm from oral sex was doing a live sex show, and that was a really shocking feeling! My whole life, you could sit me on a belt sander with a tongue on it and I wouldn't get off. But the pressure was off to be turned on by this person." Your willingness to receive these kinds of unexpected "shocks" may also be key to feeling good about working professionally with sex.

Jezebel did phone sex for a living - not surprisingly, she's an avid dirty talker now. "Doing phone sex, there were certain things that piqued my imagination, and some of my favorite phone sex customers were the fetish-freaky guys. With them I could use my imagination more. It was kind of like a training school, really. Then, in my private life, translating it into my desire: here I am, here's what I really want - I'm not playing a fantasy. The leap wasn't so big. It taught me the power of talking. The power of verbalizing things, naming things."

I noticed in the peep show that certain customers - usually the kinkier ones - were very clear about what their hot spots were and able to give me all the cues I needed in a short period of time: "I want this, this, this, this, this, and this, and string it together and make it last less than five minutes." Then there were the ones who came in who were probably just beginning to explore their alternative fantasies, and others who were simply tongue-tied. I asked Jezebel whether many of her phone sex customers were able to successfully communicate their erotic interests. "I had to draw people out a *lot*," she said. "But just asking that question is so powerful: 'What do you want?'"

ADVICE FROM THE PROS

In addition to asking my sex worker friends about their experiences in the industry, I also asked them what they had to say to non-professional exhibitionists – people who will never take their sexuality to a crowd of paying customers, but who want to hear some hints from the pros. They were most generous.

"After I read Louise Hay's book, *You Can Heal Your Life,* I said, 'Fuck it. I'm going to learn to dance,'" Annie Sprinkle says. "Every time I said something negative to myself like, 'I'm moving my ass funny' or 'I'm not good enough' or 'I'm too fat,' I would just immediately replace it with a positive affirmation. I just wouldn't let that negative voice in."

Vanessa del Rio, one of the greatest porn stars of all time, didn't grow up shy, and it shows. Her natural, passionate depictions of sexuality were not an act, and she's even a little puzzled at the degree of attention she's received over the years. "I've been trying to find out what it is that people see, because it feels natural – it doesn't feel like something that I had to go buy or look up. It just felt like, this is what sex *is!*" Her advice is simple: get into the sex. Whether you're being watched or talking dirty, start right where you are, with what you're feeling. "It's just part of sex! You start out with, 'Oh, that feels good, I love the way that feels,' and then you just go on from there."

Candye recommends that you play with erotic photography or glamour shots, perhaps moving on to video. Be playful – this is not the place to take yourself too seriously or compare yourself to a centerfold pin-up. Be ready to have fun and to accept yourself the way you are. You can do this regardless of whether you have a partner. Many reputable professional photographers are available for "boudoir" work, and if you've seen a photographer's work you love in an erotic magazine, you might want to do some research to find out whether s/he's available for private sessions. Most of these artists have websites and can be contacted through them directly.

"But first of all," Candye says, if you're experimenting with a partner, "it's important to be with somebody you feel really comfortable with." Look for someone who accepts you. When you have that partner, she suggests scripting an adventure or trying out role-play. "Don't be afraid to be something you're not. Why just be yourself? If you're going to role-play, be something you could never really be in life and try to be flamboyant about it."

It can be hard to get out of your head and into erotic adventure and exhibitionistic fun if you have issues about your body. If you are very self-conscious, try using a blindfold, concentrating on the emotions and sensations evoked when you're not looking at yourself. "It's difficult for some people to cut themselves off from their belly or their stretch marks," says Candye. "If you don't have to look at them, it can help."

Juliet is especially aware that many women hesitate to explore this way, and encourages everyone to find ways to do so that feel safe. Instead of embarking on a potentially frightening adventure, think of it more as a field trip. "Get together with a couple of women friends and go to a strip joint. Just be sure you bring some money to tip the women, because they're working!" While this is an expensive outing that's not available to everyone, window-shopping at a lingerie boutique can get your exhibitionistic juices flowing even if you're on a budget. So might renting a porn movie together, or cruising the Internet for ideas. Make popcorn and plenty of rowdy comments!

Rita encourages reading sexy books – "whether Anaïs Nin or some really raunchy magazine or one of those one-handed jerk-off books" – searching for characters and scenarios you find hot. "Masturbate to it. Explore fantasies that way. Read it out loud."

Then there's dress-up, which Rita knows a lot about. "Go buy things that feel sexy and erotic and wear them under your clothes, around the house. Look at yourself in the mirror, see what you like about it. Find clothes that really feel good on you, that make you feel sexy. Don't give up after the first stupid one-size-fits-all bustier and think 'This is never going to work.' Really take the time to find something that looks nice. Maybe have a friend go along for moral support."

Jeanna Fine's erotic power and comfort in front of the camera come from more than the ritual of makeup and fetishwear. Before she became a big star, she watched her own early movies and felt that she just blended in with all the other starlets; how could she make herself stand out? This was a business decision for her, but it also involved her pride in her work and her own sexuality. "I came to the decision that when I was on that screen, I was going to light up like a Christmas tree.

"I'd been in the business less than a year. I thought, 'I'd better get a look at what everybody else is seeing.' I watched my videos and said 'This works,' or 'That doesn't,' but then I decided I wanted to bring something more than a paint-by-numbers picture. I wanted to see what I looked like when I really came, so that I could try to bring that to my performance." She started watching herself in a mirror as she masturbated. Then she added taking dirty. "Talking to myself and masturbating in front of the mirror charged me and I thought, 'If it's working for me, it probably will work for other people.'"

It certainly did – now she's widely acknowledged as one of the hottest dirty talkers ever to hit the screen. It wouldn't have happened without the grounding in her own sexuality; she freely allows that her porn persona has affected her private life, and vice versa. "I had a partner during the time that I was evolving into the Diva. I got to practice with him. I took what we did at home and brought it to the screen, and took from the screen and brought it home.

"I found the power of my voice for orgasm myself, the first time I opened my mouth. I spoke in bed and it helped. Now if I masturbate and I'm having a really tough time, all I have to do is open my mouth and say something – and I'm coming."

Lily, too, recommends solo play for sex workers and private exhibitionists alike: "I cannot overestimate the value of private time, like the ritual of dress up, which you should never lose from your childhood – boys and butches, everybody should play dress up, it's not just the province of femmy little girls. Also masturbation. How can you have good sex with another person if you don't have a healthy, loving sexual relationship with yourself?"

EVERYBODY IS A STAR

A final – and perhaps the most important – thing we can get from the sex workers is inspiration. We may never stand in as bright a spotlight as they do; we may never share our sexually outgoing selves with strangers – or even with our partners. But that they've taken this path can give us ideas and encouragement when we experiment at home.

"I tell people, 'I want you to watch me because you know I want to be there. Go ahead and jack off to me. We're on the same wavelength,'" says Nina. "I'm not ambivalent about what I do. I have no guilt about it. That makes it very easy for me to be strong. People say, 'Nina, you're so brave, you're living your beliefs and you just do it, you don't let other people get you down, you don't let other people's opinion bother you.' I'm just doing what I thought once I had a right to do, which is to be self-actualized and to find a way to accept myself with people who wanted me to accept myself. I feel very lucky, very blessed, very charmed in that way. I still like dancing naked!"

"I think the power is in all of us" to discover our erotically powerful selves, says Jeanna, "simply by being honest. And giving it a whirl! And practice. If it doesn't work the first time, if it doesn't feel good the first time, do it again. Try it with somebody else! Maybe it's the person you were with, or the color eyeshadow you were wearing. Don't stop because it failed the first time – look at why it may have failed.

"If you can fantasize being that woman with that erotic power then you can be. I think that's a little bit of discovering the goddess inside us."

In case male readers feel that statement's not applicable to them – think again! The ability to envision becoming more sexually present and powerful has nothing to do with gender. It's just that, ironically, more women pay the rent that way – an accident of supply and demand.

Candye's story inspires especially because she wasn't welcomed into the sex business with open arms. "Society is constantly bombarding us with images that we're not okay," she says. "I ate it up; I grew up with Barbie. I was called 'Fatty' when I was still a size 12. You know, a 12 is not big! But everybody made me feel big. It's so painful when you're a kid; all you really want is to fit in. I really think it's better when you're not like everyone else. I think you can become so much more of a character. You get strength that way.

"I don't think we can get away from judging people by how they look in this society, but I do think that how you feel about yourself is everything, and however that power comes, take it. I know, because my power came in a very unconventional way – but once it came, there was no denying it."

You've met just a few of the many thousands of women and men who make up the rank and file of the sex industry. Not all sex workers are exhibitionists, and not all of those who are can articulate what it means to them; after all, the exchange of sexual energy that results doesn't even have a name in this culture, especially when it happens between strangers. It often doesn't rely on physical contact or even intimacy, as we understand it in a relationship-oriented way. Yet many sexual entertainers know it well.

Plenty of details about their lives and work are useful even to stay-at-home exhibitionists. Many of them started out ordinary, even shy. Many of them have come to relish the chance the sex business gives them to explore and be outrageous. Their larger-than-life erotic presentation is so desired – either on its own merits, or as a symbol for something else – that billions of dollars change hands every year.

What we do at home, with our lovers, in the context of a relationship, is different in many ways from what the sex workers do onstage, on screen, and on the phone – but in many ways it's just the same. Whether we do it for love, for fun, or for money, all who wish to develop strong, outgoing erotic personas must overcome any reticence we have to this kind of exploration, learn the look and the lingo that will excite a response in our lovers, customers, or fans – and most importantly in ourselves.

We stand to gain something that has nothing to do with money and everything to do with self-image. Ideally, too, whether it's a job or our weekend secret, it has a lot to do with our own sexual pleasure.

☾ 13 ❋

Exhibitionism And Your Partner

"**Y**ou can treat it like acting class if you want, but if you do it like it's work, you're kind of missing the point. Someone has to believe in you to get you started. Someone has to want it." That's what Jamie has to say about the importance of your partner's response as you begin to explore exhibitionistic play. But before you get to that point, you have to bring it up.

I've provided you with lots of ideas for hot talk and exhibitionism; now it's up to you. Maybe you've already incorporated some of these suggestions into your masturbation, your fantasy life, or erotic time with your partner. Perhaps you have a sweetie who enthusiastically welcomed the chance to play with you at exhibitionism and talking dirty. If not – if your partner seems reluctant or unenthusiastic about joining you in these new kinds of fun, or you fear talking to him or her about your desires – this chapter is for you. If you have no regular partner at the moment, you can read it for ideas about introducing exhibitionistic play when you meet your next lover or playmate.

BEING YOUR OWN LOVER

When you embrace fantasy and masturbation, part of your sex life is all your own, no matter what kind of sex you have with any other person or people. You can always enjoy exhibitionism privately. Pleasure yourself with wild fantasy scenarios – your erotic imagination doesn't have to be shackled to what's possible or likely. In your fantasies your partner (if you have one) can join you with excited relish even if s/he's completely unenthused about exhibitionism in real life. Remember that you can have sexual fantasies whether you're masturbating to them or not. You might also enjoy documenting your fantasies in a journal or writing them into erotic stories.

You can also incorporate exhibitionistic elements besides fantasies into masturbation – not just to get comfortable with the idea of sexual showing off, but to please yourself and help meet your need or desire for this kind of sex play. If anyone ever made you feel wrong or "second-best" about masturbation, start retraining yourself right now! Self-pleasuring is your birthright, a delight most people engage in. It doesn't mean you're unfaithful to your partner, it doesn't mean your sex life lacks anything; masturbation, in fact, can be a central ingredient in a perfect sex life.

I absolutely don't mean you should leave it at that. Of course you may very well want to talk to your partner about your desires, encouraging her or him to join you in your play. But your exhibitionistic pleasure need not hinge on your partner's enthusiasm – or even participation.

In the pre-orgasmic women's groups common in the 1970s, women wanting to learn to orgasm received support, information, and inspiration. Overwhelmingly, the groups worked: Women *did* learn to orgasm, even those who had never before been able to count on responding with a climax. Women who were orgasmic through masturbation were also more likely to be able to come during sex play with their partners – but if they didn't, they were still orgasmic! Their capacity to come was their own, not dependent on their partners' actions. In the same way, your partner's response to your sexual desires for exhibitionism or hot talk need not spell success or failure.

BEGINNING TO TALK WITH YOUR PARTNER: STRATEGIES AND SUGGESTIONS

Now do you feel ready to bring up your fantasies with your partner? Is your partner ready to hear them?

Consider each question separately. Just because you've gotten in touch with new or heretofore buried desires doesn't mean you must bring them up. How will you feel about yourself if your partner rejects your fantasies? Ideally you'll still feel comfortable and confident about your desires no matter how your partner reacts. If you're pretty sure a negative reaction would be a blow to your self-esteem, don't tell - at least, not yet. A few therapists on the talk-show circuit would like you to believe that any fantasy you don't share with your partner (or any fantasy about someone other than your partner) is tantamount to infidelity, but this is nonsense; you can be an open, loving, committed partner and still maintain the privacy of your erotic thoughts.

If your lover has encouraged you to talk about your fantasies and you've been reluctant, tell him or her so and say why. ("I'm afraid you'll think they're too far out." "I'm afraid you'll insist we try them and I'm not sure I want to.") The way he or she responds to your explanation can give you a clearer idea about whether your fears are warranted.

But let's get down to the business of talking to your partner - who may be even shyer than you used to be. If so, your task will be not only to express your desires, but also to support your sweetheart - perhaps in small steps - in taking some risks. That these risks are pleasure-oriented may not make them less scary, so be prepared to go slowly and give your partner plenty of positive feedback.

The way it feels to do this, and to bring up the topic in the first place, may differ according to your gender. We all grow up getting messages about what's "appropriate" to us as men or as women. Some of us have fought these gender-role imperatives, while to others they seem quite natural. So men may find it a little easier to initiate new types of play - though some may not be as comfortable actually conversing in depth about it or talking about their fears. Women may feel uneasy about initiating sexually, especially something new, and may find it harder to ask for things.

Whether you are male or female, the dynamics of your sexual relationship with your partner may change if you initiate this way, particularly if you haven't done so in the past, echoing or contradicting the power dynamics in the rest of your relationship. Whatever your ideal relationship state, learning to request new sexual activities with your partner will likely cause you to look at these dynamics with a fresh eye.

First, think about what you want to explore. It will help if you have a range of possible exhibitionistic activities for your partner and yourself. If you really want to fuck in broad daylight in the middle of Central Park, you may get there more easily by starting out by having sex with the lights on at home than by declaring "Central Park or bust!" How you get the two of you started down the right path depends upon where you are right now. Consider, given your own personal situation, the best way to get from here to there.

You can propose any one of the suggestions and exercises you've read in this book to your partner. Especially if s/he is sexually reticent, start with non-threatening, very private things – even things she or he can do alone, during masturbation. (If masturbation isn't part of your partner's life, introduce her or him to the work of Betty Dodson.) If you want your partner to be your private voyeur as you explore exhibitionism, talk about fantasy scenarios to prime the pump. Your honey can explore these mentally at whatever pace feels comfortable. Ask questions like "I'd love to dress up sexy for you. What would you like me to wear?" and "I think it would be a total turn-on to show off for you. Would you like to watch me?" This lets your lover in on your fantasy but also gives him/her a say in what might happen. The same thing goes if you want your partner to be more exhibitionistic for you.

Have specific kinds of play in mind before you approach the first conversation with your partner. If you just say, "I want to be more exhibitionistic," you might find your partner has a negative response to the word, with assumptions about its meaning that have nothing to do with your actual desires. "Does he want to flash strangers?" or "Do I have to worry about her embarrassing me at the office party?" might flit through your sweetheart's head, when all you meant was, "I want you to watch me when I come." Likewise, saying "Talk dirty to me" to a partner who has no experience with explicit language could court a colossal case of performance anxiety. Request something more specific and your partner might readily oblige.

Having specifics to discuss and request also removes your talk from the unsexy realm of the abstract. You might decide to start there – "What do you think about erotic exhibitionism?" – but please, be ready to move on to some examples so you can get out of graduate school and into bed (or out on the balcony, or wherever).

Your specifics can vary from teensy modifications of your existing sex lives to great departures; ideally you have thought of a range, so your conversation can move along your partner's comfort level rather than overshooting it entirely. Also, if s/he rejects one idea, another one might go over big, but you won't know unless you bring them both up.

Sex therapists and relationship counselors commonly recommend that you broach sexual topics, especially those dealing with things you'd like to change, outside the bedroom. When you start suggesting new and different things during sex, you risk upsetting your routine and provoking a defensive reaction. Even if you aren't in fact satisfied, and upsetting your routine is your fervent goal, give yourself a chance at success! Talking about sex at a more neutral time allows both of you a clear-headed opportunity to discuss the topic at hand.

Your chances of a successful discussion increase when you present your ideas and desires positively. Your partner won't respond any better to an accusation than you would. "You don't even *notice* when I show off for you!" may be technically true, but it doesn't give him or her much support or room to move. (It may also be quite incorrect – maybe s/he *does* notice, but is too shy or otherwise unwilling to say something about it.) How about saying instead, "I'd love to know whether it turns you on when I dress up really sexy"?

A related strategy: pair what you want to change with something you like just the way it is now. Change can feel threatening to many people, especially when they don't initiate it; it's easy to fear our lovers aren't pleased with us when they ask for something new. So reassure your partner with a statement about what delights you about sex with him or her. After all, if you don't (or didn't at one time) love *something*, what are you doing together? If you hope to construct the perfect lover out of raw material you find uninspiring, you'll need more help than you can get here. You'll have more luck if you genuinely support and encourage your lover in the direction of desired changes, reinforcing for him or her that you appreciate the things you share already.

If S/He's Uncomfortable

If this discussion proves to be difficult – if you find you've uncovered a sensitive area for either yourself or your partner, even issues you didn't know were there – be gentle with each other and try to treat it as a learning experience, an opportunity to grow. You may want to agree to talk about it later, changing the subject now to give both of you a chance to reflect on the hot spot. Don't just drop it or change the subject without acknowledging you're doing so, however – that often feels like rejection or abandonment. Instead, agree to lessen the feeling of risk now by coming back to the discussion later. It's important that each of you can feel safe.

Maybe your partner's negative or upset reaction when you bring up your desires will have nothing to do with the sexual activity itself, but with the meaning s/he attributes to it. Different people will self-talk in radically different ways: You want me to *what*? You're asking me for something different? Don't I please you? I thought I was married to a *nice* girl! What would my mother, friend, colleague, or neighbor say? This is not normal!

Your partner might simply be unable (at least right now) to tolerate the idea of being naughty, kinky, or whatever they think you're asking them to be. This may be particularly hard for you to grasp if you don't see the behavior that way, but simply as good clean experimental fun. You may be able to get a clearer idea about the sources of his or her distress by asking questions like "How would doing this activity make you feel? What meaning does it have for you?"

Take into account other possible sources of your partner's fears and hesitations. Encourage her or him to tell you what they are, and listen. Maybe your partner has unmet desires of you and feels reluctant to give you what you want without some reciprocity. Perhaps your partner doesn't experience sex in a playful way and gets a giant case of performance anxiety just hearing your request. If your lover feels stressed, overworked, or tired, any sort of request for something new may seem like just more work and stress. If so, what can you do to help ease the burdens of day-to-day life and give your partner more room to play?

Once you've decided how you'd like to approach your partner and have mustered up the courage to do so, push yourself to try at least once more if he or she doesn't respond favorably the first time. For instance, "I know last time I asked you to masturbate along with me you didn't want to, but I'd really love to try it. Would you be more willing to try it if we dimmed the lights a little?"

You might make a suggestion that your partner says "no" to automatically, without bothering to really consider it. What if you say "let's pretend" and his or her response is, "Oh, god, honey, now what?" Even if you're disheartened at your partner's response, work up the courage to ask at least a second time.

In the meantime, consider what might have caused him or her to say no. Was your timing bad? Did s/he seem to be jumping to conclusions about what you wanted? Did you ask for something too "big" in his or her eyes? Was it the very first time you'd ever tried to talk openly about sex? Any of these factors, and many others, can get in the way of your partner hearing your request favorably.

Talking, Listening, Role Modeling

If the two of you don't commonly share your feelings with each other, you may need to start learning to do so before you can navigate a hesitant partner's concerns. It's your request, so you should be prepared to role-model positive communications skills. You can model more than that – you can begin to try new things non-verbally, adding uncharacteristic activities to your repertoire. The fact that you're thinking of showing off and being looked at more may encourage your lover to pay more attention to the visual elements of your relationship. You're not only silently communicating with him or her, but with yourself – you're taking gradual steps towards your desired goal, and at the same time you're learning a new self-image. You may want to do this for a while before you talk about it, letting these changes sink in. Then you can ask, "Have you noticed that lately I've been dressing and acting differently? How do you feel about it?"

A very simple and effective way to keep communication on track is a skill called "active listening." Too often, people respond not to what their partner said, but to what they *think* they said. Furthermore, many people's tendency in conversation is to start planning their response before the other person stops talking. Sometimes they even respond to what they think their partner *meant* – whether or not they had it right. Also, defensiveness, anger, assumptions, and fear can all get in the way of clear speaking and listening. In active listening, when your partner makes a statement, try telling them what you heard them say before you press on to make your own point.

"I hear you saying that you don't want to leave the lights on when we make love," you may say, which gives your partner a chance to clarify, "No, I said I'm *afraid* to keep the lights on." You can then ask what your partner is afraid of and address her or his fears, moving the discussion along – and hopefully finding a safe way to proceed with the activity in spite of the fears.

There are so many possible reasons why we might want or not want to do something that it really pays to collect the right information. "If the lights are on, the neighbors can see in," your partner might say. "I don't want you to see my body – I'm out of shape," might be another reason to do it in the dark. "It's hard for me to fantasize when the lights are on." "The only light in the room is too bright." (Cover it with a scarf! Don't burn the house down, though.) S/he might also acknowledge that, even though it's scary, s/he wants to do it anyway, because "I want to get over being afraid of this; I think we can have more pleasure if I do" or "being scared of it is kind of a turn-on."

Encourage your partner to practice active listening as well. It will help you both keep on track, and if one of you has misunderstood or misinterpreted the other, you can clear it up right away.

If your communication is not tip-top, consider exploring ways to work on your partnered communications skills. The positive effects of doing so will extend far beyond your sex lives.

Talking about sexual fantasy is a good place to begin these initial conversations. Regardless of whether you have talked about fantasies before, you can learn more about your partner's sexual thoughts if you freely share information about your own. If your partner worries that fantasy threatens your relationship, reassure her or him that most people fantasize; perhaps you can share books about sexual fantasy to put this issue in a somewhat broader context. This gives you a chance to acknowledge that you fantasize about becoming more exhibitionistic and you want to share this sort of play with him or her, or that you have a particular fantasy you'd like to try together. Have some ready examples to illustrate what you mean.

Remember that your chances of having a successful conversation – particularly if it's the first one – increase if you *don't* have it in bed; and also if your partner is in a receptive, stress-free mood. You may want to talk about fantasies while driving in the car, in a pleasant cafe, while taking a walk, or while on vacation or a weekend getaway.

If you've found a short story or a passage of a novel you find hot, tell your partner about it and offer to read it out loud. After you've decided on a fantasy you want to explore, write it in a letter and mail it to your partner or read it to him or her on the phone. Ask what sorts of things s/he's thought about trying, what sorts of things s/he likes to think about but wants to keep on a fantasy level. Don't forget that you can have a scintillating sexual experience just talking about a fantasy while you make love. One hint, though – you probably ought to save your more forbidden fantasies until you've had some practice. In sharing fantasy, as in actual experience, if you have a reticent partner, move along with her or his comfort level in mind.

When you ask your partner's fantasies, it's very important to respect what s/he shares with you as much as you want him or her to respect your own thoughts and feelings. You don't have to act out all these fantasies; you don't *have* to do anything. Hearing about your loved one's erotic thoughts is a privilege, and if you're not ready for it, don't ask. Above all don't ridicule or reject your partner based on the things s/he thinks about. If you do, you'll send the message that it's not safe to talk to you about fantasy – or maybe about anything very private or important to him or her.

Communication, like sexual pleasure, is a two-way street. If you can't take this principle to heart, you probably will not get what you want from your partner.

WHY IT'S WORTH TRYING (EVEN IF IT'S SCARY)

Once you open the door to talking more easily about sex, you can return to the conversation again and again. Instead of seeing it as a scary effort for which you fear you'll be rejected, you can look at it as a way to become closer, share secrets, and make erotic plans. When you get ready to actually pick new things to try together, start with things that are fairly easy. No dramatic departures from your routine at first, please, unless both of you clearly feel enthusiastic about the new idea. Agree together on one or two things to try – maybe one of your fantasies and one of your partner's – and agree that you'll consider them experiments. Afterwards, compare notes. Give and listen carefully to feedback. Using this process you may be able to fine-tune your experiments until the activity appeals equally to both of you.

If you haven't been in the habit of talking frankly about sex and fantasy with your partner, her or his responses may surprise you. We might assume a partner will be reticent, only to hear "I thought you'd never ask!" Perhaps your partner has a list of things s/he'd love to try, but hasn't been willing to bring them up. If you break the ice, the two of you may move along together down such a fun-filled path of sexual experimentation that, looking back, you'll laugh at yourself for not knowing how to bring the topic up in the first place. Don't assume your partner will be much more reticent than you until you've had a real-life chance to find out. It may turn out that you're the shy one compared to him or her!

Even if your partner is very shy, however, respect that his or her life experiences and upbringing formed and shaped the sexual attitudes s/he expresses (or professes without speaking up about them). You *must* start with that – there's no getting around it. Perhaps s/he was brought up very conservatively and just needs time to get used to a new view of sex; perhaps s/he has experienced a nonconsensual sexual situation and will not feel comfortable being erotically outgoing until s/he's dealt with the past. In either case, be supportive, and know that together you can have different experiences *now*. Neither you nor your partner has finished growing.

If this book has helped you feel more comfortable about your own exhibitionistic desires and given you ideas for things you'd like to try, why not share it with your partner? Telling your partner about it or reading aloud from it can be a good way to enter the conversation. Perhaps your partner feels resistant to the idea of exhibitionism, but in fact enjoys behaviors like erotic dress, kissing in public, or talking during sex. Encourage these by responding positively to them – when you get right down to it, it doesn't matter what you call it, as long as it pushes the right erotic buttons in both of you!

Why does exhibitionism – or certain behaviors you associate with exhibitionism – appeal to you? If you can articulate this, you may be better able to interest a reluctant partner in experimenting. Do you think it will be erotically exciting? Will you feel more daring and hence better about yourself? Will you be proud to do something you've fantasized about but thought you couldn't? Examine your own assumptions about it. Finish the sentence: "Exhibitionists are...." Now bring it to the level of your own specific desires: "I want to do... because..." This helps you establish what meaning various exhibitionistic activities may have for you. Once you have a handle on this, you can share your insights with your partner. Ask how s/he would fill in those blanks.

If I were going to initiate a discussion about exhibitionism with a new partner (or one with whom I'd never talked about it), I would say something like this. "I've been thinking about something I'd love to try, and I want to know whether you think it would be fun. I really love the idea of putting on an erotic show for you. It would turn me on so much to feel your eyes on me while I strip for you and show off for you. How do you feel about that idea? I'd like to just surprise you sometime and do it. May I?" How would your approach be similar to or differ from this?

Or, if I want to be the voyeur while I encourage my partner's exhibitionism: "I've been thinking about getting you a beautiful silk robe I saw when I was out shopping. I love the idea of watching you while you run your hands all over your body, touching yourself through the silky cloth, and letting it fall open so I can see your body. Would it be sexy for you if I watched you while you touch yourself? I would keep my hands to myself until you told me to touch you too. You could just drive me crazy."

Maybe I want my lover to show off right along with me: "I was always so turned on at high school dances, but I felt like I had to act ladylike when what I really wanted to do was hump my partner's thigh. I heard about an erotic ball where people wear sexy costumes and dance as dirty as they want – would you like to go with me? We can pretend it's high school, the way it should have been!" If going out in public feels like too much of a stretch, put on some music from the decade you went to high school or college and try it at home first.

In each of these examples I give my partner information about my desire or fantasy, then ask if they'd enjoy doing it with me. As the conversation progressed I would ask whether they had any hesitations or concerns, or wanted to alter part of the scenario to make it hotter for them. If they enter into the give and take of planning a fantasy, I'll have more assurance they're truly interested in exploring and playing with me.

Besides telling your partner what you'd like to do, you can also show them. Start by being more exhibitionistic yourself. Dress in sexy ways. Buy sexy lingerie and wear it under your clothes. Make sure he or she gets to see it when the lights are on. Behave more exhibitionistically. Let her or him "catch" you masturbating or dirty dancing when s/he comes home from work.

Put on music you both like and dance at home; go out together and get a little daring on the dance floor. Take your partner shopping and buy something sexy, or ask for help choosing something s/he'd like to see you wear. Have your partner pick a sexy outfit for you from the clothes you already own. Gradually give your partner things to respond to and to join you in doing. Be your lover's role model; if you want him or her to take some erotic risks, take some yourself.

Encourage your partner to masturbate along with you. Do it side by side at first; if both you and your partner enjoy sexy movies, you can watch something together so you don't have to feel so exposed. In the periphery of your vision, though, you can see each other, and many people find this indirect vantage point highly erotic. When that has begun to feel comfortable, try sitting at opposite ends of the bed or couch and frankly watch each other. Spice up the eroticism with sex toys or dressing up. Or arrange to peep at each other; take turns masturbating while the other hides behind the door and watches.

People with both voyeuristic and exhibitionistic tendencies will get into these kinds of play more easily; encourage your partner in each as you explore your own responses.

EVALUATING YOUR EXPERIMENTS; POSSIBLE NEGOTIATIONS

How will you decide whether or not your experiments together were a success? What if you both agree they didn't work? If so, one or both of you may subsequently feel guilty, embarrassed, resentful, or foolish. Try to address how you'll deal with this ahead of time; don't attack (or deny) each other's feelings, and give each other space to feel different. Don't stop being supportive; whether or not you go back and experiment again will likely depend on how you treat each other now. Talk about what didn't work. Do something together you both enjoy. Treat it lightly – not disrespectfully, just with a sense of humor. Laughing at yourselves when something isn't working can lighten up what otherwise might seem like an unmitigated disaster – but make sure the laughter is shared.

Other possible rough spots: you find, after you decided independently to become more exhibitionistic, that your partner doesn't like you that way. Even worse – your partner encouraged you to become more bold, then decides s/he doesn't like it after all.

If after trying to interest your partner in erotic talk, showing off, dressing up, or other exhibitionistic and voyeuristic play you find you've gotten nowhere, how will you deal with your (new) desires without damaging the relationship? It's wonderful to have an enthusiastic partner, but what if yours simply isn't?

Before you give up all hope, find out whether your partner is willing to play your way sometimes even though it doesn't make her/him hot. You may be able to negotiate "scratching each other's backs" from time to time. Your partner's willingness to help you have the kind of sex you crave is a gift – respect it as such – and remember that you can probably do the same for him or her. Your partner may be a Good Samaritan or just open-minded, but if s/he seems to begrudge you this gift, see if you can get her or him to tell you why. Does he resent helping you with your fantasy because he has an unmet desire too? Does she really find it a turn-off but is trying to be accommodating nevertheless? Does he in fact think the kind of sex you want is wrong? Is she afraid you're really weird and that she hasn't known the "real you"? Is he afraid he'll like it, which would prove he's weird too? Is she worried that you might eventually embarrass her, either publicly, by your behavior, or by telling someone else what you've been up to? Fears of kinkiness and being abnormal sometimes die hard.

Maybe your partner doesn't want to play exhibitionistic games with you, but there is an exhibitionistic aspect to all sexual activity, and you may be able to reframe what you already do to find more erotic potential there. What already happens? How can you add to it via fantasy? How can you add to it in other ways like costuming? If you feel especially sexy making love in the shower, in broad daylight, near a mirror, in certain positions like doggy-style or woman astride, or making noise or talking, focus on these aspects of sex.

Maybe your partner will give you the freedom to have adventures alone. To minimize potential problems in opening up your relationship, negotiate carefully and stick to agreements. Some possible agreements to help you develop an exhibitionistically nonmonogamous lifestyle should you make this choice: engage only in visual play with others – nothing physical; engage in exhibitionistic play only with sex workers, like at a peep show; do it only when you're out of town; if you get physical with anyone else, stick to safe sex agreements; and assure yourself and your stay-at-home partner that you will not expose yourself to any sort of danger when you're out and about. Maybe computer sex or phone sex feels acceptable to your partner if nonmonogamy-in-the-flesh does not. Learning more about how others make open relationships work may also be helpful to you.

For some, nonmonogamy of any type will be out of the question. For others, trying it would lead to hurt and frustration – not everyone is cut out for it. If you decide to open a hitherto monogamous relationship, consider doing it for a pre-specified period and then re-evaluating the experiment. Are you both feeling good about the way things are going? Does either of you need to alter the agreement you originally made? You can ease into an open relationship slowly; it doesn't have to be "anything goes." Few of us are totally monogamous over the course of our lives, nor are most of us always content to be nonmonogamous. Be practical and honest about which works best for you at any given time and with any given partner. Most people will find some version of open relationship healthier for the relationship and the people in it than deception in a supposedly monogamous relationship. Some even find that partners gladly embrace polyamory or other open relationship configurations. If not, of course, another alternative is to maintain an active fantasy life with as many partners as you can imagine.

Maybe your partner will join you, but only under particular circumstances: out of town, among strangers; at Hallowe'en; at home, in private. Or perhaps your partner would like hearing about your exhibitionistic exploits, even though s/he doesn't want to join you in person. If so, you can enjoy telling tales later, and keep your sweetheart involved in your eroticism through your stories.

Maybe you can use erotic talk to good effect in other ways. Perhaps your fond fantasy – for your partner to watch while you have sex with someone else, for instance – has been rejected, but s/he will talk to you about what it would be like while the two of you make love.

When we run into difficulties negotiating the kinds of sex we want with partners, it's always wise to look at the bigger picture of the relationship. Although sometimes the only issue turns out to be our partner's distaste for a sexual style, in other cases the bottom line isn't sex at all. Increase your awareness of your relationship's patterns in and out of bed. When you talk about charged issues, what effect does it have? Look at who initiates in the relationship – not only sexually, but in all kinds of ways. How do you communicate about non-sexual issues? About sexual issues that are already part of your routine? Do you run into snags in these areas? Have you thought about getting counseling or even leaving the relationship?

If you have given an honest try and your partner remains unwilling to explore with you, you have some decisions to make. How important do you rank the sexual changes you'd like? Are your expectations realistic, your communication clean? Are you happy in the relationship in all other ways? Would you and your partner benefit from counseling, and is s/he even willing to go? Can you get the kind of sex you need outside the relationship without causing the relationship to suffer? Would you be happier without this relationship?

If you need to have this kind of conversation with yourself, I can only suggest that you be very honest. Partners do grow apart from each other (or were never very well-suited in the first place); often one partner's erotic exploration is the catalyst that ends relationships. If this happens to you, what will you do in the future to find partners who are more compatible? Getting little support for finding sexually compatible partners from society as a whole, many of us don't know how to make this a priority. If anything, we're led to believe that if we love each other or are compatible in other ways, the sex will take care of itself, but very often it doesn't work that way. Give some thought to the responses you'd like to get from a prospective partner. How will you bring up your sexual interests to new partners from now on?

Your partner's out-and-out refusal to erotically experiment with you can set off alarm bells of incompatibility, but sometimes his or her response to your sexual interests is more complicated than that. Rita found herself in such a relationship. Her first clue that something was amiss was her boyfriend's response to her desire to dress erotically. "He hated my black strapless leather mini dress," she says. "He was really upset. We fought over it. He just didn't like me in that kind of clothing. It was threatening and challenging to him if I looked sexy, put on high heels or wore makeup or tight clothes or lingerie, or talked dirty or wanted to have sex with the lights on. If I became sexual and powerful in that way he thought I would leave him." Her boyfriend's response was to go along with her desires; at the same time he treated her with increasing disdain, as though her sexual interests put her beyond the pale. He no longer felt the need to act respectful towards her.

This classic "Lady/Whore" response is more likely to come up for men when women begin to assert their desires for new erotic activities, but there are other responses. A woman may recall her mother's admonition that "men are all alike," attributing her male partner's desire for sexual experimentation to beastly male lust or assuming it means he doesn't really respect her. When partners project their discomfort and resentment about sex on each other, the entire relationship's formerly hidden power dynamics may surface. In any case such projections are a warning sign that the relationship's in danger, since a healthy relationship does not rest on projections and unacknowledged assumptions, but on good communication and real intimacy.

If a partner is pressuring you to become more exhibitionistic, there may be part of you that really wants to do it, so the line between pressure and support can become fuzzy. "It's got to keep coming back to 'What's your desire?'" says Blake. "If you're in a situation where you can't say, 'I want to do this,' anything other than 'yes' is 'no.' If you can't get to 'I want to do this,' then don't do it." Rather, try to state what kind of support you need; if your partner doesn't heed this, consider it a real warning sign. Put another way, if your partner does not care about your perspective and your needs, you are not in a truly healthy, much less compatible, relationship.

STARTING TO PLAY

If you have avoided these potential problems, you may find yourself with a willing partner but with hardly any experience between you. How do you get started?

Remember how important it can be to set time and space aside, especially if your life is already full and busy. "Most people are not sexually exhibitionistic at all," Juliet reminds us. "It's not valued in this culture." According to this view, delving deeper into our sexually playful side remains unlikely unless we make some space for it, and that's easiest to do if both you and your partner are willing to prioritize this.

"If I take the same energy I put into work and put that energy into prioritizing sex and fun, it's easy," says Jackie. "Instead of thinking, 'Oh, god, I'm so tired; I have a meeting tomorrow morning; we can't fuck now,' if I pace my day better, at eight o'clock I could be dressed up like the repairman, or handing her those gift-wrapped silk panties I just bought for her. You don't have to keep up a constant performance for your partner every day, but remember that it does take prioritizing and energy."

If you're in an experimental stage, respect that – go ahead and say out loud, "We're going to try something new and see how it feels." Respect each other for trying. If something falls flat, flexibility will make all the difference: it's okay to say, "This isn't working" or "Let's take a break" or "I do want to do this again soon, but we need to stop for now" or "I thought I was going to really enjoy this, but it's not turning out that way." It can be part of the rules that if one of you feels uncomfortable, you can call it off. Each partner in this experiment needs to take responsibility for the fact that you're weaving a new kind of sexual possibility together. It might work fabulously for both of you, or it might not, but if not it doesn't mean the experiment has failed. You can see what worked and what didn't, incorporating that knowledge next time.

Maybe you're not ready for a particular kind of play now that will be central to your sex life five years from now. Maybe you know you want to say "cunt" in bed, but not before you get comfortable saying "pussy." Maybe you ultimately want to be called "cunt" – but you definitely don't want to do it tonight! Find a language, a way to play, that's non-threatening enough that you don't scare yourself and your partner away from further exploration and risk-taking. If a type of play gives either of you access to more sexual possibility than you felt comfortable with before, you're on the right track.

Sexual experimentation requires the same sort of suspension of disbelief that theater does – each of you must decide who you want to be in the encounter and learn a new sort of erotic compatibility with the other. The scene unfolds according to its own erotic logic – just as do the sexual encounters that you're used to.

"Set it up the way you set up an SM scene," Jackie advises. "Talk about boundaries. A persona or a role can let you say or do things – 'OK, I'm the delivery man, and you're a bored housewife wearing a sheer negligee, and I'm going to fuck you from behind, and I'm going to act like a total pig.' Then you can get into it and it feels OK." In Jackie's example she illustrates naming ahead of time the things someone might object to or be afraid of. This way you can negotiate around the varying elements of the fantasy. "There's no reason why adults have to censor themselves and think, 'Oh, that's silly,'" Jackie continues. "Be as silly as you possibly can! If your partner laughs at you, good. Make it fun. The more you lighten it up, the more it's going to progress. Once you start getting validation for thinking those things, and somebody's right there with you, the more you're gonna fly with it."

The risk you run when you don't talk about the elements of your fantasy ahead of time is having the kind of experience Shar talks about – either being afraid to speak up or putting your foot in your mouth: "Although I always really liked nasty stories, I never had the courage to say that out loud. Besides whether it's embarrassing, or they laugh, or they think you're silly for telling a story, what if it out-and-out turns them off? What if they say, 'Oh, my god, that happened to me when I was five! And it doesn't turn me on at all!' Or 'That was my first girlfriend's name! Why did you have to pick the name Glenda?'"

For getting started with a partner, Rita advises us to take the experiment seriously: "You don't get into it if you're talking about the kids, or picking up the phone, or making little jokes about each other's underwear. Let a special space for sex be built; don't trivialize it. A lot of people think you're only having sex when you're fucking, but you can be having sex without even touching each other at all."

An unsupportive partner can undermine your attempts. "Make it safe. If you and I have never talked dirty before and I start talking dirty and all of a sudden you crack a joke, I may never open my mouth again." Rita acknowledges that finding your new erotic voice can feel scary and embarrassing, and warns that sometimes a couple's biggest enemy is unrealistic or unclear expectations.

Suppose I come to the door wearing only red pumps and a big smile to greet my lover, thinking it will inspire a long, languorous bout of lovemaking where I'll be rewarded with lots of sensuous attention for my bravery. If s/he reads my signal differently, as "She wants me to throw her over the back of the sofa right here and fuck her brains out," I don't get the kind of lovemaking I fantasized about. I consider the experiment a big failure, and the shoes may never be seen again. As Rita says, "If I get really brave and decide to screw up my courage and do something and I get a different reaction than I wanted, a totally different series of responses, I might just give up, feeling like I'll never get what I want."

I might have had a very different experience, though, if I'd talked to my lover about my desires ahead of time – "I have this fantasy about greeting you when you come home wearing nothing but high heels, and then you carry me into the bedroom and..." And if my lover had utilized hot talk to let me know what s/he was thinking – "Baby, you're so hot in those shoes, I just want to ravish you, is that what you want?" – I might have ended up thrilled to be thrown over the back of the sofa.

So the most effective thing you can do together is share information. Start doing this before you get to the point of sexual experimentation. Shar notes, "When you first start spending time with someone and getting to know them, whether it's a sex partner or just a friend, you find things out about each other that you wouldn't find out in ordinary conversation. 'Where do you like to eat? What are your favorite colors? What was your favorite thing to do as a kid – did you spend a lot of time alone, did you like to read?' Those kinds of things. You can make up a little quiz to learn stuff like that.

"You can still do this if you've been together for years. It can be a fun little romantic thing. Then take it a step further. Maybe one day it's finding out your favorite hiding spots to get a good view and a kiss. A romantic place where we can share a glass of wine outdoors. It's a progression. Where would be a fun place to have sex outdoors, where you could reach up under my dress without being seen? Just spark the imagination. It's getting back to that newness when you first meet someone – you are more willing to spend time and energy on things like that. You want them to be interested in you, and you want that intrigue and mystery to have the kind of power it does in the beginning.

"That could be a prelude to saying, 'Let me show you how I like you to touch my pussy.' That's a big jump. But there are little ways to get into that kind of conversation. 'What are your favorite love scenes in movies? What do they involve?' Then you can say, 'What are the biggest taboos for you? Why?' Once you start talking about something, its power to frighten you goes away."

"For people who are just coming out with their sexuality and being vocal about it, it's scary," Jackie adds. "I think the biggest antidote is remembering the child-like curiosity and innocence you once had about sex. And about your body, touching your body, touching someone else's body. Asking, 'Is this OK? Do you like this?' You can be very safe about it, start very sweet and slow. Even the slightest thing can add an extra charge. Crawling in bed, I'll start talking like she's the neighborhood kid and we're being naughty. The 'show me yours' kind of thing. That is so simple, and it's something that everybody can do.

"The flip side of 'What makes you happy?' is 'I'm going to tell you what makes me happy.' Be really clear. You can say it in a breathy voice. You don't have to be scientific about it. It comes down to clearly knowing what you want, and articulating it. If your partner cares about you, they're going to want to make you happy. If you don't let them know what you want, they're going to try what they want, and then you've got people feeling objectified and awful... People could be so much more compatible if they just started talking."

So whether you talk dirty or not, do start talking. Share fantasies and make plans together. Tell each other what scenarios and erotic roles get you hot. If one of you has misgivings about the other's desires, get more information about the contested sex-style. Find out whether any erotica or informational books dealing with that particular form of sexuality exist, and share the information with your partner. Demystify the whole topic of sex a little. Don't worry about washing the magic away by learning and talking too much about sex. Those who fear that will be the result of sexual sharing have usually not experienced the heightened comfort easy communication provides. And they don't know that, once you can talk comfortably about sex and fantasy, you can actually add heat and spice to sex.

I believe that almost everyone wants a delightful and comfortable sex life. Since you've picked up this book, you obviously do. Your partner probably does too. Even if one or both of you isn't comfortable or delighted with sex now, you need only believe that, with information, communication, and each other's support, you situation can change. Perhaps the most important step in setting out down the path of sexual experimentation together is also the simplest: acknowledge to each other that you want to continue to delight in sex with one another. Now the fun begins - divulging your fantasies and hot spots, sharing your desires, planning to act on them in ways that bring you both pleasure.

Explicit, sexy talk and exhibitionism are only two of the ways sexual energy can be played with and explored. But becoming comfortable with these kinds of sex play can provide a firm foundation for all your subsequent sexual exploration. When you indulge in exhibitionistic play - dressing up, showing off, reveling in someone else's attention - you use your body to declare that you're a proudly sexual being. You *deserve* their attention! When you use your voice to talk erotically you speak your interest in sex and pleasure loud and clear - even if you do it in a whisper. You inspire and arouse others to pleasure, too - you validate eroticism. You - yes, *you!* - model confidence, the power you've acquired by embracing sexual energy.

And to think you used to be shy.

Resources For The Recovering Shy

The dilemma of the resource compiler, especially for a book like this one, is: how long will all these places be in business? How long will these books stay in print? If you pick up a copy of *Exhibitionism For The Shy* in five years, will this guide be useful?

Resources always change, and in the dozen-plus years between the first and second editions of this book, many of the first edition's resources went stale. So I've made a website where up-to-date information can be found; please visit it, and let me know if you have additions: http://www.exhibitionismfortheshy.com

I'm especially interested in listings that will give you access to many more resources, using guidebooks, websites, and the resources of national organizations that can lead you to sources of support and places to meet people and have fun.

I'm lucky to be intimately involved with a great resource for sex-positive books and other materials – I'm the staff sexologist at Good Vibrations. But Good Vibes doesn't carry absolutely everything, and often a published resource you're interested in exploring will no longer be in print. Fortunately, out-of-print books can often be found in used bookstores or through finders' services. The Internet and the World Wide Web will continue to be ever more thorough and useful means to find resources and connect with like-minded others. Find out what your friends know about – you may get terrific references from people you know. Sleuth out books, periodicals, videos, organizations, and play venues on your own. If you find info you want to share with others, go to http://www.exhibitionismfortheshy. com – and remember to let us know if a resource you find there turns out to be a dead end. Become part of our online community of exhibitionism fans and ensure that we'll always have places to play!

Remember that prices, addresses, and phone numbers can all change over time. If you use snail mail to request a brochure or other information not available online, send a self-addressed stamped envelope with your initial enquiry and ask for updated information.

Happy hunting!

Appendix 1

"Dirty" Words and Phrases

BODY PARTS

Penis/testicles:
- cock
- balls
- joint
- prick
- dingus
- whanger
- tool
- snake
- nuts
- pecker
- rod
- skin flute
- boner
- joystick
- monster
- pud
- rod of love
- dong
- meatwhistle
- bishop (as in "beating the...")
- love muscle
- pickle
- gherkin
- wonder worm
- stick
- stem
- shaft
- root
- dick
- knob
- dork
- dong
- donacker
- wang
- schvantz
- schlong
- manfruit
- lingam
- jade stalk
- pego
- phallus
- John Thomas
- tool
- willy
- organ
- peter
- member
- meat
- third leg
- pole
- hard-on

Vulva/clitoris/vagina:
- clit
- clitty
- pearl
- man in the boat
- pussy
- love box
- cunt
- snatch
- hole
- pie
- slit
- sugar bowl
- cherry
- coozy
- love button
- bush
- poontang
- snapping pussy
- jelly roll
- twat
- snapper
- seafood
- box lunch
- hatch
- poundcake
- flower

jade gate
tail
beaver
crack
cooch
clam
gash
notch
g-spot
wipe spot
sacred spot
yoni
quim
little bud
button
bell
nookie
honeypot
happy valley
box
Cupid's highway
chalice
snatch
pumpum
oyster
cumquat
mystic grotto
love's pavilion

Anus/buttocks:
brown eye
ass
asshole
butt
butthole
bum
buns
cheeks
rump
rear
arse
backside
tail
fanny
bunghole

back passage or back
 door

Breasts:
tits
titties
nipples
bosom/s
knobs
nips
knockers
bazooms
jugs
cookies
puppies
boobs
cherries
rosebuds
coconuts
bust
melons
twins

Ejaculate:
get your rocks off
sauce
puddle
squirt
shoot
come
cum
gism (also spelled
 jism or jizz)
juice
cream
love juice
cunt juice
spend
spunk
shoot a load or a wad
fire a shot
jet the juice
come off
the big O
satisfy
pop the cork
the earth moves

load
seed
fetch
dream whip

Ways to Have Sex

Masturbate/manual:
jill off
jack off
jerk off
one man band
pound your prong
diddle
beat your meat or
 beat off
paddle the peter
wank
hand-job
whack off
pocket pool
finger fuck
finger bang
frig
fondle
pet
play with yourself
rub off
canoodle
grope
fool around
dial the czar
pet the kitty

Oral:
pearl-dive
give head
suck off
gobble
go down on
french or french job
muff-dive (or muff-
 diver)
lick my dick
blow-job

eat cunt or eat pussy
hum job
wet lips
sixty-nine
lick
lap or cunt-lap
BJ
deep throat
face fuck
service
muff-dive
tongue
face-sit
mouth music
eat at the Y
yodel in the canyon
kiss the pink
Intercourse:
fuck
screw
get it on
ream
get some nookie
lay/get laid
dip your wick
hump
bang
poke
wham
put out
pork
doggie style
ball
stick it to
stuff it
shag
get some
have it off
in and out
score
make it or make out
make love
hump
sleep with
jump your bones
shaft

get a leg over
go all the way
get a piece of ass or
  tail
shtup
pizzle
plug
tumble

Anal:
rim job
fudgepacking
cornholing
goin' up mustard
  road
fuck ass
up the old Hershey
  highway
bugger
greek
up your ass
butt fuck
ass-licking
around the world
  (ass-licking)
back-door
bit of brown
kneel at the altar
trip to the moon
felch

Other kinds of sex:
copping a feel/feel up
tribadism
dry hump
run the bases
gang-bang
quickie
fist fuck
sloppy (or slurpy)
  seconds
frottage
wet dream
circle jerk
group grope
tit fuck

daisy chain
pull a train
swing
Roman
sex sandwich
lucky Pierre
menage á trois

MISCELLANEOUS SEX
TERMS

packing
queen
piece
cocksman
blue balls
trick
lube
chicken
pecker tracks
rough trade
cunt fart
treasure trail
knock up
dew

Excretion:
golden shower
watersports
enema
scat
piddle
crap
farting
fartsniffer
pee
piss
shit

Menstruation:
on the rag
flying the flag
riding the cotton
  pony

Condom:

love glove
rubber
scum bag
raincoat
french letter
sheath

ADJECTIVES

dripping
big
hot
heaving
juicy
throbbing
hung/well-hung
cherry
stiff
piss-hard
wet
turgid
nasty
randy
horny
shivering
lusty
creamy
hungry
passionate
raunchy
kinky
wild
insatiable
gentle
tender
turned-on

THINGS TO SAY/ EXCLAMATIONS

give it to me
mow me down
please
slower
don't stop!

oh god! (or goddess!)
I die!
do me!
let me do you
harder
deeper
faster
more
put it in
push (or shove) it in
fuck me
I'm gonna come
I'm gonna squirt
I can't stop
come inside
cram it
now
put the rubber on
yes
no
get it up
sit on it
bite me
shit
eat me
stick it in
fuck you
sit on my face
fuck my face
up my ass
piss on you
stick it to me
ram it
jam it

THINGS TO CALL EACH OTHER

lover
sweetcheeks
baby
stud
slut
whore
mistress
sir
master

ma'am
officer
bitch
queer
mommy
cunt lapper
bastard
boy
girl
cocksucker
motherfucker
bulldyke
daddy
pimp
hooker
punk
piece of ass
bitch
fairy
nympho
cock-tease/cunt-tease
faggot
lesbian (or lesbo, lez, lezzie)
bastard
harlot
wild thing

FANCIFUL/CHILDISH TERMS

milking the lizard
winnebagos
pecker-breath
splurky
fur burger
hair pie
ding-a-ling
bananas and cream
one-eyed trouser snake
weenie
tuna taco
beef injection
up in the hat rack (doggy style)

Appendix 2

Chinese Taoist Sex Words

Animal in the boat, jewel terrace
– clitoris

Dark garden, divine field – hood of the
clitoris

Cinnabar grotto, jade gate, moon grotto,
yin gate – vagina

Coxcombs, scarlet pearls – labia minora

Examination hall, peach – vulva

Golden gulch – upper vulva where labia
minora meet

Jade vein – lower vulva where the labia
minora meet

Flower heart, flower pistil – cervix

Scarlet chamber – uterus

Jade fountain – lubricated vagina

Grain seed – five inches inside the vagina

Mixed rock – four inches inside the
vagina

Scented mouse – three inches inside the
vagina

Wheat bud – two inches inside the
vagina

Lute strings – one inch inside the vagina

Heavenly court, hidden valley – vaginal
vestibule

Sand mound – mons pubis

Vast fountain – female urethral opening

Twin lotus peaks – female breasts

Coral juice – breast milk

Duster handle, heavenly root, jade root,
jade spoon, jade stalk, tasseled spear,
yang implement, yang peak, yang stem
– penis

Frog mouth – male urethral opening

Drinking at the jade fountain
– cunnilingus

Playing the flute – fellatio

Water from the heavenly pool – saliva

Jade chamber – bedroom

POSITIONS:

somersaulting dragons
stepping tigers
wrestling apes
cleaving cicadas
mounting tortoises
soaring phoenix
bunny licking its fur
fish linking scales
cranes entwining necks

silkworms entangling
dragons twisting
fish eye-to-eye
swifts sharing a heart
kingfishers uniting
mandarin ducks joining
butterflies fluttering
wild ducks flying backwards
sheltering the reclining pine

bamboos by the altar
twin phoenixes dancing
wild horses leaping
white tiger jumping
jungle fowl approaching the arena
phoenix sporting in the cinnabar
 grotto
humming ape embracing the tree
cat and mouse sharing a hole

Appendix 3

Feeling and Emotion Words

adoring
adventurous
affectionate
aglow
alive
alluring
aloof
ambivalent
amused
angry
appreciative
apprehensive
apologetic
aroused
arrogant
ashamed
assertive
astonished
attracted
awed
awkward
bad
bitchy
blissful
bold
bossy
bottled up
bubbly
captivated
carefree

careless
caring
charmed
cheerful
cherished
childlike
clear
coarse
confident
considerate
consumed
contented
crazy
cruel
cuddly
daring
delighted
demanding
desirous
desperate
devoted
dirty
dominant
dominated
eager
ecstatic
effeminate
electrified
embarrassed
emotional

empathic
enchanted
energetic
enthusiastic
evil
excited
exposed
exuberant
fantastic
fascinated
fatherly
fawning
fearful
feminine
flattering/ed
floating
flustered
forceful
forward
frank
free
friendly
frightened
frivolous
frustrated
generous
gentle
genuine
giddy
giving

glad	little	pretty
gleeful	lively	prim
glowing	lonely	prissy
good	longing	proud
grateful	loose	prudish
gratified	loud	quiet
greedy	loving	rageful
grieving	low	rebellious
guilty	lustful	reckless
happy	lusty	reflective
heavenly	macho	relaxed
helpless	mad	relieved
hesitant	masculine	renewed
high	mature	reserved
honest	meek	respected
honored	melancholy	responsible
horny	mild	responsive
humiliated	mischievous	retiring
humorous	modest	reverent
hungry	motherly	rude
imaginative	mysterious	sad
in control/in charge	mystical	safe
infantile	naive	sated
infatuated	nasty	satisfied
ingenious	natural	scared
ingenuous	naughty	secretive
inhibited	nervous	secure
inspired	nice	seductive
insecure	noisy	self-centered
intelligent	obliging	self-conscious
intimidated/ing	obsessed	self-confident
intimate	open	selfish
in tune	out of control	sensitive
inventive	outspoken	sentimental
involved	outgoing	serious
irrational	overjoyed	servile
irreverent	overwhelmed	severe
jealous	pampered	sexy
joyous	patient	shaky
keyed up	peaceful	shocked
kinky	persistent	show-off
kind	pleasant	shy
kittenish	pleased	silly
lecherous	poised	sincere
leisurely	potent	slow
licentious	powerful	small
light	powerless	soft

sophisticated
special
spontaneous
spunky
steady
stern
stimulated
strong
subdued
submissive
sure
sweet
sympathetic
talkative

temperamental
tempted
tender
tentative
terrific
thankful
thrilled
tickled
timid
tired
together
tolerant
tormented
touched

tough
trusting
turned on
unaffected
understanding
uninhibited
unselfish
valued
vital
vivacious
vulnerable
warm
wholesome
wicked

Appendix 4

Some Erotic Roles

alien and earthling

biker and slut

boss and secretary/apprentice (or any subordinate)

boy and centaur

brother and sister (or sister/sister, brother/brother)

burglar and burgled

cabin boy and pirate

centerfold model and photographer

cop and robber

cowboy/girl and saloon gal

dancer and dance teacher

delivery boy and whoever he finds at home

director and starlet

doctor and patient

dominant and submissive

draq queen and unsuspecting straight man

eccentric bohemian and socialite

fair maiden and rogue

femme and butch

firefighter and rescuee

foreigner and local

gangster and gun moll

girl and her dog

hayseed and city slicker

hunter and pursued

innocent and sophisticate

jailer and prisoner

kidnapper and kidnappee

lady/lord and wench/page

Little Red Riding Hood and the wolf

master or mistress and servant/slave/maid

mechanic and opera star

mommy or daddy and girl, boy, or baby

nurse and doctor

nympho and nerdy teenager

priest and nun

priest and confessor

prince or princess and serving maid/boy

queen or king and subject

randy uncle and aunt

repairman and housewife

rock star and groupie

seducer and virgin

sergeant and recruit

strangers (on a train/in the night/...)

stripper and customer

sultan and harem dweller

swimmer and dolphin

teacher and student

top and bottom

trucker and hitch-hiker

vamp and preacher

vampire and victim

virgin and priest

voyeur and exhibitionist

whore and john

So what if you didn't find your favorite role? Add your own! Pick a movie star (be Fred and Ginger, or James Dean and Sal Mineo), an historic figure (Sappho or Casanova), or anything else that erotically inspires you. Mix the roles up. Pirate and nun... biker and headmistress... be creative and have fun!